ANTE·BELLUM

Writings of George Fitzhugh and
Hinton Rowan Helper on Slavery

———·•·———

EDITED, WITH AN INTRODUCTION, BY

HARVEY WISH

Western Reserve University

1962

CAPRICORN BOOKS

NEW YORK

CONTENTS

Library of Congress Catalog Card Number:
60-7663

MANUFACTURED IN THE UNITED STATES OF AMERICA

INTRODUCTION.

GEORGE FITZHUGH; LIFE AND WORK.

1.

THE critical decade which ended with the firing on Fort Sumter witnessed a major battle of the books over slavery which ignited the explosion of 1861. Harriet Beecher Stowe may not have been "the little lady who made this big war"—to use an expression attributed to Lincoln—but the millions of copies of her *Uncle Tom's Cabin* not only intensified antislavery feeling both here and abroad but they elicited a retaliatory "Anti-Tom literature" of Southern novels, essays, and poems. The year after Mrs. Stowe's novel, there appeared Frederick L. Olmsted's critical articles on his observations of plantation life during a fourteen-month sojourn. Olmsted offered evidence that slavery did not pay and that it retarded Southern development. One interested reader, Hinton Helper of North Carolina, drew upon Olmsted's facts and theories for his own explosive book, *The Impending Crisis* (1857). English visitors from the illustrious Charles Dickens down added their own accounts of the evils of a slave society, while theologians on both sides perused the Bible for either justification or condemnation of slavery. Talented Southern writers like William Gilmore Simms frequently diverted their creative talents into proslavery propaganda.

Not so far behind Mrs. Stowe in influence on the coming of the war were the zealous propagandists George Fitzhugh and Hinton R. Helper of North Carolina. Fitzhugh was the earnest spokesman of Virginia tidewater planters; Helper expressed the aspirations and prejudices of the non-slaveholding highlander and small farmer of the Southern Appalachian country. Fitzhugh wished the non-slaveholder to unite with the planter in a common bond of interest in the survival of slavery; Helper urged

3

all non-slaveholders to seek solidarity against the "Lord of the Lash." Fitzhugh, the Virginian, in that era of Auguste Comte's emergent social science, looked for a "sociology" that would give slave society an objective justification, while Helper the North Carolinian drew upon the significant statistics of the Census of 1850 for scientific proof that Southern backwardness, especially the depressed status of the white worker, was due to slavery alone. Both men aroused the combative spirit between the sections, stirred up congressmen in the nation's capital, and added to the certainty of an irrepressible conflict.

George Fitzhugh's paternalistic philosophy was bred in his Virginia tidewater background. He was born on November 4, 1806 in an isolated rural community along the Potomac in Prince William County, but his father, an army surgeon and planter, soon moved to King George County where the family cultivated a 500-acre plantation, presumably aided by slave labor. The Fitzhughs were hardly affluent; his father died when George was eighteen, but the young man remained wedded to the ties of the planter class; in fact, he retained a lifelong interest in genealogy which led him to trace his forebears back to the aristocratic seventeenth-century land-owner and lawyer, William Fitzhugh of Bedfordshire. The setting for his paternal race-consciousness came from the fact that both Prince William and King George counties had a slave population that substantially outnumbered the whites. When George moved to Port Royal, Caroline County, along the Rappahannock, where he spent most of his life as a lawyer and writer, he was once more in an area of a preponderant Negro population.[1]

Although Fitzhugh may have attended an academy and certainly never entered college, he read a good deal, boasted of his proficiency in Latin, and took a legal apprenticeship with "a Napoleon of the bar." But he disliked listening to the woes of clients, apparently did not attract very many, and readily took to writing pamphlets, articles, and books upon his favorite and exclusive interest —the slavery and race question. His experience in ad-

[1] This discussion of Fitzhugh is largely based on *George Fitzhugh, Propagandist of the Old South,* by Harvey Wish (Louisiana State University Press, 1943).

dressing juries undoubtedly strengthened his *ex parte* arguments for slavery. He travelled very little and never escaped a parochial outlook which judged the world by the standards of Port Royal. "We were never two weeks at a time from under the family roof," he admitted, "until we had passed middle life." His reading tastes were quite conventional and he read novels for their plots rather than for anything else. He liked the romantic historical fiction and stories of Bulwer-Lytton, Scott and Disraeli, and he condemned the realists. Once, pained by his ignorance of philosophy, he said frankly that "my pseudo-learning is all gathered from Reviews . . . Newspapers, novels, Reviews, are the sources of my information." [2]

He liked to think that he lived a quiet uneventful life in Port Royal, the "little village of flowers," where he reared a family of nine children, but he omitted the tragedies, such as the loss of most of his children early in life. His neighbors knew him as a person with a good sense of humor and a great deal of local loyalty, and as an active and "regular" county Democrat. During his early manhood, he was a Jeffersonian liberal, not altogether unlike the noted Port Royal planter and federal senator John Taylor, or the neighboring James Madison. In those early years, Virginians looked forward to the imminent extinction of slavery, and many planters, faced by a declining tobacco industry and exhausted lands, were ready to take up the liberal ideas of freeing the slaves. But by the 1850's, agricultural science and a revived plantation economy made slavery much more attractive, halted the speed of manumissions, and replaced Jeffersonianism by a reactionary paternalism. Fitzhugh changed accordingly and took up his pen to prove that slavery was eternally right.

In 1851, when Virginia politics dwelt upon the question of what to do about the free Negroes because of their allegedly incendiary effect upon the slaves, Fitzhugh took the leadership in passing county resolutions demanding harsh laws restricting the status of these former slaves and urging re-enslavement in certain cases. At the same time he published a pamphlet along these lines entitled, "What Shall be Done With the Free Negroes?" This was written

[2] George Fitzhugh to George F. Holmes, April 11, 1855 in G. F. Holmes Letter Book (Manuscript in the Duke University Library).

while the newspapers reported slave plots in the state and told of the sharp drop in plantation production in the West Indies that had come with Britain's emancipation of her slaves. California, Illinois, and other states in the North as well as in the South had passed laws forbidding free Negroes to come within their borders. Southerners had long stressed the lesson of Haiti where the slaves had won freedom by killing their masters or driving them to the United States mainland. Virginia counted two well-authenticated slave insurrections—Gabriel's attack in 1800 and Nat Turner's uprising in 1831. Fitzhugh's solution was to establish some type of peonage for the freedmen or to send them back to Africa. He urged the state to hire out those free Negroes who did not earn enough to support themselves. Some of these suggestions resembled measures that Virginia actually did carry out.

During the spring and summer of 1854, Fitzhugh acted as a contributing editor for the *Richmond Examiner,* which claimed the largest newspaper circulation in the South. The editor then was the fire-eating Robert William Hughes, who enthusiastically encouraged his associates to take up the offensive against Northern abolitionism. Many of Fitzhugh's articles were to be reprinted in his book, *Sociology for the South* (1854), but they had already attracted wide notice. He challenged the Garrisons and the Greeleys: "We have stood on the defensive long enough. We can throw fire-brands as well as the abolitionists; and the poor in the free states are much more ready for insurrection than the slaves of the South." Like the South Carolina extremist, John C. Calhoun, he too urged Northern industrialists to join hands with the planters in order to head off any class uprising of factory workers or slaves.

Sociology for the South was published by a leading Richmond bookseller, job printer and importer of foreign books, Adolphus Morris. Its title shared honors with *A Treatise on Sociology* (1854) by Henry Hughes of Mississippi as the first volume in America to carry the word "sociology" on its title page. Hughes' work was also pro-slavery propaganda, but its use of pseudo-scientific jargon was more deliberate and consistent than Fitzhugh's.

The idea of a new social science as a solvent of social ills was usually inspired by the writings of Francis Bacon.

One of Fitzhugh's correspondents, the talented George Frederick Holmes, who became a professor of history and literature at the University of Virginia, used Bacon's ideal as expressed in the *New Atlantis* as a starting point for his own theories of a social science. Holmes also found in Aristotle not only a justification of slavery but an organic theory to the effect that the family and human society were of natural and organic origin and growth. This observation was applied by Holmes to the plantation society. In fact, Holmes was to publish in 1883 the first college textbook in sociology, not following the line of Herbert Spencer, emphasizing free competition in the manner of English and Northern writers, but along organic Aristotelian lines (even if he had to drop slavery by then). Fitzhugh and Holmes broached the idea of creating a new sociology to a Northern abolitionist and eccentric, Stephen Pearl Andrews, who had published a brochure on a science of society. However, this dream of inventing a scientific solution to the slavery controversy came to nothing.[3]

Sociology for the South came from the presses in the fateful year of 1854 when Douglas secured the Kansas-Nebraska Act and overthrew almost the last vestiges of the Compromise of 1850, opened the door to that miniature civil war, Bleeding Kansas, and helped to split the Democratic Party. Partly as a result, the Republican Party was born that year, and its very name as well as its reaffirmation of the language of the Declaration of Independence meant the resurgence of Jeffersonian liberalism. This was the intellectual strain of individualism that Fitzhugh was trying to destroy.

Naturally, the book pleased the South, which had smarted under the taunts of the abolitionists, and correspondingly angered the North, which was directly attacked. Its sales, according to the author, were excellent, though largely confined to Richmond, Fredericksburg and Washington. The Richmond papers of course took the lead in enthusiasm. Holmes was a host in himself, for he extolled the work not only in the *Richmond Examiner*, but also in the *Southern Literary Messenger* and the *Quarterly*

[3] Harvey Wish, "George F. Holmes and the Genesis of American Sociology," *American Journal of Sociology*, XXXIX (1941), 698-707; *id.*, "Stephen Pearl Andrews, Pioneer American Sociologist," *Social Forces*, XIX (1941), 477-482.

Review of the Methodist Episcopal Church South; in fact,
he almost certainly did the review in the *Southern Quarterly Review* of which he had once been an assistant editor, and from time to time he added friendly comments on
the book in his articles for *De Bow's Review.* Since the
ideas of the two men were so similar, it was not difficult
for Holmes to praise *Sociology for the South* as "a bold
assertion of universal principles." For such valuable services, Fitzhugh reciprocated by campaigning in the *Richmond Enquirer* to secure for Holmes a vacant professorship at the University of Virginia. Southern newspapers
liked Fitzhugh's tactic of taking the offensive against the
antislavery forces. The distinguished Edmund Ruffin of
Virginia, who combined great acumen as a scientific agri-
culturalist with fire-eating politics, praised the author's
"novel and profound views on the comparison of slavery
with what is miscalled 'free society'." Ruffin, it will be
noted, later claimed the credit for firing the first gun of
the Civil War.

While Northern newspapers tended at first to ignore the
book, emphatic rejoinders came from Horace Greeley's
antislavery *New York Tribune* and from several abolitionist papers. Greeley wrote a caustic editorial upon "The
Dawn of a New Literature," and dwelt on the barrenness
of Southern letters and the peculiar beginnings of "a coming race of proslavery poets, historians, philosophers, and
artists." Fitzhugh, glad to get any publicity, promptly replied to this attack in a letter published in the *Tribune.*
He argued that Greeley himself had been the first to proclaim that free or competitive society was a failure and
that this view was apparent in his cooperative experiments
such as the Fourierite Phalansteries.

Fitzhugh was sometimes invited to lecture in nearby
Fredericksburg, but the most exciting invitation came at
this time from the New Haven Lyceum. The managers
wished the Virginian to speak upon his favorite subject,
"The Failure of Free Society" and then planned to have
Wendell Phillips, the abolitionist, prepare a reply. Fitzhugh managed to undertake this arduous journey, arduous
for him, although he was financially embarrassed by a lawsuit in the Circuit Court of Caroline County for a debt of
$530 and he lacked sufficient funds even to make his long-
deferred visit to his friend Holmes.

Many of his auditors were Yale professors—one was Professor Benjamin Silliman, the noted chemist—who listened politely to an unusually long discourse and wondered how so genial a personality could take so extremist a stand on the failures of modern capitalist society. The next day, when Phillips arrived after a delay due to a lawsuit of his own, the New Englander had several pointed observations to make: "When I and many more like me are welcomed to Richmond to defend New England and her institutions, without danger of the penitentiary, then may Massachusetts and Connecticut be weighed in the balance with Virginia."

Fitzhugh's stay in New Haven proved both pleasant and enlightening. He was taken for a carriage tour of the town by Samuel Foote, the favorite uncle of Harriet Beecher Stowe, and even met one of Harriet's talented sisters. The trip revealed to the Southerner that ordinary Northern workmen could afford to live in attractive cottages. However, he soon explained this phenomenon to himself and to his readers that New England's prosperity was unsubstantial and temporary because it hung upon the erratic fluctuations of capital and commerce in foreign trade. The comfortable homes that he saw were due to the exploitation of the farmer by parasitic trade. Never would Fitzhugh look upon the Cotton Kingdom as a capitalistic institution.

During the exciting Buchanan-Frémont presidential campaign of 1856, the sage of Port Royal became a contributing editor for the militant *Richmond Enquirer,* one of whose recent editors had killed the editor of the *Richmond Whig* in a duel. (Fortunately, Fitzhugh was too mild-mannered a man, even a bit absent-minded, to involve himself in journalistic controversies on the duelling field). This time his articles were to make up the substance of a second book, *Cannibals All! or Slaves Without Masters,* a detailed attack upon the exploitation of labor in competitive (i.e., non-slaveholding) societies. One of Fitzhugh's most extreme *Enquirer* statements, divorced of its explanatory context, was seized upon and widely circulated in Frémont Republican Club leaflets of that year: "Slavery is the natural and normal condition of the laboring man, whether white or black." This implied that the author would enslave all workmen—which Fitzhugh explicitly denied.

One of the interesting paradoxes of American history is the fact that Lincoln based one of his most striking antitheses, "A House Divided Against Itself Cannot Stand," upon one of Fitzhugh's editorial statements. The Southerner had stated on May 6, 1856, "Social forms so widely differing as those of domestic slavery and (attempted) universal liberty cannot long co-exist in the Great Republic of Christendom. They cannot be equally adapted to the wants and interests of society." He had added that "each one should be governed according to his wants and moral and intellectual capacities." Lincoln, as Americans learned, also doubted the prolonged coexistence of slavery and freedom side by side, but he believed that a peaceful transformation through public opinion would insure the coming victory of freedom. Stephen Douglas charged that Lincoln had uttered an incendiary idea leading to irrepressible conflict in his House-Divided speech but the future president denied the charge and pointed out that the same idea had appeared in the *Richmond Enquirer,* a paper to which Lincoln subscribed to learn the Southern point of view. He had also read carefully in *Sociology for the South,* where similar phrases declaring irrepressible conflict had been printed. Fitzhugh too, it should be noted, did not believe that the coexistence of slavery and freedom would be disrupted by violence. But Illinois newspapers which were well-known as Lincoln organs sometimes chose to borrow Fitzhugh's extreme statements as proof of the new, implacable position of the Southern extremists.

Meanwhile Fitzhugh had begun a permanent literary connection with the influential *De Bow's Review* and formed a long friendship with its energetic editor. James D. B. De Bow edited a magazine which stressed Southern nationalism in the economic and cultural spheres. When he became a prime mover for the revival of the African slave trade—then regarded as piracy in the eyes of the law—and converted the Southern Commerical Conventions to a course of action to change the federal and state laws, Fitzhugh reversed his previous opposition to this project. De Bow was also the superintendent of the Fed-

eral Census and had the painful duty of compiling facts
that too frequently showed how badly the South was los-
ing out currently in the economic rivalry of the sections.
Perhaps the mid-twentieth-century analogy between the
US-Soviet rivalry and that between North and South is
not out of place here. De Bow and his contributors added
to the sectional tensions; he was to precede Fitzhugh in
the final demand for secession.

From his former home in Charleston, where militancy
unfortunately lacked the material resources of the new
Southwest tributary to New Orleans, De Bow had carried
on the tradition of Nullification and extreme States Rights
that brought South Carolina finally to attack Fort Sumter.
His contributors included the leading Southern militants
—Fitzhugh, Holmes, William Grayson (a Charleston author of an interminable poem on "The Hireling and the
Slave"), and a number of racist anthropologists who made
the infant science a proslavery tool. For a time De Bow
held the title of professor of political economy at the University of Louisiana and urged Southerners to awake to
the importance of modern business and commercial subjects instead of clinging to the English emphasis on the
classics. Shortly before the Civil War, he published a pamphlet, *The Interest in Slavery of the Southern Non-Slaveholder* (1860), apparently intended as an indirect reply to
Helper's *The Impending Crisis*. De Bow argued that the
great Southern staples could not grow without slavery,
that Britain's emancipation policy had failed and had prospered her slaveholding competitors, that Santo Domingo
emancipation meant race wars, and that no actual competition existed between plantation slaveholders and white
independent farmers.[4]

One of De Bow's noted protegés among the rising anthropologists, Dr. Josiah C. Nott, was a professor of anat-
omy at the University of Louisiana and had also come from
South Carolina. In collaboration with George R. Gliddon
of Mobile, he published the racist interpretation of permanent Negro inferiority in *Types of Mankind* (1856) and

[4] Ottis C. Skipper, *J. D. B. De Bow, Magazinist of the Old
South* (University of Georgia Press, 1958); Robert F. Durden,
"J. D. B. De Bow: Convolutions of a Slavery Expansionist,"
The Journal of Southern History, XVII (1951), 441-461.

even edited an early English translation of the notorious
racist book of Count Joseph Arthur de Gobineau, *The
Moral and Intellectual Diversity of Races*. This extolled
"Aryan" superiority and racial determinism in history;
"Aryanism" was then a novel term outside of the realm
of philology. Gobineau, it will be recalled, was one of the
chief ideological ancestors of Hitler's National Socialism.
Fitzhugh had at first rejected this Aryanism because it
conflicted with the Bible, but he too came around to the
Nott-Gobineau way of thinking and proclaimed these
truths of permanent Negro backwardness in *De Bow's
Review*.

By mid-century, racial thought in both Europe and
America divided between monogenists who believed in a
single creation of all races of men and polygenists who
held that God created each race of men separately. The
pseudo-science of the polygenists satisfied American racists
who were embarrassed by the notion of a common origin
for Negroes and whites; empire-builders abroad also liked
to think of the lesser breeds as destined forever to be hew-
ers of wood and drawers of water for the better-endowed
white man.

Cannibals All! was issued in 1857 by the same publishers who had printed Fitzhugh's previous book. It appeared
in time to heighten the prevailing tension. The South was
shaken by a unique large-scale insurrection panic which
may have been based on imaginary events but it swept almost every slaveholding state beginning with Texas and
led the planters to organize vigilante committees after the
popular California model to compel slaves under torture
to confess to insurrection plots. Southerners believed that
the slaves were incited by the prospects of Frémont's presidential victory over Buchanan and consequent freedom;
since Frémont failed, it was suspected that the slaves
would try to win freedom by themselves. Fitzhugh, of
course, dismissed the possibility of slave uprisings in his
writings.

The new book tried to prove that capital exploited labor
in nonslaveholding societies and dwelt upon the shocking
evidence taken by the sensational parliamentary investigations into labor abuses in factories and mines. In many respects, this work duplicated the earlier arguments of

Sociology for the South, but it took a much more militant stand against the North.

Again, Southern reviewers heartily endorsed his work although De Bow added some qualifications that Fitzhugh was "one of the truest philosophers of the age, but like all other philosophers, a little fond of paradoxes, a little inclined to run a theory into extremes, and a little impractical." Garrison, who had characterized *Sociology for the South* as "a shallow, impudent, and thoroughly satanic work," declared in a lengthy vituperative review in the *Liberator*:

> Mr. Fitzhugh is the Don Quixote of Slavedom— only still more demented than his illustrious predecessor. As the latter saw in a harmless windmill a giant of frightful aspect, and lustily assailed it with all the success possible under the circumstances, so the former sees in freedom a terrific monster which is devouring its millions, and valiantly essays to drive it from the earth.

Noted English travelers like Charles Mackay, novelist and poet, took Fitzhugh as typical of the new militant pro-slavery school. Frederick L. Olmsted, then engaged in publishing a trilogy on his journey in the South, agreed in his later edition, *The Cotton Kingdom,* with such estimates:

> Nothing but a reversal of the current of our Northern history for half a century, nothing in fact but the enslavement of labour at the North, could in the nature of things give that security even temporarily to the capitalists of labour at the South which they need.

In his material affairs, Fitzhugh had begun to prosper in a modest way. To his growing earnings from publications in 1857 was now added a small salary of $1600 as a law clerk in the office of Attorney General Jeremiah S. Black —altogether an annual income of about $3000. His letter of application to President Buchanan asserted that he had always been a Democratic regular, a devoted supporter of the President, an ardent Unionist (he did not specify his peculiar methods of achieving this goal), and that now he was poor and needed office for its emoluments as well as for the access to books that a Washington post afforded.[5] Fitzhugh admired the capital as the "only practically democratic city" in America because of the wise paternalistic policy of the federal government in the District of Columbia, especially the generous provisions for popular recreation, intellectual improvement and relief. De Bow, then in Washington as the Census Superintendent, afterwards recalled Fitzhugh's pleasant stay in the city: ". . . we have seen that philosopher deport himself in the courtly saloons of the Capital in other days, imbibe the wines of France, and puff the regalias of Habana and occasionally indulge himself in a broad cloth suit, which however never retained very long its finish."

By 1858, Fitzhugh's books, articles, and newspaper writings had attained wide notoriety in the North, although the custom of leaving articles unsigned gave the impression that many Southern writers rather than a few subscribed to his belligerent views of free society. United States congressmen from the North frequently cited Fitzhugh's extreme statements as evidence that the South was now committed to the new idea that not only African slavery but slavery as a principle, black or white, was right *per se*.

Senator Charles Sumner of Massachusetts chose Fitzhugh as a major target in his angry speech of June 4, 1860, "The Barbarism of Slavery." He dwelt upon the Southerner's references to the rightness of slavery regardless of complexion as expressed in the *Richmond Enquirer*, the *Charleston Mercury*, and in *Sociology for the South*. These abhorrent views he thought were the intellectual counterpart of Southern lynchings, duels, bowie knives, the degradation of women, and the absolutism of the slaveholder. Among others, as already noted, Abraham Lincoln had reacted vehemently to Fitzhugh's ideas. Southern Senators, particularly extremists like Robert M. T. Hunter of Virginia (after whom Fitzhugh had named his eldest son) now liked to speak of slavery as "the normal condition of human society" and Senator James M. Mason of the same

[5] G. Fitzhugh to G. F. Holmes, July 27, 1857 in Holmes Letter Book; Fitzhugh to President James Buchanan, March 24, 1857, Files of the Attorney General (in The National Archives).

state asserted that slavery was "ennobling to both races, the white and the black." [6]

On the eve of the Civil War, Fitzhugh felt lukewarm about secession and urged "disunion within the union" instead; this was a program of non-intercourse aimed at Massachusetts which would tax products of that state and cease cultural contacts as much as possible. De Bow sniffed at this mild measure. When war actually began, Fitzhugh was ready to rationalize in *De Bow's Review* that war elevated the sentiments and ennobled character by stamping out the spirit of gain. He accepted a clerkship in the Auditor's Office of the Confederate Department of the Treasury. His son, Robert Hunter, an engineering graduate of the University of Virginia, took charge of a Confederate engineering corps and won praise for meritorious service. Another son, George Stuart, fought in the battle of Antietam and earned promotion to a lieutenancy. Port Royal itself was too close to the firing lines to escape bombardment; one Union shell crashed into the old mansion of the Fitzhughs, but the family had already left.

After the war, the Virginian took defeat gracefully and wrote in a conciliatory vein, hoping to soften the mood of the victors. He was appointed by the Freedmen's Bureau as a local court agent to supervise labor contracts between freedmen and farm employers. For a year he was an associate judge of the Freedmen's Court and decided Negro cases on an informal paternalistic basis rather than on technical grounds. The Fitzhughs then lived comfortably at Camp Lee in an imposing brick residence.

However, Radical Reconstruction antagonized Fitzhugh just as it did most Southern whites. In Caroline County, where Negro sharecroppers outnumbered whites, race relations were tense. The Virginian, writing at various times in *De Bow's Review* and *Lippincott's Magazine*, charged the Radicals at aiming at racial amalgamation and ridiculed the current efforts to educate the Negroes as incredibly naive, an encouragement to idleness. Social equality, he held, was an impossibility. But by 1872, he felt again in a

[6] For this and other congressional reactions, see *Congressional Globe*, 35 Cong., 2 Sess., Appendix, 224, 236-237, 284-285, 300; 36 Cong., 1 Sess., 224-225, 571, 931, 2601; Appendix, 104-109, 172, 354, 375.

conciliatory mood toward the North: "Community of interests and like social and industrial systems will bind us
together in the future." He was even ready to praise the
rise of industrial and commercial monopolies. A monopolistic capitalism embodied the attractive feudal ideals that
he admired.

In 1878, now an ailing invalid of 72, his wife dead, and
his surviving children grown up and dispersed, he left his
Virginia home to live in Frankfort, Kentucky, with his son,
Robert Hunter, a construction engineer. Then in 1880, he
moved to Huntsville, Texas, where a daughter was married to a wounded Confederate veteran from Tennessee.
Their son, Marcellus E. Foster, became the crusading editor of the *Houston Press*, a Scripps-Howard paper. Finally,
on July 29, 1881, George Fitzhugh died, forgotten by the
antebellum generation who were now occupied with ad-
justment to a new order that the proslavery propagandists
had tried to avert.[7]

Sociology for the South and Cannibals All!

2.

BOTH of Fitzhugh's books as well as his other writings deal
with the proslavery theme from a consistent anti-liberal
viewpoint. The gist of the argument may be found as early
as 1849 in his pamphlet *Slavery Justified*—the idea that
slavery or serfdom was the norm in human development,
freedom the exception:

> Liberty and equality are new things under the sun.
> The free states of antiquity abounded with slaves.
> The feudal system that supplanted Roman institutions
> changed the form of slavery but brought with it nei-
> ther liberty or equality. France and the Northern
> States of our Union have alone fully and fairly tried
> the experiment of a social organization founded upon
> universal liberty and equality of rights.

This liberal system had failed. Liberty meant a bitter competition between the strong and the weak and as in the
plant kingdom, no resulting improvement could be dis-
cerned in the species. Laissez-faire hurt laborers as a class

[7] Fredericksburg (Va.) *News,* August 15, 1881.

because merchants and employers lacked the kindly sympathies of planters. The remedy for these new evils lay in identifying the interests of the weak and the strong, the poor and the rich—a result that could be reached through slavery or feudalism. He apologized for using the term "sociology" but explained that the ailments of a competitive order now required doctors of society.

Sociology for the South began with an unusual argument for a champion of the Southern planter—an arraignment of free trade as well as classical economics in general. The revolutionary maxims of free competition, he said, came into existence only after the overthrow of Greek and Roman slavery, feudal serfdom, and the Catholic social order. With the Reformation, the world outlook changed. "Men were suddenly called on to walk alone, to act and work for themselves without guide, advice or control from superior authority."

Adam Smith and his *Wealth of Nations* (1776) had formulated unworkable laissez-faire doctrines. "For writing a one-sided philosophy, no man was better fitted than Adam Smith. He possessed extraordinary powers of abstraction, analysis, and generalization. He was absent, secluded, and unobservant." Fitzhugh, as his various writings indicated, stressed experience, especially historical facts, rather than *a priori* logic or abstractions. To the Virginian, all trade, domestic and foreign, was a "war of the wits" in which the stronger prevailed. Besides, he believed, the products of farm labor were at a great discount in an exchange for those of industrial labor. Thus England robbed Ireland and the North drained the wealth of the South. Privately Fitzhugh explained to George F. Holmes: "Again, I like a good deal of free competition, but would relieve the weak and poor and ignorant from its crushing operations—confine it to the rich, skilful, and professional."

Instead of free trade, Fitzhugh hoped for more self-sufficiency in a state like Virginia, not only in economic affairs but also in politics and culture within a loose federal union. He would expand and strengthen the state banks through branch banking and more currency control. To encourage the growth of moderate-sized towns he would stimulate internal improvements and plan railroads and highways along strategic lines that would penetrate the

Western part of the state and cut off the Northern influence. He hoped that such a program of economic nationalism would prevent southern states from becoming colonies of the North. A diversified South could afford to build schools and colleges of its own.

Most interesting is his argument for mass education among whites as a means of winning over the loyalty of the nonslaveholder. Since the poorer classes constituted Virginia's militia and police and protected property, they must be educated. Besides, these classes "secure[d] men in possession of a kind of property which they [the slave-owners] could not hold for a day but for the supervision and protection of the poor." Slavery, he conceded, was itself responsible for rendering the South exclusively agricultural, keeping her population too sparse for neighborhood schools, preventing diversity of occupations, and cutting off the poor from the means of education. To head off more drastic steps by the forces of universal suffrage, he would begin with the distribution of a large weekly newspaper to poor families at less than one dollar a year. Other gradual (and apparently equally modest) steps would be added later. Government sponsorship of public works would provide employment. Economic rivalry between the races might be curbed by confining Negroes to farm work and coarse mechanical labor. In later years the South was to crusade for a textile industry as a means of elevating the poor white and highlanders while excluding the competition of Negroes. Fitzhugh's program aimed at a new white solidarity based on the union of interest between non-slaveholder and planter.

A large part of *Sociology for the South* consisted of an arraignment of liberal Jeffersonian theories. This served as a weapon against the rising Republican Party with its Jeffersonian tenets, attacked the abolitionists who adhered to higher law doctrines above the Constitution itself, and berated the surviving remnants of old-fashioned Virginia liberalism. Fitzhugh blamed Locke and the Enlightenment *philosophes* for introducing a mechanistic interpretation of the world which overthrew the divine right of kings and the ideals of prescriptive government. "They confounded the moral with the physical world, and this was not strange, because they had begun to doubt whether there was any other than a physical world."

Jefferson's Declaration made no sense to him. Men were not born equal, physically, morally or intellectually, and the environment accentuated these natural differences. Some were born with saddles on their backs and others booted and spurred to ride them—"and the riding does them good." No institution could prevent the powerful few from acquiring rule over the masses. Life and liberty were not inalienable rights as was evident from the examples of history, the armed forces, and incarcerated prisoners. Under the liberal competitive system most men's happiness consisted of destroying the happiness of other people. He made equally short shrift of the famous Virginia Bill of Rights which rested on similar glittering fallacies. As governor of Virginia, Jefferson overthrew the props of a sound conservative and traditional order by eliminating primogeniture and entail in the state. Such liberal steps both here and elsewhere merely replaced a moderate and stable small aristocracy by monopolistic bankers and hereditary plutocrats. Thus Jefferson was responsible for "a total revolution"—a startlingly modern phrase—and not a loose series of social reforms. As for the American Revolution itself, no one should reckon it to be more than an act of separation, of independence—not a social revolution.

The assault on liberalism was also extended to the contemporary "isms" such as feminism and cooperative Utopianism. Bluestockings such as Mrs. Stowe, Harriet Martineau and Frances Wright were abhorrent to him, for Woman's true strength lay in the domestic sphere. Liberalism was also responsible for gross utilitarianism and the absence of such sound standards as prevailed in classical times. "There is not a poet, an orator, or painter in the world," he asserted rhetorically. Finally, he rejected the Enlightenment idea of progress which was a passing illusion that would soon yield to a universal form of paternalism. "One set of ideas will govern and control after awhile the civilized world," he concluded. "Slavery will everywhere be abolished or everywhere be reinstituted." Of the outcome he had no doubt.

He dwelt upon the laissez-faire industrialism which exploited women and children under the heel of the industrial classes. From the Parliamentary Reports and the social protest literature of the Christian Socialists he culled numerous examples of such abuses. Rewriting history, he

argued that pauperism and beggary in England were unknown until the villeins began to escape from their masters to engage in a nomadic predatory life. Liberty had
bred the French Revolution and the successive Paris
struggles at the barricades. Now the able and paternalistic dictator Louis Napoleon sought to remedy these consequences of freedom through socialistic measures. "He is
a socialist, and socialism is the new fashionable name of
slavery." Elsewhere, trade unionism was another socialistic institution created by the need to cope with the
ravages of laissez-faire. But socialism produced its own
evils which could be solved only by the Southern slavery
principle of mutual interest.

He drew a romantic picture of the happy-go-lucky slave
living on an efficient plantation system. The Southerner
was the Negro's best friend, not the meddling abolitionist. However, Fitzhugh admitted in a letter to Holmes that
he had retouched the facts a little, "I assure you, Sir, I
see great evils in Slavery, but in a controversial work I
ought not to admit them." Finally, he added the usual Bible
arguments for slavery, adding that the Scriptures justified
all slavery regardless of race and hence supported his general theory of the universal character of slavery.

The second book, *Cannibals All! or Slaves Without Masters,* took its title and certain of its ideas from Carlyle's
Latter-Day Pamphlets (1850) and elaborated upon the
anti-liberal attack of the previous book. Its style, like that
of *Sociology for the South,* was polemical, repetitious and
ill-organized. Some of its half-plausible arguments and
reactionary conservatism suggested the propaganda of
twentieth-century totalitarianism. "My chief aim," he said,
"has been to shew that Labor makes values and Wit exploitates and accumulates them; and hence to deduce the
conclusion that the unrestricted exploitation of so-called
free society is more oppressive to the laborer than domestic slavery." Once more he drew from the intellectual ar-
senal of the socialists to attack industrial capitalism whose
practices were "little better than moral Cannibalism."

This time he argued that rents and interest are the
means by which Capital masters labor. Only under slavery
did the increase of a master's capital benefit the slave because he was a member of the plantation family. After all,
the author could say that Southerners commonly referred

to their slaves as "my people." Efforts by the Utopian communities to halt exploitation through cooperation had
failed because their prescriptions would cure the disease
by killing the patient. Capitalistic oppression did not take
its full toll in the North because of temporary exceptional
conditions, the safety valve afforded by the unoccupied
frontier—"in forty-eight hours laborers may escape to the
West and become proprietors." This formulation long
preceded the frontier theory of Frederick Jackson Turner
expressed in 1893. Furthermore, the incidence of all taxation fell upon the laborer who could not escape it; in fact,
capital accumulation worsened laboring conditions. "Thus
the poor are continually forging new chains for themselves." Possibly Fitzhugh knew of the *Communist Mani-
festo* of 1848 where some of his choice phrases had already appeared. Naturally he denied that the South shared
in the depressed condition of labor and he never considered the economic effects of race prejudice under ideals
of white supremacy upon the Negro worker.

He added many fresh illustrations of the evils of free
society, of the jungle atmosphere of a war of the classes,
and of the assumption that might makes right. In England economic and constitutional changes had enhanced
these injustices. The advance of the House of Commons
and the Bank of England meant the growth of the capitalist and moneyed interests, while the gains of the middle
class had been at the expense of the Tories, the Crown,
and the Church, all allies and guardians of the laboring
class. Fitzhugh ignored the true capitalistic economics of
the plantation system and the rising capitalistic spirit of
New Orleans, Richmond and Savannah.

Elsewhere *Cannibals All!* revived Edmund Burke's theory of virtual representation of the masses by a natural
elite. The ruling classes, so the author believed, must act
in the general interest according to their best lights. "The
mass of mankind," he held, "cannot be governed by law.
More of despotic discretion and less of law is what the
world wants." Liberty in the modern sense was unattain-
able and undesirable because its realization meant class
oppression; but a "true democracy" would equalize the
burdens of life according to capacity and ability. Presumably the pleasant arrangements of the Southern plantation amounted to a true democracy. Altogether, the tra-

ditionalistic arguments of Fitzhugh were not new and the illustrations were the common property of the mid-century, but his application of the socialistic indictments of liberalism as a Southern defense did have many elements of novelty. He raised certain fundamental issues of human freedom—which he scarcely solved—that have direct relevance today.

HINTON ROWAN HELPER AND *The Impending Crisis.*

3.

WHILE George Fitzhugh and James D. B. De Bow urged the solidarity of all white southerners, Hinton R. Helper of North Carolina called upon the nonslaveholding high-landers of the Southern Appalachians and on the small farmers to throw off the dominance of the planters. (None of these men, however, were concerned with the welfare of the Negro.)

Helper was born on December 27, 1829 in Rowan (now Davie) County, western North Carolina, on a small farm along the Yadkin River where nonslaveholders predominated, although Negroes were substantial in number. The large planters of the middle counties contested for power against the nonslaveholders. After 1850, Democrats from the eastern part of the state pressed for state's rights and even secession against western nationalist Whigs like the Helper family. By 1860, the year that Helper's book, *The Impending Crisis,* startled North Carolina especially as well as the nation, less than 28 per cent of Carolina families owned slaves and even this class averaged less than ten slaves per planter.[8]

[8] The most useful accounts of Helper are those of Theodore V. Theobald, "Hinton Rowan Helper and *The Impending Crisis,*" Master's Thesis, Political Science Department, Columbia University Library (June, 1949); Hugh T. Lefler, *Hinton Rowan Helper, Advocate of a White America* (Southern Sketches, No. 1, Charlottesville, Va., 1935); Benjamin F. Gilbert, "The Life and Writings of Hinton R. Helper," The register of the Kentucky Historical Society, 53 (1955), 58-75; William Polk, "The Hated Helper," *South Atlantic Quarterly,* XXX (1931), 177-189; and David R. Barbee, "Hinton Rowan Helper," *Tyler's Quarterly Historical and Genealogical Magazine,* XV (July,

In the Yadkin Valley, where Daniel Boone had once settled, many of the farmers were descendants of Scotch-Irish, Scotch and German pioneers, and Hinton's father, too, was a German migrant of colonial times. Jacob Helfer (as the family name appeared originally) came in 1752 from a rural area near Heidelberg, acquired a small farm, and left one 200-acre tract to two sons, one of which was Hinton. (Hinton was a fifth son and the seventh child). The youth afterwards recalled that he had plowed and harrowed many a long summer in the field—an implied rebuke to the proslavery tenet that only Negroes could adjust to manual field work in the South. Yet he claimed that his father had owned several slaves.

During the long winter nights, he read avidly in a cabin by the light of pine knots and thus escaped what he called "the prison grounds of those loathsome dungeons of illiteracy in which it has been the constant policy of the oligarchy to keep the masses, the nonslaveholding whites and the negroes, forever confined." This reference to the Negro however is misleading for he shared the common anti-Negro prejudices of so many of the small farmers and workers who regarded Negroes as competitors and beings of a low order. He attended a small academy and thus went far beyond his fellow North Carolinian, Andrew Johnson, in formal schooling, though both shared the common antagonism toward the large planters and (in greatly varying degrees) the white-man-supremacy emphasis. In Reconstruction years, Helper became a strong supporter of Johnson against the Radicals. The Helpers advanced rapidly up the ladder of middle-class respectability, for one brother became a newspaper editor, another a professor at the democratic citadel of Davidson College, and others succeeded in business.

For several years Helper worked as a clerk in a Salisbury bookstore and later became a partner in another book firm. Subsequently, he admitted to his employer that he had stolen small sums from the till, altogether about $300, but promised to make good on this theft. In 1850, Hinton went to New York where he was infected with the current gold fever, embarked on a clipper ship for California, and

1933), 145-172; and James G. de R. Hamilton, "Hinton R. Helper," *Dictionary of American Biography*, VIII, 517-518.

sailed around Cape Horn, acquiring a lasting interest, while cruising along the coast of South America, in the future of that continent.

His three years in California were very disappointing, for he failed to mine enough gold even to meet his expenses, but he took his revenge on this state by publishing a severely condemnatory book, *The Land of Gold* (1855). So extreme is its tone that a leading publisher even reproduced it in 1948 as a hoax under the title, *Dreadful California*.[9] He berated the state's urban squalor, crime, whisky-tippling, and even the climate, although he liked the Vigilante system and "the best people" who belonged to it. All Chinese looked alike to him and thrived on the traffic in immoral women, bad eating habits, filth, duplicity, extreme clannishness, and a superiority-complex toward whites. He concluded that Chinese immigration was undesirable and that all "inferior races" must become subordinate to the will of the Anglo-Saxon. The inferior peoples included not only the Chinese but the Irish, the American Indians and the Jews. In describing the California Jews, he revealed much more about his own crude antisemitic stereotypes of greed and depravity than about the Jews of California.

One passage in *The Land of Gold* which dealt with his return passage across Nicaragua was later singled out by his proslavery critics as evidence of his inconsistency and lack of integrity on the slavery issue:

> Nicaragua can never fulfill its destiny until it introduces negro slavery. Nothing but slave labor can ever subdue its forests and cultivate its unlimited lands. White men may live upon its soil with an umbrella in one hand and a fan in the other, but they can never unfold or develop its resources . . .

> The time may come when negro slaves will no longer be profitable in the United States, and it is also possible that the descendants of Ham may finally work their way beyond the present limits of our country.

Far from seeing any inconsistency between *The Land of Gold* and *The Impending Crisis* on the slave issue, Helper

---

[9] This book, edited by Lucius Beebe and Charles M. Clegg, was published in 1948 by Bobbs-Merrill.

later tried to bring out a new single edition of both volumes. He felt no compassion for Negroes, only a keen desire to eliminate slave competition and planter monopoly for the benefit of the Anglo-Saxon American worker and farmer. Slavery was doomed economically in the United States, but it had a future in Latin America. He did mention several instances of California slaves who were worse off in freedom than in bondage, but this meant only that while Negroes could adjust themselves to slavery, this was no argument for the perpetuation of the institution in the United States.

Back in Salisbury in 1854, the same year that Fitzhugh's *Sociology for the South* appeared, he too decided to enter the slavery controversy. He sniffed at propaganda novels such as *Uncle Tom's Cabin* as excellent for women, but held that only facts would do for men. The latest literary fashion in the controversy over slavery was for writers to arm themselves for the fray with economic statistics, and this tendency received a major impetus from De Bow's revealing Census of 1850.[10] This shocked proslavery men and correspondingly elated their foes because of the overwhelming evidence (which De Bow never quite explained away) that the Northern rate of material progress far exceeded that of the Cotton Kingdom. Here were the abundant statistics that Helper needed to make his case against the planter by attributing Southern backwardness and the depressed condition of the poorer whites entirely to slavery. He disregarded the fact that many nonslaveholders acted upon a belief that they held a decided stake in slavery because it served to police four million Negroes and maintained white supremacy, particularly in the hundreds of counties where Negroes outnumbered whites. Unlike Frank Owsley and the modern Vanderbilt University group of historians,[11] he overlooked the effect of Southern rural clannishness in mitigating the explosive possibilities of class wars between planters and

[10] Howard C. Perkins, "A Neglected Phase of the Movement for Southern Unity, 1847-1852," *The Journal of Southern History*, XII (1946), 153-203.

[11] Frank Owsley, *The Plain Folks of the Old South* (Louisiana State University Press, 1949); Guion G. Johnson, *Ante-Bellum North Carolina: A Social History* (University of North Carolina Press, 1937).

small farmers. Unfortunately for his purpose, he directed his appeal to a Southern class that was notoriously illiterate and could scarcely imbibe his arguments directly. A handful of Antislavery pulpits and the grapevine were not enough.

After a brief stay in North Carolina, he left for the North to complete and publish his manuscript. This was 1856, just before the Republicans met in their first presidential convention and stirred the South with the spectre of domination by a purely sectional party and a candidate devoted to the antislavery cause. In Baltimore Helper finished his manuscript and found time to organize a local Republican club, but a local mob dispersed the group. Politically he had long been a nationalist Whig of the Henry Clay school up to the time that he became a Republican, a shift that millions were to make. But the large publishers refused to take so belligerent a manuscript which they feared would antagonize their important Southern clientele; even abolitionist editors did not like its tone. Finally, the Burdick Brothers of New York agreed to issue the book if Helper would guarantee them against loss. In June, 1857, this 420-page book, *The Impending Crisis of the South: How to Meet It*, appeared in a substantial attractive format at the moderate price of one dollar.

He dedicated it to the nonslaveholding whites of the South and disavowed any desire to cast "unmerited opprobrium" upon slaveholders or "to display any special friendliness or sympathy for the blacks." His expressed intention was to concentrate upon the economic aspects of slavery insofar as the whites were concerned and only incidentally on the humanitarian side. This antislavery presentation he hoped would elevate the South to an honorable and powerful position among the enlightened quarters of the globe.

The main argument centered about the fact that the North and the South had been about equal in importance at the time that the Constitution was adopted, but that their relative position had been greatly changed since in favor of the North. Thus Massachusetts and North Carolina in 1790 had populations and economic output of similar size, but in 1850 the former greatly excelled in population, manufactures, farm and real-estate values, and in the extent of mass literacy. Southern dependence upon the North for almost everything had grown to absurd dimensions. For every article of utility and adornment, the South was compelled to go North—for matches and paintings, for steamships and statuary. Only the North had foreign trade, vast domestic markets and notable artists, for the South contributed nothing to literature, invention and the arts and failed to patronize its own manufacturers and mechanics. Once he completed this rather exaggerated indictment, he reduced the causes to one single factor—"slavery, and nothing but slavery, has retarded the progress and prosperity of our portion of the Union." Certainly, Frederick Law Olmsted, in his current writings which Helper knew at least at second-hand, had also believed that slavery held the South back, but he had avoided an unequivocal position except for the idea that slavery did not pay even for the master class.

As a confirmed racist, Helper ignored the rôle of anti-Negro prejudices in retarding the incentives and productivity of one-third of the South's total population. He gave no thought to the fact that relatively few suitable occupations were open even to the most gifted Negro—if he conceded the possibility that such able persons existed among that race. "To say nothing of the sin and shame of slavery," asserted the author, who did indeed say nothing on this score, "we believe it a most expensive and unprofitable institution." He singled out the miserably low status of the poor whites among nonslaveholders, attacked the proslavery apologists, and constantly reiterated his bitter scorn and contempt for the mind and conscience of "the lords of the lash."

In handling statistics for the two sections, he used the propagandist's prerogative of selecting those states whose development bolstered his thesis. Thus he compared unlike states such as Massachusetts with North Carolina, and Pennsylvania with South Carolina, and ignored the obvious evidences of the great internal migrations from the border states which led to the rapid growth of the vast Black Belt of the Deep South. In overstressing the dependence of the South upon the North, he did not allow for the usual reciprocal relationship between modern rural and urban areas. As for the question as to whether slavery paid in a purely economic sense, there are still able historians like Kenneth Stampp, author of *The Peculiar Institution,* who contend that it did.

Like other antislavery writers, he gave considerable attention to the weight of authorities against slavery, an emphasis that Republican campaigners thought especially useful. His challenging chapter on the barrenness of Southern literary genius and the scarcity of publishers offered some relevant, if not altogether adequate observations. "What has produced this literary pauperism of the South?" he demanded and of course the answer was always the same—the economic impoverishment due to slavery. Helper expressed his caustic disagreement with proslavery writers like De Bow (although he praised his statistical compilation), Fitzhugh, and William Gilmore Simms who urged the creation of a native Southern literature. "Thank God," said Helper, "a 'Southern literature' in the sense intended by the champions of slavery is a simple impossibility, rendered such by that exility of mind which they demand in its producers as a prerequisite to admission into the guild of Southern authorship." Finally, Helper offered a solution: Organize a nonslaveholders' party, tax slaveholding so heavily that it would cease to be profitable to anyone, and use certain other forms of pressure. He closed with a threat of mass action against the planter class.

THE RECEPTION AND INFLUENCE
OF *The Impending Crisis*

Helper's book sold well during the first year, aided generously by Horace Greeley and his *New York Tribune* which devoted no less than eight columns—a unique record—to what the reviewer described as one of the most remarkable antislavery works. Most of the review consisted of copious extracts from the book.[12] That conservative organ of the Boston Brahmins, *The North American Review,* stated that while it was an arresting fact that such a book should be written by the son of a slaveholder, the results were disappointing because the opprobrious

[12] New York *Weekly Tribune,* July 4, 1857; see digest of reviews in T. V. Theobald, *op. cit.;* for a critical attitude toward Helper see the New York *Herald,* November 26, 1859 and October 20, 1860.

rhetoric would neutralize its effect. All of the impressive statistics were offset by the terms of contempt for the slaveholder and the solution offered amounted to the instigation of civil war among Southerners. A violent emancipation could only leave the ex-slaves to face the wrongs of serfdom without protection.

William Lloyd Garrison of the *Liberator* liked Helper as much as he disliked Fitzhugh and praised the arguments of the North Carolinian as irrefutable and the facts unimpeachable. Extreme rhetoric of course did not disturb Garrison. Correspondingly, Southerners felt outraged and the North Carolina newspapers led all the rest in denouncing Helper as a traitor and renegade of the South. The *Raleigh Standard* of September 16, 1857 apostrophized, "Throw yourself into the arms of Fred Douglass, Hinton, and mingling, mix with that dark, infidel, and traitorous crew upon whose purses all your highest hopes now depend." This charge was most unfair since no white supremacist hated amalgamation more than Helper. Other North Carolina newspapers opened an attack upon Helper's integrity, particularly concentrating upon the story of Helper's early act of embezzlement.

By the end of the first year, *The Impending Crisis* had sold between thirteen and fourteen thousand copies, a rather high figure for a current work of non-fiction. It could scarcely compare of course with the millions of copies of novels written by "the scribbling women", to use Hawthorne's bitter phrase—Stowe, E.D.E.N. Southworth, and Maria S. Cummins, but then women accounted for so many of the readers of fiction. Republican leaders quickly saw the high propaganda value of an ardent antislavery book written by a Southerner and planned to issue an abbreviated edition or "Compendium" of 100,000 copies to spread the message of *The Impending Crisis*. Although the panic of 1857 discouraged subscribers to the publication fund and the Republicans were unable to use the *Compendium* in time for the Congressional elections, the project materialized in 1859, bringing a flood of Helper literature to the aid of the Republican candidate for the presidency. This was fortunate for the book because the year 1858 saw few sold and it seemed on the way to extinction. Some stimulus had to save it.

North Carolina proslavery politicians and journalists

kept the Helper agitation alive. In Congress, Senator Asa Briggs of that state struck back on April 3, 1858 against Republicans like the abolitionist senator from Massachusetts, Henry Wilson, who drew enthusiastically upon *The Impending Crisis* for antislavery ammunition. Briggs dwelt at length upon the facts of Helper's embezzlement and also charged him with robbing a bookstore partner in Salisbury:

> He is a dishonest, degraded and disgraced man and although—much to be regretted—a native of the State, yet he is an apostate son, ruined in fortune and character, and catering to a diseased appetite at the North to obtain a miserable living by slanders upon the land of his birth—had left the land of his birth for the good of the State.

This severe attack aroused Helper to take revenge upon his enemies and he rushed to the floor of the Senate and then the House, but did not find Briggs. He turned upon the North Carolina congressman from Salisbury, whom he assumed was Briggs' informant. One Southern spectator described him as "a tall, slim, peculiar-looking person, with short black hair, whiskers and mustaches, a very bronzed complexion, and a fierce military expression." On a nearly empty floor, the two men met, exchanged insults, and engaged in a rough-and-tumble fight which was definitely going in Helper's favor at the time that he was pulled away from the congressman. Helper, it was discovered, had taken no chances upon the outcome, for he carried on his person—like so many congressmen of that critical decade—a revolver and a bowie knife. However, no charges were pressed and the $1000 bond imposed on him to keep the peace was promptly paid by several Republican leaders.

North Carolina, then ruled by strict State Rights Democrats, campaigned to oust antislavery agitators like Helper. Quakers, antislavery Germans, college professors, and clergymen produced many rebels but their influence was almost extinguished by a growing intellectual and legislative blockade of free speech. At the University of North Carolina, Professor Benjamin S. Hedrick of the Chemistry Department had gone so far in his antislavery sentiments as to state publicly that he would vote for the

Republican presidential nominee if Frémont's name appeared on the state ticket. Innumerable letters and editorials in the North Carolina press demanded Hedrick's resignation, college alumni denounced him as a traitor, and some Southerners threatened to tar and feather him. Hedrick lost his post, but he continued to express antislavery views after leaving the state and even wrote that Helper's book was a study in economics which represented "perfectly the point of view of the educated and thinking non-slaveholder."[13]

When copies of *The Impending Crisis* were surreptitiously brought into the state, possessors were treated as guilty of incendiary activity. Local residents of High Point, North Carolina, seized a consignment of 150 copies and threw these into a bonfire in the public square. South Carolina and other Southern states reported similar incidents. When political enemies charged the governor of North Carolina with possession of the dangerous book, he explained that he had thrown one out of the window and used another to light his pipe!

North Carolina officials drove four ministers out for circulating *The Impending Crisis*. Of these cases, the *cause célèbre* was the trial of an aged Methodist minister, Daniel Worth, who was convicted of circulating the Helper book—a felony punishable by jail for not less than a year* and a public whipping; a second offense could mean the death penalty. Worth did receive the year's sentence, although the court remitted the public whipping because of his advanced age. He appealed to the state supreme court, but lost, since the judges were convinced that the book was incendiary. The elderly prisoner then spent a winter in jail, was released on bond, but decided to forfeit it and to go North where he might lecture upon the evils of slavery and earn enough to repay the bondsmen. From all this Southern ferment, Helper discreetly absented himself because, as one newspaper of his state put it, if he did return "North Carolina would make a home for him in the bosom of his native soil."

By the spring of 1859, Horace Greeley and other Re-

[13] William H. Gehrke, "Negro Slavery Among the Germans in North Carolina," *The North Carolina Historical Review*, XIV (1937), 307-324; Kenneth M. Stampp, "The Southern Refutation of the Proslavery Argument," *ibid.*, XXI (1944), *passim.*

publicans had financed the original project for 100,000
copies of the *Compendium* and were able to issue the book
at a trifling cost, in fact for nothing at all in many instances. The *Compendium* was a 214-page paper-bound
book whose small print compressed a large part of the
original work; it was quickly circulated through numerous
agents and bookstores which responded to the appeal of
the *New York Tribune* and active Republicans like Joseph
Medill of the *Chicago Tribune*. Although the sponsors
eliminated the originally extreme epithets and added
(through Helper) fresh material on "witnesses against
slavery," James Gordon Bennett's anti-reformist *New
York Herald* denounced the *Compendium* as "the text
book of Revolution" and even charged that Greeley and
his staff had themselves concocted *The Impending Crisis*.

Sixty-eight influential Republicans and Whigs, among
them John Sherman, William H. Seward and Joshua Gid-
dings, hastened to indorse the book publicly and to circulate it under the congressional frank. Antislavery writers
added to the tension by writing books, pamphlets and
articles to refute him. One of the most vehement anti-
Helper books was Samuel Wolfe's *Helper's Impending
Crisis Dissected* (Philadelphia, 1860), which dwelt upon
Helper's carelessness in handling statistics. By this time, the
Democrats understood how effective the Helper book was
as propaganda for the presidential election.

John Brown's startling attack on Harper's Ferry and
his hanging on Friday, December 2, 1859, pushed the lines
of tension to the breaking point. Southerners charged that
the North was instigating race war, but the New Eng-
landers of Ohio's Western Reserve went into mourning for
John Brown, and Emerson himself dropped his cautious
attitude toward sectional controversy by declaring that
Brown would make the gallows as glorious as the Cross.
On Monday, December 5, the House of Representatives
met with many of their members equipped with pistols
and bowie knives. One group of Democrats were determined to press for a showdown with those who had indorsed *The Impending Crisis*. This title had now become
grimly prophetic, although surprisingly few had actually
read the work before making up their minds that it was
actually an incendiary book.

The House was in no mood for the prosaic tempo of

law-making and the 109 Republicans who held a plurality were regarded with deep suspicion and fear by their opponents. The Democrats, it is true, had their own quarrel over the leadership of Stephen A. Douglas regarding slavery in Kansas; and a small number of Know-Nothings (the American Party) held the balance of power. Southerners talked of secession in the event a Republican became president and hot-headed members shouted challenges to a duel. An Illinois congressman replied menacingly to the angry Southerners, "By God, if I can't talk, I can do something else."

The first great test of partisan strength came over the choice of a Speaker of the House who, it had formerly been expected, would be John B. Sherman of Ohio. However a political bombshell came in the resolution of John B. Clark of Missouri:

> Resolved, That the doctrines and sentiments of a certain book called "The Impending Crisis of the South—How to Meet It," purporting to have been written by one Hinton R. Helper, are insurrectionary and hostile to the domestic peace and tranquility of the country, and that no member of this House who has endorsed and recommended it, or the Compend from it, is fit to be Speaker of this House.

Clark went on for two days to denounce Sherman as an indorser of the book and read extracts to prove its dangerous character. A supporter of the Clark resolution from Virginia argued that indorsers of the book were "not fit to live."

From December 5, 1859 to February 1, 1860, a fierce congressional debate raged, one of the bitterest in the memory of the oldest congressmen, while the prolonged voting on the speakership failed to give Sherman the few additional votes that he needed. This Ohio congressman was indeed embarrassed by being caught in an unusual predicament for so cautious a politician. He admitted to his brother, the illustrious William T. Sherman, that he had not read the book but had relied upon the fact that even a slaveholder had indorsed it. "It was a thoughtless, foolish, and unfortunate act." Everyone, he thought, knew his own moderate sentiment and firm opposition to anything that would drive the South to desperation. Other indorsers tried to escape the storm by denying that they subscribed to all of the Helper doctrines.

The excitement was transmitted to the country through detailed first-page coverage in the newspapers. Even the dignified Senate picked up the quarrels of the House while Southern leaders like Robert Toombs of Georgia and Alexander Stephens assailed "Helferism". The immediate excitement was lost amid other pressing issues on February 1, 1860 when Sherman gave up the fight and withdrew his name from the speakership contest, leaving the field to a compromise candidate free of Helperism.[14]

The last battle of *The Impending Crisis* was fought in a victorious cause which it substantially promoted. Republicans urging the election of Abraham Lincoln found the Helper appeal to the white farmer useful in the doubtful counties of the Old Northwest where the animosity for the planter was accompanied by no sympathy for the Negro. In those states where Negro migrants were not welcome, it was difficult to use antislavery arguments based on humanitarian grounds, but the small farmer could understand the monopolistic power of the planter as it cast its shadow across vast unused lands in the West. The bloody contest for free labor in Kansas had made the issue of slavery in the territories of immediate concern to the Old Northwest as well as to the North East.

Republicans estimated that the Helper book played a major part in winning certain doubtful areas for Lincoln, but the candidate himself deplored the extreme language of Helper as unwise and charged that Southern leaders had tried to use the book during the speakership contest as a clever tactic to split the young Republican party. Antislavery leaders such as Cassius M. Clay of Lexington helped to circulate Helper's book in the Southern Appalachians, but the pall of illiteracy and the organized proslavery forces hampered this effort.

[14] Ollinger Crenshaw, "The Speakership Contest of 1859-1860," *Mississippi Valley Historical Review*, XXIX (1942), 323-338; Emerson D. Fite, *The Presidential Campaign of 1860* (Macmillan, 1911), 33-46; W. G. Bean, "John Letcher and the Slavery Issue in Virginia's Gubernatorial Contest of 1858-1859," *The Journal of Southern History*, XX (1954), 22-49; James F. Rhodes, *History of the United States*, II, 417; Letters of John Sherman, *Century Magazine* (November, 1892), 90.

Democrats countered with anti-Helper literature such as Samuel Wolfe's book, *Helper's Impending Crisis Dissected*. It seemed particularly *apropos* to pit a Northerner, Gilbert J. Beebe, against Helper. Beebe's *A Review and Refutation of Helper's Impending Crisis* attacked the North Carolinian's statistics, his alleged falsehoods, his twisted logic which ignored such facts as that Boston had fallen from first place in population to seventh and was now outstripped by three Southern cities—surely not in keeping with the idea of slavery's all-destructive powers. Beebe charged that the North Carolinian had deliberately ignored the sensational growth in population since 1820 of Alabama, Mississippi and Missouri. If the Negroes were excluded from the reckoning, and he assumed that they should be, per capita figures on production and wealth would favor the South in many areas.

HELPER'S LATER CAREER.

Helper was indeed impressed by the turmoil that he had caused and watched the sales of his *Compendium* soar to 142,000 copies, but his book did not enrich him because this edition was not contracted upon a royalty basis. He tried to earn a living by public lecturing, but few people came to hear him and trouble-makers drove off some of his would-be auditors. Not even the encouragement and advertising of Horace Greeley's powerful newspaper, the *New York Tribune,* could fill the lecture-halls. As a result, Helper turned to his Republican friends to obtain some political office for him.

On November 13, 1861, Lincoln appointed him as consul to Buenos Aires. This afforded him a commercial background for the suits that he was later to bring against Latin American debtors on behalf of American claimants. He not only married a local Catholic lady but even submitted to a Catholic ceremony despite his vitriolic anti-Catholicism and he dwelt among a people whom he always regarded as racially inferior. Apparently his official activities left something to be desired, for his accounts showed a shortage of $6000 when he resigned on October 20,1866; but the tolerant Grant Administration indicated its forgiveness after its advent in 1869.

Once home, Helper reacted violently to the program of Radical Reconstruction which meant to him a program

of social and political equality for the races ending in amalgamation. He turned his prolific pen to a trilogy which
was essentially anti-Negro as well as anti-Radical and
pleased the Democrats so much that they used extracts for
propaganda just as the Republicans did in 1860. The
first book, *Nojoque: A Question for a Continent* (New
York, 1867), frankly asserted a primary object "to write
the negro out of America" and secondly "to write him out
of existence." He proposed that Negroes be removed to
Africa and that the Chinese must go too by 1900; in fact
he hoped that the entire world could in some way be left
to the dominion of the pure white races. Therefore, he
condemned all concessions to an inferior race, like those
presumably made by the Radicals, as stupidity and
knavery. To advance his ideal of white imperialism he
wished to redivide the world among twenty-one large
nations. This post-Civil War generation, not Helper alone,
had its virulent racist movements like the first Ku Klux
Klan, the lynching outbreaks of the 1880's and 1890's,
and the anti-Chinese agitation culminating in the Chinese
Exclusion Act. Abroad, imperialism was in full flower and
racist doctrines flourished as a justification for the domination of Asia and Africa by the West.

Many of the same racist ideas, only with fresh illustrations added, appear in his second anti-Negro book, *The
Negroes in Negroland* (New York, 1868), just in time to
aid the Democrats in the presidential race. By 1868 Helper
was strongly supporting his fellow-North Carolinian repre-
sentative of the small farmer, Andrew Johnson, now the
foe of the Radicals. The next book, *Noonday Exigencies
in America* (New York, 1871) tied his racist prejudices to
a program for a new political party which would overthrow the Radicals and save the South from hybridization.
Helper would "Americanize" the South by bringing in
Northern and European immigrants and by excluding
"inferior" races. Under a new constitution he would also
establish an honest Civil Service (like the Mugwumps or
Independents), strengthen the legal status of women,
punish drunkenness, and do much more to renovate a
White America. Other ideas suggested that this would
actually be a White Protestant nation.

Always vigorously active, he looked about for new

causes, stayed briefly in North Carolina, then moved to
the nation's capital where he became a lobbyist for claims
against South American countries. Many of these activities are set forth in great detail through his published
letters, official briefs, and general discussions in *Oddments
of Andean Diplomacy* (St. Louis, 1879). A very large
part of the book contained his insistent memorials to Congress on behalf of his clients against impecunious Latin
American governments. In his flamboyant style he denounced Bolivia for twenty years of procrastination in
paying a $25,000 claim whose legality and justice were
fully admitted by that government. He indicted Bolivia
as "the Insidious Author and Persistent Perpetrator of a
New International Crime." Civil wars in Bolivia, changes
of government, and national poverty accounted for most
of the delay and for a modest final settlement that did
not cover all of the accrued interest. In fighting Bolivia,
Helper importuned the successive Secretaries of State,
numerous congressmen, and prominent national figures for
aid, even urging the State Department to resort to force
if persuasion failed. In another protracted case, this time
against Brazil, he exploded against the "servile and sable subjects, jesuitry, bi-colored hybridity" of these people; but he finally won.

The greatest project of his life, the idea of a double-
track steel railway running through the length of the entire hemisphere along the Andes to the tip of South America is fully covered in *Oddments of Andean Diplomacy.*
This Three Americas Railway would connect the Southern Pacific Railway with a line through Mexico and Central
America, and then along a mountain chain to Cuzco,
Peru, and Santiago, Chile. Helper pursued every likely
sponsor—Carnegie, Rockefeller, Dom Pedro of Brazil—
took five trips to Latin America, and aroused public opinion through an essay contest which paid $5000 to the
winners, who could best depict the advantages of the
Railway. Apparently the scheme was not without merit,
for this was the day of the great transcontinental railroads,
and it had been indorsed by the United States representa-
tive to Peru and sympathetic congressional investigators.
But despite this constructive effort for Latin America's
future, Helper did not give up his dislike of what he re-

garded as a mongrel people—"a largely preponderating,
idle, vicious, and worthless population of negroes, Indians,
and bi-colored hybrids" living under the "fanatical sway
of Roman Catholicism."

But disappointments clung to him; others went ahead
with his projects and ignored him. In 1899, Helper's wife
deserted him while he was suffering declining fortunes,
though no shortage of grandiose plans. His old antislavery
friends apparently had long shunned him for what must
have been his racist ideas—although anti-Negro sentiments also appeared in blunt form in the writings of the
noted antislavery historians, James Ford Rhodes, John W.
Burgess, and others. Helper continued to attract attention in Washington and one correspondent described him
as a tall broad-shouldered man with florid large features
and a white beard. The reporter insisted that Charles
Dickens had immortalized Helper as the eccentric Grad-
grind of *Hard Times*, but the resemblance between the
North Carolinian and the Dickensian character is difficult
to perceive.[15]

Eventually, even the hardy Hinton Helper had to yield
to the inroads of old age—he was eighty in 1909. His
blandishments failed him in his efforts to solicit funds
from congressmen and friends and he was forced to live
abjectly under an assumed name in a cheap rooming house
on Pennsylvania Avenue. Finally, his mind gave way and
he committed suicide in his room on March 9, 1909.

Thus ended the life of an eccentric genius, steeped in
bigotry, erratic in his social solutions, yet hopeful of raising the status of millions of underprivileged Southern
whites. Like the Southern small farmers of the 1880's and
1890's who struggled against the power of the Bourbon
planters and industrialists, he would eliminate the Negro
as a factor by disfranchising or expelling him. Many
thousands had gone so far as to sanction the lynching of
Negroes—at least they did so by participating in the white
mobs who took justice into their own hands. Helper's own
racial bigotries are similar to those of the Dixie demagogues who retained power by capitalizing upon the feelings of racial insecurity as well as the economic weaknesses

[15] Hugh T. Lefler, *op. cit.*, passim; J. S. Bassett, "Anti-Slavery
Leaders of North Carolina," John Hopkins Studies, Series XVI,
No. 6, 15-23; Washington *Post*, March 10, 1909.

of the Southern rural white. The small farmer's battle against the Bourbon at the end of the nineteenth century bore some resemblance to Helper's war upon the Lords of the Lash despite the earlier question of slavery.

SOCIOLOGY FOR THE SOUTH

OR THE

FAILURE OF FREE SOCIETY.

BY GEORGE FITZHUGH.

THE THING THAT HAS BEEN, IT IS THAT WHICH SHALL BE;
AND THAT WHICH IS DONE IS THAT WHICH SHALL BE DONE;
AND THERE IS NO NEW THING UNDER THE SUN.—ECC. 1 9.

Naturam expelles furca, tamen usque recurret—Horace.

RICHMOND, VA.
A. MORRIS, PUBLISHER.
1854.

TO THE PEOPLE OF THE SOUTH.

WE DEDICATE this little work to you, because it is a zealous and honest effort to promote your peculiar interests. Society has been so quiet and contented in the South—it has suffered so little from crime or extreme poverty, that its attention has not been awakened to the revolutionary tumults, uproar, mendicity and crime of free society. Few are aware of the blessings they enjoy, or of the evils from which they are exempt.

From some peculiarity of taste, we have for many years been watching closely the perturbed workings of free society. Its crimes, its revolutions, its sufferings and its beggary, have led us to investigate its past history, as well as to speculate on its future destiny. This pamphlet has been hastily written, but is the result of long observation, some research and much reflection. Should it contain suggestions that will enlist abler pens to show that free society is a failure and its philosophy false, our highest ambition will be gratified. Believing our positions on these subjects to be true, we feel sanguine they are destined to final vindication and triumph. We should have written a larger work, had not our inexperience in authorship warned us that we had better await the reception of this. We may again appear in the character of writer before the public; but we shall not intrude, and would prefer that others should finish the work which we have begun. Treating subjects novel and difficult of comprehension, we have designedly indulged in iteration; for we preferred offending the ear and the taste of the reader, to confounding or confusing him by insufficient elaboration. In truth, fine finish and rotundity are not easily attained in what is merely argumentative and controversial.

On all subjects of social science, Southern men, from

their position, possess peculiar advantages when they undertake discussion. History, past and contemporaneous, informs them of all the phenomena of other forms of society, and they see every day around them the peculiarities and characteristics of slave society, of which little is to be learned from books. The ancients took it for granted that slavery was right, and never attempted to justify it. The moderns assume that it is wrong, and forthwith proceed to denounce it. The South can lose nothing, and may gain, by the discussion. She has, up to this time, been condemned without a hearing.

With respect, your fellow-citizen,
GEO. FITZHUGH.

PREFACE.

WE HESITATED some time in selecting the title of our work. We did not like to employ the newly-coined word Sociology. We could, however, find none other in the whole range of the English language, that would even faintly convey the idea which we wished to express. We looked to the history of the term. We found that within the last half century, disease, long lurking in the system of free society, had broken out into a hundred open manifestations. Thousands of authors and schemers, such as Owen, Louis Blanc and Fourier, had arisen proposing each a different mode of treatment for the disease which all confessed to exist. Society had never been in such a state before. New exigencies in its situation had given rise to new ideas, and to a new philosophy. This new philosophy must have a name, and as none could be found ready-made to suit the occasion, the term Sociology was compounded, of hybrid birth, half Greek and half Latin, as the technical appellative of the new-born science. In Europe, the term is familiar as "household words." It grates harshly, as yet, on Southern ears, because to us it is new and superfluous— the disease of which it treats being unknown amongst us. But as our book is intended to prove that we are indebted to domestic slavery, for our happy exemption from the social afflictions that have originated this philosophy, it became necessary and appropriate that we should employ this new word in our title. The fact that, before the institution of Free Society, there was no such term, and that it is not in use in slave countries, now, shows pretty clearly that Slave Society, ancient and modern, has ever been in so happy a condition, so exempt from ailments, that no doctors have arisen to treat it of its complaints, or to propose remedies for their cure. The term, therefore, is not only appropriate to the subject and the occasion, but pregnantly suggestive of facts and arguments that sustain our theory.

CHAPTER I.

FREE TRADE.

POLITICAL economy is the science of free society. Its theory and its history alike establish this position. Its fundamental maxims, *Laissez-faire* and *"Pas trop gouverner,"* are at war with all kinds of slavery, for they in fact assert that individuals and peoples prosper most when governed least. It is not, therefore, wonderful that such a science should not have been believed or inculcated whilst slavery was universal. Roman and Greek masters, feudal lords and Catholic priests, if conscientious, must have deemed such maxims false and heretical, or if unconscientious, would find in their self-interest sufficient reasons to prevent their propagation. Accordingly we find no such maxims current, no such science existing, until slavery and serfdom were extinct and Catholicism maimed and crippled, in the countries that gave them birth. Men belonging to the higher classes of society, and who neither feel nor apprehend the ills of penury or privation, are very apt to think little of those ills, and less of the class who suffer them. Especially is this the case with unobservant, abstract thinkers and closet scholars, who deal with little of the world and see less of it. Such men judge of mankind, their progress and their happiness, by the few specimens subjected to the narrow range of their experience and observation. After the abolition of feudalism and Catholicism, an immense amount of unfettered talent, genius, industry and capital, was brought into the field of free competition. The immediate result was, that all those who possessed either of those advantages prospered as they had never prospered before, and rose in social position and intelligence. At the same time, and from the same causes, the aggregate wealth of society, and probably its aggregate intelligence, were rapidly increased. Such was no doubt

part of the effects of unfettering the limbs, the minds and
consciences of men. It was the only part of those effects
that scholars and philosophers saw or heeded. Here was
something new under the sun, which refuted and rebuked
the wisdom of Solomon. Up to this time, one-half of mankind had been little better than chattels belonging to the
other half. A central power, with branches radiating
throughout the civilized world, had trammeled men's
consciences, dictated their religious faith, and prescribed
the forms and modes of worship. All this was done away
with, and the new world just started into existence was
certainly making rapid progress, and seemed to the ordinary observer to be very happy. About such a world,
nothing was to be found in books. Its social, its industrial
and its moral phenomena, seemed to be as beautiful as
they were novel. They needed, however, description,
classification and arrangement. Men's social relations and
moral duties were quite different under a system of universal liberty and equality of rights, from what they had
been in a state of subordination and dependence on the
one side, and of power, authority and protection on the
other. The reciprocal duties and obligations of master and
slave, of lord and vassal, of priest and layman, to each
other, were altogether unlike those that should be practiced between the free and equal citizens of regenerated
society. Men needed a moral guide, a new philosophy of
ethics; for neither the sages of the Gentiles, nor the Apos-
tles of Christianity, had foreseen or provided for the great
light which was now to burst upon the world. Moses, and
Solomon, and Paul, were silent as Socrates, Plato and Aristotle, as to this social Millenium, and the moral duties and
obligations it would bring in its train.

Until now, industry had been controlled and directed
by a few minds. Monopoly in its every form had been rife.
Men were suddenly called on to walk alone, to act and
work for themselves without guide, advice or control
from superior authority. In the past, nothing like it had
occurred; hence no assistance could be derived from
books. The prophets themselves had overlooked or
omitted to tell of the advent of this golden era, and were
no better guides than the historians and philosophers. A
philosophy that should guide and direct industry was
equally needed with a philosophy of morals. The occasion

found and made the man. For writing a one-sided philosophy, no man was better fitted than Adam Smith. He possessed extraordinary powers of abstraction, analysis and generalization. He was absent, secluded and unobservant. He saw only that prosperous and progressive portion of society whom liberty or free competition benefitted, and mistook its effects on them for its effects on the world. He had probably never heard the old English adage, "Every man for himself, and Devil take the hindmost." This saying comprehends the whole philosophy, moral and economical, of the "Wealth of Nations." But he and the political economists who have succeeded him, seem never to have dreamed that there would have been any "hindmost." There can never be a wise moral-philosopher, or a sound philosophy, till some one arises who sees and comprehends all the "things in heaven and earth." Philosophers are the most abstracted, secluded, and least observant of men. Their premises are always false, because they see but few facts; and hence their conclusions must also be false. Plato and Aristotle have to-day as many believers as Smith, Paley or Locke, and between their times a hundred systems have arisen, flourished for a time, and been rejected. There is not a true moral philosophy, and from the nature of things there never can be. Such a philosophy has to discover first causes and ultimate effects, to grasp infinitude, to deal with eternity at both ends. Human presumption will often attempt this, but human intellect can never achieve it. *We* shall build up no system, attempt to account for nothing, but simply point out what is natural and universal, and humbly try to justify the ways of God to man.

Adam Smith's philosophy is simple and comprehensive, (*teres et rotundus.*) Its leading and almost its only doctrine is, that individual well-being and social and national wealth and prosperity will be best promoted by each man's eagerly pursuing his own selfish welfare unfettered and unrestricted by legal regulations, or governmental prohibitions, farther than such regulations may be necessary to prevent positive crime. That some qualifications of this doctrine will be found in his book, we shall not deny; but this is his system. It is obvious enough that such a governmental policy as this doctrine would result in, would stimulate energy, excite invention and industry,

and bring into livelier action, genius, skill and talent. It
had done so before Smith wrote, and it was no doubt the
observation of those effects that suggested the theory.
His friends and acquaintances were of that class, who, in
the war of the wits to which free competition invited, were
sure to come off victors. His country, too, England and
Scotland, in the arts of trade and in manufacturing skill,
was an over-match for the rest of the world. International
free trade would benefit his country as much as social free
trade would benefit his friends. This was his world, and
had it been the only world his philosophy would have
been true. But there was another and much larger world,
whose misfortunes, under his system, were to make the fortunes of his friends and his country. A part of that world,
far more numerous than his friends and acquaintance was
at his door, they were the unemployed poor, the weak
in mind or body, the simple and unsuspicious, the prodi-
gal, the dissipated, the improvident and the vicious. *Laissez-faire* and *pas trop gouverner* suited not them; one
portion of them needed support and protection; the other,
much and rigorous government. Still they were fine subjects out of which the astute and designing, the provident
and avaricious, the cunning, the prudent and the industrious might make fortunes in the field of free competition.
Another portion of the world which Smith overlooked,
were the countries with which England traded, covering
a space many hundred times larger than England herself.
She was daily growing richer, more powerful and intellectual, by her trade, and the countries with which she
traded poorer, weaker, and more ignorant. Since the vast
extension of trade, consequent on the discoveries of Co-
lumbus and Vasco de Gama, the civilized countries of
Europe which carried on this trade had greatly prospered,
but the savages and barbarians with whom they traded
had become more savage and barbarous or been exterminated. Trade is a war of the wits, in which the stronger
witted are as sure to succeed as the stronger armed in a
war with swords. Strength of wit has this great advantage
over strength of arm, that it never tires, for it gathers new
strength by appropriating to itself the spoils of the vanquished. And thus, whether between nations or individuals, the war of free trade is constantly widening the relative abilities of the weak and the strong. It has been

justly observed that under this system the rich are continually growing richer and the poor poorer. The remark is true as well between nations as between individuals. Free trade, when the American gives a bottle of whiskey to the Indian for valuable furs, or the Englishman exchanges with the African blue-beads for diamonds, gold and slaves, is a fair specimen of all free trade when unequals meet. Free trade between England and Ireland furnishes the latter an excellent market for her beef and potatoes, in exchange for English manufactures. The labor employed in manufacturing pays much better than that engaged in rearing beeves and potatoes. On the average, one hour of English labor pays for two of Irish. Again, manufacturing requires and encourages skill and intelligence; grazing and farming require none. But far the worst evils of this free trade remain to be told. Irish pursuits depressing education and refinement, England becomes a market for the wealth, the intellect, the talent, energy and enterprise of Ireland. All men possessing any of these advantages or qualities retreat to England to spend their incomes, to enter the church, the navy, or the army, to distinguish themselves as authors, to engage in mechanic or manufacturing pursuits. Thus is Ireland robbed of her very life's blood, and thus do our Northern States rob the Southern.

Under the system of free trade a fertile soil, with good rivers and roads as outlets, becomes the greatest evil with which a country can be afflicted. The richness of soil invites to agriculture, and the roads and rivers carry off the crops, to be exchanged for the manufactures of poorer regions, where are situated the centres of trade, of capital and manufactures. In a few centuries or less time the consumption abroad of the crops impoverishes the soil where they are made. No cities or manufactories arise in the country with this fertile soil, because there is no occasion. No pursuits are carried on requiring intelligence or skill; the population is of necessity sparse, ignorant and illiterate; universal absenteeism prevails; the rich go off for pleasure and education, the enterprising poor for employment. An intelligent friend suggests that, left to nature, the evil will cure itself. So it may when the country is ruined, if the people, like those of Georgia, are of high character, and betake themselves to other pursuits than mere agriculture,

and totally repudiate free trade doctrines. Our friends'
objection only proves the truth of our theory. We are very
sure that the wit of man can devise no means so effectual
to impoverish a country as exclusive agriculture. The ravages of war, pestilence and famine are soon effaced; centuries are required to restore an exhausted soil. The more
rapidly money is made in such a country enjoying free
trade, the faster it is impoverished, for the draft on the soil
is greater, and those who make good crops spend them
abroad; those who make small ones, at home. In the absence of free trade, this rich region must manufacture for
itself, build cities, erect schools and colleges, and carry on
all the pursuits and provide for all the common wants of
civilized man. Thus the money made at home would be
spent and invested at home; the crops would be consumed
at home, and each town and village would furnish manure
to fertilize the soil around it. We believe it is a common
theory that, without this domestic consumption, no soil
can be kept permanently rich. A dense population would
arise, because it would be required; the rich would have
no further occasion to leave home for pleasure, nor the
poor for employment.

The valley of the Great Salt Lake is cut off by mountains from the rest of the world, except for travel. Suppose
it to continue so cut off, and to be settled by a virtuous,
enlightened people. Every trade, every art, every science,
must be taught and practiced within a small compass and
by a small population, in order to gratify their wants and
their tastes. The highest, most diffused and intense civilization, with great accumulation of wealth, would be the
necessary result. But let a river like the Mississippi pass
through it. Let its inhabitants become merely agricultural,
and exchange their products for the manufactures of
Europe and the fruits of Asia, and would not that civilization soon disappear, and with it the wealth and capital
of the country? Mere agriculture requires no skill or education, few and cheap houses, and no permanent outlay
of capital in the construction of the thousand edifices
needed in a manufacturing country. Besides, the consumption of the crops abroad would be cheating their
lands of that manure which nature intended for them.
Soon the rich and enlightened, who owned property there,

would, like Irish landlords, live and spend their incomes elsewhere.

The profits of exclusive agriculture are not more than one-third of those realized from commerce and manufactures. The ordinary and average wages of laborers employed in manufactures and mechanic trades are about double those of agricultural laborers; but, moreover, women and children get good wages in manufacturing countries, whose labor is lost in agricultural ones. But this consideration, great as it is, shrinks to insignificance compared with the intellectual superiority of all other pursuits over agriculture.

The centralizing effects of free trade alone would be sufficient to condemn it. The decline of civilization under the Roman Empire was owing solely to centralization. If political science has at all advanced since the earliest annals of history, that advance is the discovery that each small section knows best its own interests, and should be endowed with the most of the functions of government. The ancients, in the days of Herodotus, when the country around the Levant and the Islands in the Mediterranean were cut up into hundreds of little highly enlightened independent States, seem to have understood the evils of centralization quite as well as the moderns. At least their practice was wiser than ours, whatever may have been their theory. Political independence is not worth a fig without commercial independence. The tribute which the centres of trade, of capital, and of mechanical and artistic skill, such as England and the North exact from the nations they trade with, is more onerous and more destructive of civilization than that exacted from conquered provinces. Its effects everywhere are too obvious to need the citation of proofs and instances. Social centralization arises from the *laissez-faire* system just as national centralization. A few individuals possessed of capital and cunning acquire a power to employ the laboring class on such terms as they please, and they seldom fail to use that power. Hence, the numbers and destitution of the poor in free society are daily increasing, the numbers of the middle or independent class diminishing, and the few rich men growing hourly richer.

Free trade occasions a vast and useless, probably a very

noxious waste of capital and labor, in exchanging the
productions of different and distant climes and regions.
Furs and oils are not needed at the South, and the fruits
of the tropics are tasteless and insipid at the North. Providence has wonderfully adapted the productions of each
section to the wants of man and other animals inhabiting
those sections. It is probable, if the subject were scienti-
fically investigated, it would be found that the productions
of one clime when used in another are injurious and deleterious. The intercourse of travel and the interchange of
ideas it occasions advances civilization. The intercourse of
trade, by accustoming barbarous, savage and agricultural
countries to depend daily more and more on the centres
of trade and manufactures for their supplies of every thing
requiring skill or science for its production, rapidly depresses civilization. On the whole subject of civilization
there is a prevalent error. Man's necessities civilize him, or
rather the labor, invention and ingenuity needed to supply them. Relieve him of the necessity to exert those qualities by supplying through trade or other means his wants,
and he at once begins to sink into barbarism. Wars are fine
civilizers, for all men dread violent death; hence, among
barbarians, the implements of warfare are far superior to
any other of their manufactures, but they lead the way to
other improvements. The old adage, that "necessity is the
mother of invention," contains our theory; for invention
alone begets civilization. Civilization is no foreign hot-bed
exotic brought from distant climes, but a hardy plant of
indigenous birth and growth. There never was yet found a
nation of white savages, their wants and their wits combine to elevate them above the savage state. Nature,
that imposed more wants on them, has kindly endowed
them with superior intelligence to supply those wants.

Political economy is quite as objectionable, viewed as a
rule of morals, as when viewed as a system of economy.
Its authors never seem to be aware that they are writing
an ethical as well as an economical code; yet it is probable
that no writings, since the promulgation of the Christian
dispensation, have exercised so controlling an influence on
human conduct as the writings of these authors. The morality which they teach is one of simple and unadulterated
selfishness. The public good, the welfare of society, the
prosperity of one's neighbors, is, according to them, best

promoted by each man's looking solely to the advancement of his own pecuniary interests. They maintain that national wealth, happiness and prosperity being but the aggregate of individual wealth, happiness and prosperity, if each man pursues exclusively his own selfish good, he is doing the most he can to promote the general good. They seem to forget that men eager in the pursuit of wealth are never satisfied with the fair earnings of their own bodily labor, but find their wits and cunning employed in over-reaching others much more profitable than their hands. *Laissez-faire,* free competition begets a war of the wits, which these economists encourage, quite as destructive to the weak, simple and guileless, as the war of the sword.

In a book on society, evincing much power and originality of thought, by Stephen Pearl Andrews, this subject is well handled. We annex a short extract: "It follows, from what has been said, that the value principle is the commercial embodiment of the essential element of conquest and war—war transferred from the battle-field to the counter—none the less opposed, however, to the spirit of christian morality, or the sentiment of human brotherhood. In bodily conflict, the physically strong conquer and subject the physically weak. In the conflict of trade, the intellectually astute and powerful conquer and subject those who are intellectually feeble, or whose intellectual development is not of the precise kind to fit them for the conflict of wits in the matter of trade. With the progress of civilization and development, we have ceased to think that superior strength gives the *right* of conquest and subjugation. We have graduated in idea out of the period of physical dominion. We remain, however, as yet, in the period of intellectual conquest or plunder. It has not been questioned hitherto, as a general proposition, that the man who has superior intellectual endowments to others, has a right resulting therefrom to profit thereby at the cost of others. In the extreme applications of the admission only is the conclusion denied. (That is, as he had before said, 'You must not be too bad.' 'Don't gouge too deep.') In the whole field of what are denominated the legitimate operations of trade, there is no other law recognized than the relative 'smartness' or shrewdness of the parties, modified at most by the sentimental precept stated above."

It begets another war in the bosom of society still more

terrible than this. It arrays capital against labor. Every
man is taught by political economy that it is meritorious
to make the best bargains one can. In all old countries,
labor is superabundant, employers less numerous than
laborers; yet all the laborers must live by the wages they
receive from the capitalists. The capitalist cheapens their
wages; they compete with and underbid each other, for
employed they must be on any terms. This war of the rich
with the poor and the poor with one another, is the morality which political economy inculcates. It is the only morality, save the Bible, recognized or acknowledged in
free society, and is far more efficacious in directing worldly
men's conduct than the Bible, for that teaches self-denial,
not self-indulgence and aggrandizement. This process of
underbidding each other by the poor, which universal
liberty necessarily brings about, has well been compared
by the author of *Alton Locke** to the prisoners in the Black
Hole of Calcutta strangling one another. A beautiful system of ethics this, that places all mankind in antagonistic
positions, and puts all society at war. What can such a war
result in but the oppression and ultimate extermination
of the weak? In such society the astute capitalist, who is
very skilful and cunning, gets the advantage of every one
with whom he competes or deals; the sensible man with
moderate means gets the advantage of most with whom he
has business, but the mass of the simple and poor are outwitted and cheated by everybody.

Woman fares worst when thrown into this warfare of
competition. The delicacy of her sex and her nature pre-
vents her exercising those coarse arts which men do in the
vulgar and promiscuous jostle of life, and she is reduced
to the necessity of getting less than half price for her work.
To the eternal disgrace of human nature, the men who
employ her value themselves on the Adam Smith principle
for their virtuous and sensible conduct. "Labor is worth
what it will bring; they have given the poor woman more
than any one else would, or she would not have taken the
work." Yet she and her children are starving, and the employer is growing rich by giving her half what her work
is worth. Thus does free competition, the creature of free
society, throw the whole burden of the social fabric on
the poor, the weak and ignorant. They produce every

* A famous novel of working-class life, by Charles Kingsley
(1850).

thing and enjoy nothing. They are "the muzzled ox that treadeth out the straw."

In free society none but the selfish virtues are in repute, because none other help a man in the race of competition. In such society virtue loses all her loveliness, because of her selfish aims. Good men and bad men have the same end in view: self-promotion, self-elevation. The good man is prudent, cautious, and cunning of fence; he knows well, the arts (the virtues, if you please) which enable him to advance his fortunes at the expense of those with whom he deals; he does not "cut too deep"; he does not cheat and swindle, he only makes good bargains and excellent profits. He gets more subjects by this course; everybody comes to him to be bled. He bides his time; takes advantage of the follies, the improvidence and vices of others, and makes his fortune out of the follies and weaknesses of his fellow-men. The bad man is rash, hasty, unskilful and impolitic. He is equally selfish, but not half so prudent and cunning. Selfishness is almost the only motive of human conduct in free society, where every man is taught that it is his first duty to change and better his pecuniary situation.

The first principles of the science of political economy inculcate separate, individual action, and are calculated to prevent that association of labor without which nothing great can be achieved; for man isolated and individualized is the most helpless of animals. We think this error of the economists proceeded from their adopting Locke's theory of the social contract. We believe no heresy in moral science has been more pregnant of mischief than this theory of Locke. It lies at the bottom of all moral speculations, and if false, must infect with falsehood all theories built on it. Some animals are by nature gregarious and associative. Of this class are men, ants and bees. An isolated man is almost as helpless and ridiculous as a bee setting up for himself. Man is born a member of society, and does not form society. Nature, as in the cases of bees and ants, has it ready formed for him. He and society are congenital. Society is the being—he one of the members of that being. He has no rights whatever, as opposed to the interests of society; and that society may very properly make any use of him that will redound to the public good. Whatever rights he has are subordinate to the good of the whole; and he has never ceded rights to it, for he was born its slave, and had no rights to cede.

Government is the creature of society, and may be said to derive its powers from the consent of the governed; but society does not owe its sovereign power to the separate consent, volition or agreement of its members. Like the hive, it is as much the work of nature as the individuals who compose it. Consequences, the very opposite of the doctrine of free trade, result from this doctrine of ours. It makes each society a band of brothers, working for the common good, instead of a bag of cats biting and worrying each other. The competitive system is a system of antagonism and war; ours of peace and fraternity. The first is the system of free society; the other that of slave society. The Greek, the Roman, Judaistic, Egyptian, and all ancient polities, were founded on our theory. The loftiest patrician in those days, valued himself not on selfish, cold individuality, but on being the most devoted servant of society and his country. In ancient times, the individual was considered nothing, the State every thing. And yet, under this system, the noblest individuality was evolved that the world has ever seen. The prevalence of the doctrines of political economy has injured Southern character, for in the South those doctrines most prevail. Wealthy men, who are patterns of virtue in the discharge of their domestic duties, value themselves on never intermeddling in public matters. They forget that property is a mere creature of law and society, and are willing to make no return for that property to the public, which by its laws gave it to them, and which guard and protect them in its possession.

All great enterprises owe their success to association of capital and labor. The North is indebted for its great wealth and prosperity to the readiness with which it forms associations for all industrial and commercial purposes. The success of Southern farming is a striking instance of the value of the association of capital and laborers, and ought to suggest to the South the necessity of it for other purposes.

The dissociation of labor and disintegration of society, which liberty and free competition occasion, is especially injurious to the poorer class; for besides the labor necessary to support the family, the poor man is burdened with the care of finding a home, and procuring employment, and attending to all domestic wants and concerns. Slavery relieves our slaves of these cares altogether, and slavery is a form, and the very best form, of socialism. In fact, the ordinary wages of common labor are insufficient to keep up separate domestic establishments for each of the poor, and association or starvation is in many cases inevitable. In free society, as well in Europe as in America, this is the accepted theory, and various schemes have been resorted to, all without success, to cure the evil. The association of labor properly carried out under a common head or ruler, would render labor more efficient, relieve the laborer of many of the cares of household affairs, and protect and support him in sickness and old age, besides preventing the too great reduction of wages by redundancy of labor and free competition. Slavery attains all these results. What else will?

We find in the days of Sir Matthew Hale, a very singular pamphlet attributed to him. It was an attempt to prove that two healthy laborers, marrying and having in the usual time four children, could not at ordinary labor, and with ordinary wages, support their family. The nursing, washing, cooking and making clothes, would fully occupy the wife. The husband, with the chances of sickness and uncertainty of employment, would have to support four. Such is the usual and normal condition of free laborers. With six children, the oldest say twelve years of age, their condition would be worse. Or should the husband die, the family that remained would be still worse off. There are large numbers of aged and infirm male and female laborers, so that as a class, it is obvious, we think, that under ordinary circumstances, in old countries, they are incapable of procuring a decent and comfortable support. The wages of the poor diminish as their wants and families increase, for the care and labor of attending to the family leaves them fewer hours for profitable work. With negro slaves, their wages invariably increase with their wants. The master increases the provision for the family as the family increases in number and helplessness. It is a beautiful example of communism, where each one receives not according to his labor, but according to his wants.

A maxim well calculated not only to retard the progress

of civilization, but to occasion its retrogression, has grown out of the science of political economy. "The world is too much governed," has become quite an axiom with many politicians. Now the need of law and government is just in proportion to man's wealth and enlightenment. Barbarians and savages need and will submit to but few and simple laws, and little of government. The love of personal liberty and freedom from all restraint, are distinguishing traits of wild men and wild beasts. Our Anglo-Saxon ancestors loved personal liberty because they were barbarians, but they did not love it half so much as North American Indians or Bengal tigers, because they were not half so savage. As civilization advances, liberty recedes, and it is fortunate for man that he loses his love of liberty just as fast as he becomes more moral and intellectual. The wealthy, virtuous and religious citizens of large towns enjoy less of liberty than any other persons whatever, and yet they are the most useful and rationally happy of all mankind. The best governed countries, and those which have prospered most, have always been distinguished for the number and stringency of their laws. Good men obey superior authority, the laws of God, of morality, and of their country; bad men love liberty and violate them. It would be difficult very often for the most ingenious casuist to distinguish between sin and liberty; for virtue consists in the performance of duty, and the obedience to that law or power that imposes duty, whilst sin is but the violation of duty and disobedience to such law and power. It is remarkable, in this connection, that sin began by the desire for liberty and the attempt to attain it in the person of Satan and his fallen angels. The world wants good government and a plenty of it—not liberty. It is deceptive in us to boast of our Democracy, to assert the capacity of the people for self-government, and then refuse to them its exercise. In New England, and in all our large cities, where the people govern most, they are governed best. If government be not too much centralized, there is little danger of too much government. The danger and evil with us is of too little. Carlyle says of our institutions, that they are "anarchy plus a street constable." We ought not to be bandaged up too closely in our infancy, it might prevent growth and development; but the time is coming when we shall need more of government, if we would secure the permanency of our institutions.

All men concur in the opinion that some government is necessary. Even the political economist would punish murder, theft, robbery, gross swindling, &c.; but they encourage men to compete with and slowly undermine and destroy one another by means quite as effective as those they forbid. We have heard a distinguished member of this school object to negro slavery, because the protection it afforded to an inferior race would perpetuate that race, which, if left free to compete with the whites, must be starved out in a few generations. Members of Congress, of the Young American party, boast that the Anglo-Saxon race is manifestly destined to eat out all other races, as the wire-grass destroys and takes the place of other grasses. Nay, they allege this competitive process is going on throughout all nature; the strong are everywhere devouring the weak; the hardier plants and animals destroying the weaker, and the superior races of man exterminating the inferior. They would challenge our admiration for this war of nature, by which they say Providence is perfecting its own work—getting rid of what is weak and indifferent, and preserving only what is strong and hardy. We see the war, but not the improvement. This competitive, destructive system has been going on from the earliest records of history; and yet the plants, the animals, and the men of to-day are not superior to those of four thousand years ago. To restrict this destructive, competitive propensity, man was endowed with reason, and enabled to pass laws to protect the weak against the strong. To encourage it, is to encourage the strong to oppress the weak, and to violate the primary object of all government. It is strange it should have entered the head of any philosopher to set the weak, who are the majority of mankind, to competing, contending and fighting with the strong, in order to improve their condition.

Hobbes maintains that "a state of nature is a state of war." This is untrue of a state of nature, because men are naturally associative; but it is true of a civilized state of universal liberty, and free competition, such as Hobbes saw around him, and which no doubt suggested his theory. The wants of man and his history alike prove that slavery has always been part of his social organization. A less degree of subjection is inadequate for the government and protection of great numbers of human beings.

An intelligent English writer, describing society as he saw it, uses this language:

"There is no disguishing from the cool eye of philosophy, that all living creatures exist in a state of natural warfare; and that man (in hostility with all) is at enmity also with his own species; man is the natural enemy of man; and society, unable to change his nature, succeeds but in establishing a hollow truce by which fraud is substituted for violence."

Such is free society, fairly portrayed; such are the infidel doctrines of political economy, when candidly avowed. Slavery and Christianity bring about a lasting peace, not "a hollow truce." But we mount a step higher. We deny that there is a society in free countries. They who act each for himself, who are hostile, antagonistic and competitive, are not social and do not constitute a society. We use the term free society, for want of a better; but, like the term free government, it is an absurdity: those who are governed are not free—those who are free are not social.

CHAPTER II.

FAILURE OF FREE SOCIETY AND
RISE OF SOCIALISM.

THE phenomena presented by the vassals and villiens of Europe after their liberation, were the opposite of those exhibited by the wealthy and powerful classes. Pauperism and beggary, we are informed by English historians, were unknown till the villiens began to escape from their masters, and attempted to practise a predatory and nomadic liberty. A liberty, we should infer from the descriptions we can get of it, very much like that of domestic animals that have gone wild—the difference in favor of the animals being that nature had made provision for them, but had made none for the villiens. The new freemen were bands of thieves and beggars, infesting the country and disturbing its peace. Their physical condition was worse than when under the rule of the Barons, their masters, and their moral condition worse also, for liberty had made them from necessity thieves and murderers. It was necessary to retain them in slavery, not only to support and sustain them and to prevent general mendicity, but equally necessary in order to govern them and prevent crime. The advocates of universal liberty concede that the laboring class enjoy more material comfort, are better fed, clothed and housed, as slaves, than as freemen. The statistics of crime demonstrate that the moral superiority of the slave over the free laborer is still greater than his superiority in animal well-being. There never can be among slaves a class so degraded as is found about the wharves and suburbs of cities. The master requires and enforces ordinary morality and industry. We very much fear, if it were possible to indite a faithful comparison of the conduct and comfort of our free negroes with that of the runaway Anglo-Saxon serfs, that it would be found that the negroes have fared better and committed much less crime than the whites. But those days, the 14th and 15th centuries, were the halcyon days of vagabond liberty. The few that had escaped from bondage found a wide field and plenty of subjects for the practice of theft and mendicity. There was no law and no police adequate to restrain them, for until then their masters had kept them in order better than laws ever can. But those glorious old times have long since passed. A bloody code, a standing army and efficient police keep them quiet enough now. Their numbers have multiplied a hundred fold, but their poverty has increased faster than their numbers. Instead of stealing and begging, and living idly in the open air, they work fourteen hours a day, cooped up in close rooms, with foul air, foul water, and insufficient and filthy food, and often sleep at night crowded in cellars or in garrets, without regard to sex.

In proceeding to prove that this is a correct account of the effects in England of liberating the laboring class, we are at much difficulty how to select from the mass of testimony that at every turn presents itself to us. We are not aware that any one disputes the fact that crime and pauperism throughout Western Europe increased *pari passu* with liberty, equality and free competition. We know of but a single respectable authority that disputes the fact that this increase is directly attributable to free competition or liberty. Even the Edinburgh Review, hitherto the great champion of political economy and free competition, has been silent on the subject for several years. With strange inconsistency, the very men who assert that universal liberty has, and must ever, from the nature of things, increase crime, mendicity and pauperism among the laboring class, maintain that slavery degrades this very class whom it preserves from poverty and crime. The elevation of the scaffold is the only moral or physical elevation that they can point to which distinguishes the condition of the free laborer from his servile ancestor. The peasantry of England, in the days of Cressey, Agincourt and Shrewsbury, when feudalism prevailed, were generally brave, virtuous, and in the enjoyment of a high degree of physical comfort—at least, that comfort differed very little from that of their lords and masters. This same peasantry, when Charles Edward with three thousand

Highlanders invaded England, had become freemen and cowards. Starving Frenchmen will at least fight, but starving Chartists only bluster. How slavery could degrade men lower than universal liberty has done, it is hard to conceive; how it did and would again preserve them from such degradation, is well explained by those who are loudest in its abuse. A consciousness of security, a full comprehension of his position, and a confidence in that position, and the absence of all corroding cares and anxieties, makes the slave easy and self-assured in his address, cheerful, happy and contented, free from jealousy, malignity, and envy, and at peace with all around him. His attachment to his master begets the sentiment of loyalty, than which none more purifies and elevates human nature. This theory of the moral influences of slavery is suggested and in part borrowed from Alexandre Dumas' "French Milliner." He, descended from a negro slave, and we may presume prejudiced against slavery, speaks in glowing terms of its happy influence on the lives and manners of the Russian serfs. He draws a contrast between their cheerfulness and the wretchedness of the French laboring class, and attributes solely to the feeling of security which slavery induces, their enviable cheerfulness.

The free laborer rarely has a house and home of his own; he is insecure of employment, sickness may overtake him at any time and deprive him of the means of support; old age is certain to overtake him, if he lives, and generally finds him without the means of subsistence; his family is probably increasing in numbers, and is helpless and burdensome to him. In all this there is little to incite to virtue, much to tempt to crime, nothing to afford happiness, but quite enough to inflict misery. Man must be more than human, to acquire a pure and a high morality under such circumstances.

In free society the sentiments, principles, feelings and affections of high and low, rich and poor, are equally blunted and debased by the continual war of competition. It begets rivalries, jealousies and hatreds on all hands. The poor can neither love nor respect the rich, who, instead of aiding and protecting them, are endeavoring to cheapen their labor and take away their means of subsistence. The rich can hardly respect themselves, when they reflect that wealth is the result of avarice, caution, circumspection and hard dealing. These are the virtues which free society in its regular operation brings forth. Its moral influence is therefore no better on the rich than on the poor. The number of laborers being excessive in all old countries, they are continually struggling with, scandalizing and underbidding each other, to get places and employment. Every circumstance in the poor man's situation in free society is one of harassing care, of grievous temptation, and of excitement to anger, envy, jealousy and malignity. That so many of the poor should nevertheless be good and pure, kind, happy and high-minded, is proof enough that the poor class is not the worst class in society. But the rich have their temptations, too. Capital gives them the power to oppress; selfishness offers the inducement, and political economy, the moral guide of the day, would justify the oppression. Yet there are thousands of noble and generous and disinterested men in free society, who employ their wealth to relieve, and not to oppress the poor. Still these are exceptions to the general rule. The effect of such society is to encourage the oppression of the poor.

The ink was hardly dry with which Adam Smith wrote his Wealth of Nations, lauding the benign influences of free society, ere the hunger and want and nakedness of that society engendered a revolutionary explosion that shook the world to its centre. The starving artisans and laborers, and fish-women and needle-women of Paris, were the authors of the first French revolution, and that revolution was everywhere welcomed, and spread from nation to nation like fire in the prairies. The French armies met with but a formal opposition, until they reached Russia. There, men had homes and houses and a country to fight for. The serfs of Russia, the undisciplined Cossacks, fought for lares and penates, their homes, their country, and their God, and annihilated an army more numerous than that of Xerxes, and braver and better appointed than the tenth legion of Caesar. What should Western European poor men fight for? All the world was the same to them. They had been set free to starve, without a place to rest their dying heads or to inter their dead bodies. Any change they thought would be for the better, and hailed Buonaparte as a deliverer. But the nature of the evil was not understood: there were some remnants of feudalism, some vigor in the Catholic church; these Buonaparte swept away, and left the poor without a stay or a hope. Buonaparte is conquered and banished, universal peace restored: commerce, mechanic arts, manufactures and agriculture revive and flourish; invention is stimulated, industry urged on to its utmost exertion. Never seemed the world so prosperous, so happy, so progressive. But only seemed! Those awful statistics unfold the sad tale that misery and crime and poverty are on the increase still. The prisons are filled, the poor houses and the penal colonies supplied too fast, and the gallows ever pendant with its subject. In 1830, Paris starves again, builds barricades, continues hungry, and hesitates what next to do. Finally sets up a new king, no better than the one she has expelled. Revolution follows revolution with electric speed throughout a great part of Western Europe. Kings are deposed, governments changed; soon new kings put in their places, and things subside—not quietly—into the *status quo ante bellum*. All this, while millions of the poor are fleeing from Europe as men fly from an infected plague spot, to seek their fortunes in other climes and regions. Another eighteen years of hunger, of crime, of riots, strikes, and trades unions, passes over free society. In 1848 the drama of 1830 is almost literally re-enacted. Again Paris starves, builds barricades, and expels her king. Again Western Europe follows her example. By this time, however, men had discovered that political changes would not cure the diseases of society. The poor must have bread; government must furnish it. Liberty without bread was not worth fighting for. A Republic is set up in Paris that promises employment and good wages to every body. The experiment is tried and fails in a week. No employment, except transplanting trees and levelling mounds, could be found, and the treasury breaks. After struggling and blundering and staggering on through various changes, Louis Napoleon is made Emperor. He is a socialist, and socialism is the new fashionable name of slavery. He understands the disease of society, and has nerve enough for any surgical operation that may be required to cure it. His first step in socialism was to take the money of the rich to buy wheat for all. The measure was well-timed, necessary and just. He is now building houses on the social plan for working men, and his Queen is providing nurseries and nurses for the chil-

dren of the working women, just as we Southerners do for
our negro women and children. It is a great economy. Fourier suggested it long after Southerners had practiced it.
During these times there was a little episode in Ireland—
Ireland, the freest country in the world, where law is vio-
lated every day, mocked at and derided, whence the rich
and the noble have emigrated, where all are poor, all
equal, and all idle. A few thousands only had usually
starved annually; but the potatoe crop failed; they had no
feudal lords to buy other food for them, and three hundred
thousand starved in a single season. No slave or serf ever
did starve, unless he were a runaway. Irishmen, although
they love liberty to distraction, have lost their taste for
starving. They are coming *en masse* to America, and in a
few years, at the present rate of emigration, will leave the
island without inhabitants. The great and increasing emigration from free society in Europe can only be accounted
for on the ground that they believe their social system so
rotten that no mere political change can help them—for a
political revolution can be had on twenty-four hours' notice.

The Chartists and Radicals of England would in some
way subvert and re-construct society. They complain of
free competition as a crying evil, and may be classed with
the Socialists. The high conservative party called Young
England vainly endeavors, by preaching fine sentiments,
to produce that good feeling between the rich and the
poor, the weak and the powerful, which slavery alone can
bring about. Liberty places those classes in positions of
antagonism and war. Slavery identifies the interests of rich
and poor, master and slave, and begets domestic affection
on the one side, and loyalty and respect on the other.
Young England sees clearly enough the character of the
disease, but is not bold enough to propose an adequate
remedy. The poor themselves are all practical Socialists,
and in some degree pro-slavery men. They unite in strikes
and trades unions, and thus exchange a part of their liberties in order to secure high and uniform wages. The exchange is a prudent and sensible one; but they who have
bartered off liberty, are fast verging towards slavery.
Slavery to an association is not always better than slavery
to a single master. The professed object is to avoid ruinous
underbidding and competition with one another; but this

competition can never cease whilst liberty lasts. Those who wish to be free must take liberty with this inseparable burden. Odd-Fellows' societies, temperance societies, and all other societies that provide for sick and unfortunate members, are instances of Socialism. The muse in England for many years has been busy in composing dissonant laborer songs, bewailing the hardships, penury and sufferings of the poor, and indignantly rebuking the cruelty and injustice of their hard-hearted and close-fisted employers.

Dickens and Bulwer denounce the frame-work of society quite as loudly as Carlyle and Newman, the two latter of whom propose slavery as a remedy for existing evils. A large portion of the clergy are professed Socialists, and there is scarcely a literary man in England who is not ready to propose radical and organic changes in her social system. Germany is full of Communists; social discontent is universal, and her people are leaving *en masse* for America—hopeless of any amelioration at home for the future. Strange to tell, in the free States of America too, Socialism and every other heresy that can be invoked to make war on existing institutions, prevail to an alarming extent. Even according to our own theory of the necessity of slavery, we should not suppose that that necessity would be so soon felt in a new and sparsely-settled country, where the supply of labor does not exceed the demand. But it is probable the constant arrival of emigrants makes the situation of the laborer at the North as precarious as in Europe, and produces a desire for some change that shall secure him employment and support at all times. Slavery alone can effect that change; and towards slavery the North and all Western Europe are unconsciously marching. The master evil they all complain of is free competition—which is another name for liberty. Let them remove that evil, and they will find themselves slaves, with all the advantages and disadvantages of slavery. They will have attained association of labor, for slavery produces association of labor, and is one of the ends all Communists and Socialists desire. A well-conducted farm in the South is a model of associated labor that Fourier might envy. One old woman nurses all the children whilst the mothers are at work; another waits on the sick, in a house set aside for them. Another washes and cooks, and a fourth makes and mends the clothing. It is a great economy of labor, and is a good idea

of the Socialists. Slavery protects the infants, the aged and
the sick; nay, takes far better care of them than of the
healthy, the middle-aged and the strong. They are part of
the family, and self-interest and domestic affection combine
to shelter, shield and foster them. A man loves not only
his horses and his cattle, which are useful to him, but he
loves his dog, which is of no use. He loves them because
they are his. What a wise and beneficent provision of
Heaven, that makes the selfishness of man's nature a protecting ægis to shield and defend wife and children, slaves
and even dumb animals. The Socialists propose to reach
this result too, but they never can if they refuse to march
in the only road Providence has pointed out. Who will
check, govern and control their superintending authority?
Who prevent his abuse of power? Who can make him
kind, tender and affectionate, to the poor, aged, helpless,
sick and unfortunate? *Quis custodiet custodes?* Nature es-
tablishes the only safe and reliable checks and balances in
government. *Alton Locke* describes an English farm, where
the cattle, the horses and the sheep are fat, plentifully fed
and warmly housed; the game in the preserves and the
fish in the pond carefully provided for; and two freezing,
shivering, starving, half-clad boys, who have to work on
the Sabbath, are the slaves to these animals, and are
vainly endeavoring to prepare their food. Now it must
have occurred to the author that if the boys had belonged
to the owner of the farm, they too would have been well-
treated, happy and contented. This farm is but a miniature
of all England; every animal is well-treated and provided
for, except the laboring man. He is the slave of the brutes,
the slave of society, produces everything and enjoys nothing. Make him the slave of one man, instead of the slave of
society, and he would be far better off. None but lawyers
and historians are aware how much of truth, justice and
good sense, there is in the notions of the Communists, as to
the community of property. Laying no stress on the too
abstract proposition that Providence gave the world not
to one man, or set of men, but to all mankind, it is a fact
that all governments, in civilized countries, recognize the
obligation to support the poor, and thus, in some degree,
make all property a common possession. The poor laws
and poor houses of England are founded on communistic
principles. Each parish is compelled to support its own

poor. In Ireland, this obligation weighs so heavily as in many instances to make farms valueless; the poor rates exceeding the rents. But it is domestic slavery alone that can establish a safe, efficient and humane community of property. It did so in ancient times, it did so in feudal times, and does so now, in Eastern Europe, Asia and America. Slaves never die of hunger; seldom suffer want. Hence Chinese sell themselves when they can do no better. A Southern farm is a sort of joint stock concern, or social phalanstery, in which the master furnishes the capital and skill, and the slaves the labor, and divide the profits, not according to each one's in-put, but according to each one's wants and necessities.

Socialism proposes to do away with free competition; to afford protection and support at all times to the laboring class; to bring about, at least, a qualified community of property, and to associate labor. All these purposes, slavery fully and perfectly attains.

To prove the evil effects, moral, social and economic, of the emancipation of feudal slaves or villiens, and how those evil effects gave birth to Socialism, we quote first from the Pictorial History of England:

"To the period (15th century) immediately preceding the present, belongs the origin of English pauperism, as well as of the legislation on the subject of the poor. So long as the system of villienage was maintained in its integrity, there could be no paupers in the land; that is to say, no persons left destitute of the means of subsistence, except beggary or public alms. The principle of that institution was, that every individual who had nothing else, had at least a right of food and shelter from the landed proprietor whose bondsman he was. The master was not more entitled to the services of his villien, than the villien was to the maintenance of himself and his family, at the expense of his master. This has of absolute necessity been the law in every country in which slavery has existed. * * * * But as soon as the original slavery of the English laboring population begun to be exchanged for freedom, and villienage gradually, and at last generally passed away in the manner stated in the last book, the working man, now his own master, was of course left in all circumstances to his own resources; and when either want of employment, or sickness, or the helplessness of old

age came upon him, if he had not saved something from
his former earnings, and had no one to take care of him
from motives of affection or compassion, his condition was
as unprovided for as that of the fowls of the heavens. But
men will not starve, whilst they can either beg or steal;
hence, the first appearance that the destitute poor, as a
class of the community, make in our annals, is in the character of *thieves* and mendicants, sometimes enforcing their
demands by threats or violence."—Vol. 2d, pages 262,
263.

Such is the description of free society at its birth, by
authors who hate and denounce slavery. We will proceed
to prove from like authority, that the number of mendicants and thieves has increased with accelerating speed
from that day to this.

We find in Hume's History of England, treating of the
discontents of the people in the reign of Edward VI., the
following language:

"There is no abuse in civil society so great as not to be
attended with a variety of beneficial consequences; and in
the beginnings of reformation, the loss of these advantages
is always felt very sensibly, while the benefit resulting
from the change is the slow effect of time, and is seldom
perceived by the bulk of the nation. Scarce any institution
can be imagined less favorable in the main to the interests of mankind, than that of monks and friars; yet was it
followed by many good effects, which having ceased by
the suppression of the monasteries, were much regretted
by the people of England. The monks always residing in
their convents in the centre of their estates, spent their
money in the provinces, and among their tenants, afforded
a ready market for commodities, and were a sure resource
to the poor and indigent; and though their hospitality and
charity gave too much encouragement to idleness and prevented the increase of public riches, yet did it provide to
many a relief from the extreme pressure of want and necessity."

In the Pictorial History of England, under the head of
the Condition of the People, about the 16th and 17th centuries, we find crime and pauperism still on the increase,
and hundreds of essays and books written and many acts
of Parliament passed on this perplexing and growing evil
in free society. But it was after Napoleon had made a dead

level of Western European society, a sort of *"tabula raza,"*
by destroying the remnants of feudalism and crippling and
cramping the Catholic Church, that liberty and free competition were first given free scope and elbow-room. Not
till then had the doctrines, that "might makes right" and
"every man for himself, and devil take the hindmost," been
brought into full play. The natural consequence was, that
the strong conquered and devoured the weak much faster
than they had ever done before. The world of the political economists, the rich, the astute, the avaricious, the prudent, the circumspect and hard-hearted, started forward
with railroad speed and railroad recklessness. The world
of the Socialists, (vastly increased in numbers,) the poor,
the weak, ignorant, generous and improvident, ran backwards quite as fast as the other world went forward. Almost every middle-aged man who can read a newspaper
is aware, that whilst the aggregate wealth of civilized mankind has increased more rapidly since the fall of Napoleon
than it ever did before, and whilst the discoveries and inventions in physical science have rapidly lessened the
amount of labor necessary to procure human subsistence
and comfort, yet these advantages have been monopolized by the few, and the laboring millions are in worse
condition (in free society) than they ever were before. On
this subject we shall quote from two able articles in Blackwood, not because our positions need proof, but because
these quotations will throw much light on the character of
the disease under which free society is suffering, and show
that protection of some kind is imperiously demanded to
shield the masses from the grinding oppression of universal
liberty, free competition and *laissez-faire,* and to show that
it is the carrying into practical operation the theories of the
political economists, or free trade men, that has occasioned
the unexampled progress and prosperity of the few who
are strong, and the appalling and increasing crime and
destitution of the many, who are weak. Further, these
quotations will sustain and illustrate our doctrine that the
political economists have taken partial views of society,
and have mistaken the good luck and success of their
friends for the general condition and fortune of mankind.
Blackwood seems to contemplate protection against foreign competition as an adequate remedy. We leave it to
the intelligent reader to say, whether protection against

social and domestic competition is not quite as necessary
—and nothing but slavery can afford this latter protection.

In a review of *Alton Locke* in Blackwood, Nov. No.
1850, the following passages will be found:

"No man with a human heart in his bosom, unless that
heart is utterly indurated and depraved by the influence of
mammon, can be indifferent to the fate of the working
classes. Even if he were not urged to consider the awful
social questions which daily demand our attention in this
perplexing and bewildered age, by the impulses of humanity or by the call of Christian duty, the lower motive of interest alone should incline him to serious reflection on a
subject which involves the well-being, both temporal and
eternal, of thousands of his fellow-beings, and possibly the
permanence of order and tranquility in this realm of Great
Britain. Our civil history during the last thirty years of
peace, resembles nothing which the world has yet seen or
which can be found in the records of civilization. The
progress which has been made in the mechanical sciences
is of itself almost equivalent to a revolution. The whole
face of society has been altered; old employments have
become obsolete, old customs have been altered or remodelled, and old institutions have undergone innovation.
The modern citizen thinks and acts differently from his fathers. What to them was object of reverence, is to him
subject of ridicule; what they were accustomed to prize
and honor, he regards with undisguised contempt. All this
we call improvement, taking no heed the while whether
such improvement has fulfilled the primary condition of
contributing to and increasing the welfare and prosperity
of the people. Statistical books are written to prove how
enormously we have increased in wealth; and yet, side by
side with Mr. Porter's bulky tome, you will find pamphlets
containing ample and distinct evidence that hundreds of
thousands of our industrious fellow-countrymen are at this
moment famishing for lack of employment, or compelled
to sell their labor for such wretched compensation, that
the pauper's dole is by many regarded with absolute envy.
Dives and Lazarus elbow one another in the street, *and
our political economists select Dives as the sole type of the
nation.* Sanitary commissioners are appointed to whiten the
outside of the sepulchre; and during the operation their

stomachs are made sick by the taint of the rottenness
within. The reform of Parliament is, comparatively speaking, a matter of yesterday; and yet the operatives are peti-
tioning for the charter!

These are stern realities, grave facts, which it is impossible to gainsay. What may be the result of them, unless
some adequate remedy can be provided, it is impossible
with certainty to predict; but unless we are prepared to
deny the doctrine of that retribution which has been directly revealed to us from above, and of which the history
of neighboring states affords us so many striking examples,
we can hardly expect to remain unpunished for what is
truly a national crime. The offence, indeed, according to
all the elements of human calculation, is likely to bring
its own punishment. It cannot be that society can exist in
tranquility, or order be permanently maintained, so long
as a large portion of the working classes, of the hard-
handed men whose industry makes capital move and multiply itself, are exposed to the operation of a system that
makes their position less tolerable than that of Egyptian
bondsmen. To work is not only a duty, but a privilege; but
to work against hope, to toil under the absolute pressure
of despair, is the most miserable lot that the imagination
can possibly conceive. It is, in fact, a virtual abrogation
of that freedom which every Briton is taught to consider
his birthright, but which now, however well it may sound
as an abstract term, is practically, in the case of thousands,
placed utterly beyond their reach.

We shall not probably be suspected of any intention to
inculcate radical doctrines. We have no sympathy, but the
reverse, with the quacks, visionaries and agitators, who
make a livelihood by preaching disaffection in our towns
and cities, and who are the worst enemies of the people
whose cause they pretend to advocate. We detest the selfish views of the Manchester school of politicians, and we
loathe that hypocrisy which, under the pretext of reform-
ing, would destroy the institutions of the country. But,
if it be true, as we believe it to be, that the working and
producing classes of the community are suffering unexampled hardship, and that not of a temporary and exceptional kind, but from the operation of some vicious and
baneful element that has crept into our social system, it
then becomes our duty to attempt to discover the actual

nature of the evil; and, having discovered that, to consider seriously what cure it is possible to apply." * * *
"Here is a question urgently presenting itself to the consideration of all thinking men; a question which concerns the welfare of hundreds of thousands; a question which has been evaded by statesmen so long as they dared to do so with impunity; but which now can be no longer evaded: that question being, whether any possible means can be found for ameliorating and improving the condition of the working classes of Great Britain, by rescuing them *from the cruel effects of that competition which makes each man the enemy of his fellow; which is annually driving from our shores crowds of our best and most industrious artisans; which consigns women from absolute indigence to infamy; dries up the most sacred springs of affection in the heart; crams the jail and the poor-house; and is eating like a fatal canker into the very heartblood of society.*" This subject was deemed by Blackwood so important, that it was resumed in a subsequent number of that review, "The Dangers of the Country," March 1851. We will not fatigue the reader's attention with extracts from that article, which is a most able and interesting one; but will merely state that, after giving tedious and careful statistics, showing the rapid and unexampled increase of crime and pauperism in Great Britain since 1819, a period in which the prosperity of the upper classes was as remarkable as the continually increasing debasement and misery of the lower, the Reviewer concludes with these emphatic words: "But this we do say, and with these words we nail our colors to the mast, PROTECTION MUST BE RESTORED, OR THE BRITISH EMPIRE WILL BE DISSOLVED." Now the evil complained of is free competition, and nothing short of some modification of slavery can give protection against free competition. To leave no room for cavil or doubt as to the truth of our positions, that pauperism commenced and crime was increased with the birth of the liberty of the laboring class, and that each extension of liberty has immediately occasioned an accelerated increase of poverty and crime, we wish to adduce authorities, not only of the highest character, but representing all parties and shades of opinion. We now quote from the April number, 1854, of the Westminster Review on "The Results of the Census." After treating of the breaking up

of the feudal system and dissolution of the Catholic church, the writer thus proceeds: "These interests having gone down and another class having arisen, is there any other to be considered? Yes, an enormous one—an appalling one—the pauper interest. Long before the dissolution of the monasteries, the pauperism of the country had become an almost unmanageable evil. *It began with the abolition of serfage;* and the monasteries absorbed as much as they could of an existing evil, increasing it all the while. From the fourteenth century there had been laws to restrain vagrancy; and in the sixteenth it had increased 'to the marvellous disturbance of the common weal of this realm.' Beggars went about, 'valiant and sturdy,' in great 'routs and companies.' The vagrants were to be put in prison, branded and whipped; the clergy were to press all good citizens to give alms; and all who were able must find employment for those who could work. Then came the compulsory tax: and then the celebrated 43d Elizabeth; and all apparently in vain. The lower class had not risen, generally speaking, with the middle; and there was as wide an interval between that middle class and the pauper banditti of the realm, as there once was between the landed class and the serfs." Pauper banditti! And this is what two hundred years of liberty makes of white laborers. And now four hundred years have passed over, and their condition is getting daily worse; they are quitting their homes—no, not homes, for they have none—but flying from the land that has persecuted them to every wild and desert corner of the earth.

The contemporaneous appearance of *Alton Locke* and a vast number of pamphlets and essays on the subject of the sufferings and crimes of the laboring class in Great Britain, forms a most interesting epoch in the history of social science. No one who pays the least attention to the subject, will doubt that the doctrines and philosophy of socialism or communism, which just then became rife in England, owed their birth to the increased and increasing sufferings of the poor, which that philosophy proposes to remove. The Edinburgh Review, in its January number, 1851, discourses as follows: "As long as socialism was confined to the turbulent, the wild and the disreputable, and was associated with tenets which made it disgusting and disreputable, perhaps the wisest plan was to pass it over in silence, and suffer it to die of its own inherent weakness. But now, when it has appeared in a soberer guise and purified from much of its evil intermixtures; when it has shown itself an actual and energetic reality in France; when it has spread among the intelligent portions of the working classes in our own country more extensively than is commonly believed; when it raises its head under various modifications, and often as it were unconsciously, in the disquisitions which issue from the periodical press; when a weekly journal, conducted with great ability as to every thing but logic, is devoted to its propagation; and when clergymen of high literary reputation give in their scarcely qualified adherence, and are actively engaged in reducing to practice their own peculiar modification of the theory, it would be no longer kindly or decorous to ignore a subject which is so deeply interesting to thousands of our countrymen." In speaking of the doctrines of the socialists, the writer goes on to say: "The position they take is this: Society is altogether out of joint. Its anomalies, its disfigured aspect, its glaring inequalities, the sufferings of the most numerous portions of it, are monstrous, indefensible, and yearly increasing. Mere palliations, mere sham improvements, mere gradual ameliorations will not meet its wants; it must be remodelled, not merely furbished up. Political economy has hitherto had it all its own way; and the shocking condition into which it has brought us, shews that its principles must be strangely inadequate or unsound. The miseries of the great mass of the people, the inability to find work, or to obtain in return for such work as can be performed in reasonable time and by ordinary strength a sufficiency of the comforts and necessaries of life, may all be traced to one source—competition instead of combination. The antagonistic and regenerative principle which must be introduced, is association." No association, no efficient combination of labor can be effected till men give up their liberty of action and subject themselves to a common despotic head or ruler. This is slavery, and towards this socialism is moving. The above quotation and the succeeding one go to prove the positions with which we set out: that free trade or political economy is the science of free society, and socialism the science of slavery. The writer from whom we are quoting sees and thus exposes the tendency of socialism to slavery: "There is the

usual jumble between the fourteenth century and the nineteenth; the desire to recall the time when the poor were at
once the serfs and the proteges of the rich, and to amal-
gamate it with the days of chartism, when the poor assert their equality and insist upon their freedom. It is not
thus that irritation can be allayed or miseries removed or
wrongs redressed. The working classes and their advocates
must decide on which of the two positions they will take
their stand: whether they will be cared for as dependents
and inferiors, or whether, by wisdom, self-control, frugal-
ity and toil, they will fight their independent way to dignity and well-being; whether they will step back to a
stationary and degraded past, or strive onward to the assertion of their free humanity? But it is not given to them,
any more than to other classes, to combine inconsistent
advantages: they cannot unite the safety of being in leading strings, with the liberty of being without them; the
right of acting for themselves, with the right to be saved
from the consequences of their actions; they must not
whine because the higher classes do not aid them, and refuse to let these classes direct them; they must not insist
on the duty of government to provide for them, and deny
the authority of government to control them; they must
not denounce *laissez-faire*, and denounce a paternal despotism likewise." The greatest of all communists, if communist he be, Proudhon, has also seen and exposed this
tendency of socialism to slavery. He is a thorough-going
enemy of modern free society; calls property a thief; and
would, he says, establish anarchy in place of government.
But we have not been able to understand his system, if
any he has.

The North British Review stands probably as high for
its ability, sound political views and literary integrity, as
any other periodical whatever. We will cite copiously from
its article on "Literature and the Labor Question," February No. 1851, not merely for the weight of its authority
and the force of its arguments, but chiefly because the
writer of that article sums up with some fulness and great
ability the proofs of the failure of society as now constituted in Western Europe, and of the almost universal
abandonment of political economy, the philosophy of that
society:

"Servants of this class, and constituting by far the most

numerous portion of every community, are the *prolétaires,* or speaking more restrictedly, the working men, who earn to-day's bread by to-day's labor. They are the veritable descendants of those who in ancient times were the slaves; with but few differences their social position is the same. Despite saving banks, temperance societies, and institutions for mutual improvement, the characteristics of this class, like that of the literary class, is, and probably ever will be, pecuniary *insouciance.* From week to week, these thousands live, now in work and now out of work, as careless of to-morrow as if Benjamin Franklin had never lived, entering at one end of the journey of existence and issuing at the other, without ever having at any one moment accumulated five superfluous shillings."

A beautiful commentary on the dignity of labor.

As to the prevalence of discontent with free society, and of socialistic and revolutionary doctrines in France, the writer employs the following language:

"One cannot now take up a French book-seller's list of advertisements, without seeing the titles of publications of all kinds and sizes devoted to the elucidation of social questions. 'L'Organization du Travail;' 'Destinée Sociale;' 'Études sur les causes principales de la Misère;' 'De la condition physique et morale des jeunes Ouvriers.' Such are some of the titles of a class of French books sufficient already to form a library. The thing, in fact, has become a profession in France. Men of all kinds and of all capacities—men who do not care one farthing about the condition of the people, or about the condition of any body except themselves, as well as men of real goodness and philanthropy, now write books full of statistics about the working classes, and of plans for diminishing the amount of social evil. And so too in this country. The 'Condition of England Question' has become the target at which every shallow witling must aim his shaft. All literature seems to be flowing towards this channel, so that there seems to be a likelihood that we shall soon have no literature at all but a literature of social reference."

Whilst all this hubbub and confusion is going on in France and England, occasioned by the intensest suffering of the free laborers, we of the South and of all slaveholding countries, have been "calm as a summer's evening," quite unconscious of the storm brewing around us. Yet those people who confess that their situation is desperate, insist that we shall imitate their institutions, starve our laborers, multiply crime, riots and pauperism, in order, we suppose, to try the experiment of Mormonism, Socialism or Communism. Try it first, yourselves!

The following passage—and we have quoted a similar one from Blackwood—is a distinct assertion of the complete failure of free society. It is the admission of witnesses of the highest character, corroborated by the testimony of all classes of society—for the poor, by their strikes, trade unions, temperance societies, odd-fellow societies, and insurance societies, speak as eloquently on this subject as the rich and the learned.

"*Alton Locke* is, upon the whole, as powerful a literary expression as exists of the *general conviction*, shared by all classes alike, that the country has arrived at a condition when something extraordinary, whatever it is, must be decided on and done, if society is to be saved in Great Britain. As such, therefore, it is a book that should be welcome to all parties."

Now listen to the conclusion, and see whether the practical remedy proposed be not SLAVERY. We believe there is not an intelligent reformist in the world who does not see the necessity of slavery—who does not advocate its reinstitution in all save the name. Every one of them concurs in deprecating free competition, and in the wish and purpose to destroy it. To destroy it is to destroy Liberty, and where liberty is destroyed, slavery is established.

"At what conclusion have we arrived? We have pointed out as one of the most remarkable signs of the times, the appearance of a literature of social reference, originating in and then farther promoting a *rapprochement* between the two extremes of society, men of letters and the working classes. We have examined, and to some extent analyzed, the two most conspicuous examples that have been recently furnished in this country, of this new direction and intention of literature. And what has been the result? The result has been, that in both cases, we have found ourselves conducted by the writers in question to one point: the pronunciation of the terrible phrase, 'Organization of Labor,' and the contemplation of a possible exodus, at no very distant period, out of the Egypt of our present system, of *competition* and *laissez-faire*, into a compara-

tive Canaan of some kind of co-operative socialism. Such
is the fact: startling it may be, but deserving to be fairly
stated and apprehended. Right or wrong, we believe this
to be a true version and fair history of our current social
literature. We have elicited it from an examination of but
two examples; but we believe the most extensive examination would not invalidate it. Collect all the books, pamphlets and papers that constitute our literature of social
reference, or assemble all our men of letters, who have
contributed to that literature, so as to learn their private
aspirations and opinions with respect to the social problem, and the last word, the united note would still be:
'The Organization of Labor on the associative principle.'
There are of course dissentients, but such is the note of
the majority; and so far as the note is of value, it may be
asserted that a decree of the literary faculty of the country has gone forth, declaring the avatar of political economy, if not as a science of facts, at least as a supreme rule
of government, to be near its close."

Now strip these and the extracts from Blackwood of
their pompous verbiage, and they become express asser-
tions that free society has failed, and that that which is
not free must be substituted. Every Southern slave has an
estate in tail, indefeasible by fine and recovery, in the lands
of the South. If his present master cannot support him, he
must sell him to one who can. Slaves, too, have a valuable
property in their masters. Abolitionists overlook this—
overlook the protective influence of slavery, its distinguishing feature, and no doubt the cause of its origin and continuance, and abuse it as a mere engine of oppression. Infant negroes, sick, helpless, aged and infirm negroes, are
simply a charge to their master; he has no property in them
in the common sense of the term, for they are of no value
for the time, but they have the most invaluable property
in him. He is bound to support them, to supply all their
wants, and relieve them of all care for the present or future. And well, and feelingly and faithfully does he discharge his duty. What a glorious thing to man is slavery,
when want, misfortune, old age, debility and sickness
overtake him. Free society, in its various forms of insurance, in its odd-fellow and temperance societies, in its social and communistic establishments, and in ten thousand
other ways, is vainly attempting to attain this never-failing

protective, care-taking and supporting feature of slavery.
But it will blunder and flounder on in vain. It cannot put
a heart and feeling into its societies and its corporations.
God makes masters and gives them affections, feelings and
interests that secure kindness to the sick, aged and dying
slave. Man can never inspire his ricketty institutions with
those feelings, interests and affections. Say the Abolitionists—"Man ought not to have property in man." What a
dreary, cold, bleak, inhospitable world this would be with
such a doctrine carried into practice. Men living to themselves, like owls and wolves and lions and birds and beasts
of prey? No: "Love thy neighbor as thyself." And this
can't be done till he has a property in your services as well
as a place in your heart. *Homo sum, humani nihil a me
alienum puto!* This, the noblest sentiment ever uttered by
uninspired man, recognises the great truth which lies at
the foundation of all society—*that every man has property
in his fellow-man!* It is because that adequate provision is
not made properly to enforce this great truth in free society, that men are driven to the necessity of attempting to
remedy the defects of government by voluntary associations, that carry into definite and practical operation this
great and glorious truth. It is because such defects do
not exist in slave society, that we are not troubled with
strikes, trade unions, phalansteries, communistic establishments, Mormonism, and the thousand other isms that de-
face and deform free society. Socialism, in some form or
other, is universal in free society, and its single aim is to
attain the protective influence of slavery. St. Simon would
govern his social establishments by savants, more despotic
than masters. He would have no law but the will of the
savant. He would have a despot without the feelings and
the interests of a master to temper his authority. Fourier
proposes some wild plan of passional attraction as a substitute for government, and Louis Blanc is eloquent about
"attractive labor." All human experience proves that society must be ruled not by mere abstractions, but by men
of flesh and blood. To attain large industrial results, it must
be vigorously and severely ruled. Socialism is already slavery in all save the master. It had as well adopt that feature
at once, as come to that it must to make its schemes at once
humane and efficient. Socialism in other forms than that
of slavery is not a new thing. It existed in Crete, in Sparta,

in Peru, and was practiced by the Essenes in Judea. All ancient institutions were very much tinged with its doctrines and practices, not only in the relation of master and slave, which was universal, but in the connection of the free citizens to one another and to the government. The doctrines of individuality, of the social contract and of *laissez-faire,* had not then arisen. Our only quarrel with Socialism is, that it will not honestly admit that it owes its recent revival to the failure of universal liberty, and is seeking to bring about slavery again in some form.

The little experiment of universal liberty that has been tried for a little while in a little corner of Europe, has resulted in disastrous and appalling failure. Slavery has been too universal not to be necessary to nature, and man struggles in vain against nature. "Expel nature with a fork, and she will again return;" or, in the eloquent language of Solomon—"The thing that hath been, it is that that shall be; and that which is done, is that which shall be done; and there is no new thing under the sun."

No one who reads a newspaper can but have observed that every abolitionist is either an agrarian, a socialist, an infidel, an anti-renter, or in some way is trying to upset other institutions of society, as well as slavery at the South. The same reasoning that makes him an abolitionist soon, carries him further, for he finds slavery in some form so interwoven with the whole frame-work of society, that he invariably ends by proposing to destroy the whole edifice and building another on entirely new principles. Some, like Fourier, are honest enough to admit that it must also be built with new materials. There is too much human nature in man for their purposes. Part of that nature is the continual effort to make others work and support him whilst he is idle; in other words, to enslave them, and yet not be charged with their support. But Fourier and his disciples promise most positively that their system will in a few generations cleanse mankind of their mundane dross, expel every particle of human nature, and that then their system will work admirably. Until then, we would advise them to procure good practical overseers from Virginia to govern their phalanxes and phalansteries; and we venture to affirm, if they try one, they will never be willing to exchange him for that whip-syllabub, sentimental ruler, "passional attraction." Passional attraction is the very thing government has chiefly to check and punish, and we suspect it will be so to the end of the chapter. The argument seems fairly, however, to have arrived at this point: All concur that free society is a failure. We slave-holders say you must recur to domestic slavery, the old-est, the best and most common form of Socialism. The new schools of Socialism promise something better, but admit, to obtain that something, they must first destroy and eradi-cate man's human nature.

CHAPTER III.

THE TWO PHILOSOPHIES.

IN THE three preceding chapters we have shewn that the world is divided between two philosophies, the one, the philosophy of free trade and universal liberty—the philosophy adapted to promote the interests of the strong, the wealthy and the wise, the other, that of socialism, intended to protect the weak, the poor and the ignorant. The latter is almost universal in free society; the former prevails in the slaveholding States of the South. Thus we see each section cherishing theories at war with existing institutions. The people of the North and of Europe are pro-slavery men in the abstract; those of the South are theoretical abolitionists. This state of opinions is readily accounted for. The people in free society feel the evils of universal liberty and free competition, and desire to get rid of those evils. They propose a remedy, which is in fact slavery; but they are wholly unconscious of what they are doing, because never having lived in the midst of slavery, they know not what slavery is. The citizens of the South, who have seen none of the evils of liberty and competition, but just enough of those agencies to operate as healthful stimulants to energy, enterprise and industry, believe free competition to be an unmixed good.

The South, quiet, contented, satisfied, looks upon all socialists and radical reformers as madmen or knaves. It is as ignorant of free society as that society is of slavery. Each section sees one side of the subject alone; each, therefore, takes partial and erroneous views of it. Social science will never take a step in advance till some Southern slaveholder, competent for the task, devotes a life-time to its study and elucidation; for slavery can only be understood by living in its midst, whilst thousands of books daily exhibit the minutest workings of free society.

The knowledge of the numerous theories of radical reform proposed in Europe, and the causes that have led to their promulgation, is of vital importance to us. Yet we turn away from them with disgust, as from something unclean and vicious. We occupy high vantage ground for observing, studying and classifying the various phenomena of society; yet we do not profit by the advantages of our position. We should do so, and indignantly hurl back upon our assailants the charge, that there is something wrong and rotten in our system. From their own mouths we can show free society to be a monstrous abortion, and slavery to be the healthy, beautiful and natural being which they are trying, unconsciously, to adopt.

CHAPTER IV.

NEGRO SLAVERY.

WE HAVE already stated that we should not attempt to introduce any new theories of government and of society, but merely try to justify old ones, so far as we could deduce such theories from ancient and almost universal practices. Now it has been the practice in all countries and in all ages, in some degree, to accommodate the amount and character of government control to the wants, intelligence, and moral capacities of the nations or individuals to be governed. A highly moral and intellectual people, like the free citizens of ancient Athens, are best governed by a democracy. For a less moral and intellectual one, a limited and constitutional monarchy will answer. For a people either very ignorant or very wicked, nothing short of military despotism will suffice. So among individuals, the most moral and well-informed members of society require no other government than law. They are capable of reading and understanding the law, and have sufficient self-control and virtuous disposition to obey it. Children cannot be governed by mere law; first, because they do not understand it, and secondly, because they are so much under the influence of impulse, passion and appetite, that they want sufficient self-control to be deterred or governed by the distant and doubtful penalties of the law. They must be constantly controlled by parents or guardians, whose will and orders shall stand in the place of law for them. Very wicked men must be put into penitentiaries; lunatics into asylums, and the most wild of them into strait-jackets, just as the most wicked of the sane are manacled with irons; and idiots must have committees to govern and take care of them. Now, it is clear the Athenian democracy would not suit a negro nation, nor will the government of mere law suffice for the individual negro. He is but a grown up child, and must be governed as a child, not as a lunatic or criminal. The master occupies towards him the place of parent or guardian. We shall not dwell on this view, for no one will differ with us who thinks as we do of the negro's capacity, and we might argue till dooms-day, in vain, with those who have a high opinion of the negro's moral and intellectual capacity.

Secondly. The negro is improvident; will not lay up in summer for the wants of winter; will not accumulate in youth for the exigencies of age. He would become an insufferable burden to society. Society has the right to prevent this, and can only do so by subjecting him to domestic slavery. In the last place, the negro race is inferior to the white race, and living in their midst, they would be far outstripped or outwitted in the chase of free competition. Gradual but certain extermination would be their fate. We presume the maddest abolitionist does not think the negro's providence of habits and money-making capacity at all to compare to those of the whites. This defect of character would alone justify enslaving him, if he is to remain here. In Africa or the West Indies, he would become idolatrous, savage and cannibal, or be devoured by savages and cannibals. At the North he would freeze or starve.

We would remind those who deprecate and sympathize with negro slavery, that his slavery here relieves him from a far more cruel slavery in Africa, or from idolatry and cannibalism, and every brutal vice and crime that can disgrace humanity; and that it christianizes, protects, supports and civilizes him; that it governs him far better than free laborers at the North are governed. There, wife-murder has become a mere holiday pastime; and where so many wives are murdered, almost all must be brutally treated. Nay, more: men who kill their wives or treat them brutally, must be ready for all kinds of crime, and the calendar of crime at the North proves the inference to be correct. Negroes never kill their wives. If it be objected that legally they have no wives, then we reply, that in an experience of more than forty years, we never yet heard of a negro man killing a negro woman. Our negroes are not only better off as to physical comfort than free laborers, but their moral condition is better.

But abolish negro slavery, and how much of slavery

still remains. Soldiers and sailors in Europe enlist for life;
here, for five years. Are they not slaves who have not only
sold their liberties, but their lives also? And they are worse
treated than domestic slaves. No domestic affection and
self-interest extend their ægis over them. No kind mistress,
like a guardian angel, provides for them in health, tends
them in sickness, and soothes their dying pillow. Wellington at Waterloo was a slave. He was bound to obey,
or would, like admiral Byng, have been shot for gross misconduct, and might not, like a common laborer, quit his
work at any moment. He had sold his liberty, and might
not resign without the consent of his master, the king. The
common laborer may quit his work at any moment, whatever his contract; declare that liberty is an alienable
right, and leave his employer to redress by a useless suit
for damages. The highest and most honorable position on
earth was that of the slave Wellington; the lowest, that
of the free man who cleaned his boots and fed his hounds.
The African cannibal, caught, christianized and enslaved,
is as much elevated by slavery as was Wellington. The
kind of slavery is adapted to the men enslaved. Wives and
apprentices are slaves; not in theory only, but often in
fact. Children are slaves to their parents, guardians and
teachers. Imprisoned culprits are slaves. Lunatics and idiots are slaves also. Three-fourths of free society are slaves,
no better treated, when their wants and capacities are
estimated, than negro slaves. The masters in free society,
or slave society, if they perform properly their duties, have
more cares and less liberty than the slaves themselves. "In
the sweat of thy face shalt thou earn thy bread!" made all
men slaves, and such all *good men* continue to be.

Negro slavery would be changed immediately to some
form of peonage, serfdom or villienage, if the negroes were
sufficiently intelligent and provident to manage a farm. No
one would have the labor and trouble of management, if
his negroes would pay in hires and rents one-half what free
tenants pay in rent in Europe. Every negro in the South
would be soon liberated, if he would take liberty on the
terms that white tenants hold it. The fact that he cannot
enjoy liberty on such terms, seems conclusive that he is
only fit to be a slave.

But for the assaults of the abolitionists, much would
have been done ere this to regulate and improve Southern

slavery. Our negro mechanics do not work so hard, have many more privileges and holidays, and are better fed and clothed than field hands, and are yet more valuable to their masters. The slaves of the South are cheated of their rights by the purchase of Northern manufactures which they could produce. Besides, if we would employ our slaves in the coarser processes of the mechanic arts and manufacturers, such as brick making, getting and hewing timber for ships and houses, iron mining and smelting, coal mining, grading railroads and plank roads, in the manufacture of cotton, tobacco, &c., we would find a vent in new employments for their increase, more humane and more profitable than the vent afforded by new states and territories. The nice and finishing processes of manufactures and mechanics should be reserved for the whites, who only are fitted for them, and thus, by diversifying pursuits and cutting off dependence on the North, we might benefit and advance the interests of our whole population. Exclusive agriculture has depressed and impoverished the South. We will not here dilate on this topic, because we intend to make it the subject of a separate essay. Free trade doctrines, not slavery, have made the South agricultural and dependent, given her a sparse and ignorant population, ruined her cities, and expelled her people.

Would the abolitionists approve of a system of society that set white children free, and remitted them at the age of fourteen, males and females, to all the rights, both as to person and property, which belong to adults? Would it be criminal or praiseworthy to do so? Criminal, of course. Now, are the average of negroes equal in formation, in native intelligence, in prudence or providence, to well-informed white children of fourteen? We who have lived with them for forty years, think not. The competition of the world would be too much for the children. They would be cheated out of their property and debased in their morals. Yet they would meet every where with sympathizing friends of their own color, ready to aid, advise and assist them. The negro would be exposed to the same competition and greater temptations, with no greater ability to contend with them, with these additional difficulties. He would be welcome nowhere; meet with thousands of enemies and no friends. If he went North, the white laborers would kick him and cuff him, and drive him out of employment. If he went to Africa, the savages would cook him and eat him. If he went to the West Indies, they would not let him in, or if they did, they would soon make of him a savage and idolater.

We have a further question to ask. If it be right and incumbent to subject children to the authority of parents and guardians, and idiots and lunatics to committees, would it not be equally right and incumbent to give the free negroes masters, until at least they arrive at years of discretion, which very few ever did or will attain? What is the difference between the authority of a parent and of a master? Neither pay wages, and each is entitled to the services of those subject to him. The father may not sell his child forever, but may hire him out till he is twenty-one. The free negro's master may also be restrained from selling. Let him stand *in loco parentis,* and call him papa instead of master. Look closely into slavery, and you will see nothing so hideous in it; or if you do, you will find plenty of it at home in its most hideous form.

The earliest civilization of which history gives account is that of Egypt. The negro was always in contact with that civilization. For four thousand years he has had opportunities of becoming civilized. Like the wild horse, he must be caught, tamed and domesticated. When his subjugation ceases he again runs wild, like the cattle on the Pampas of the South, or the horses on the prairies of the West. His condition in the West Indies proves this.

It is a common remark, that the grand and lasting architectural structures of antiquity were the results of slavery. The mighty and continued association of labor requisite to their construction, when mechanic art was so little advanced, and labor-saving processes unknown, could only have been brought about by a despotic authority, like that of the master over his slaves. It is, however, very remarkable, that whilst in taste and artistic skill the world seems to have been retrograding ever since the decay and abolition of feudalism, in mechanical invention and in great utilitarian operations requiring the wielding of immense capital and much labor, its progress has been unexampled. Is it because capital is more despotic in its authority over free laborers than Roman masters and feudal lords were over their slaves and vassals?

Free society has continued long enough to justify the

attempt to generalize its phenomena, and calculate its moral and intellectual influences. It is obvious that, in whatever is purely utilitarian and material, it incites invention and stimulates industry. Benjamin Franklin, as a man and a philosopher, is the best exponent of the working of the system. His sentiments and his philosophy are low, selfish, atheistic and material. They tend directly to make man a mere "featherless biped," well-fed, well-clothed and comfortable, but regardless of his soul as "the beasts that perish."

Since the Reformation the world has as regularly been retrograding in whatever belongs to the departments of genius, taste and art, as it has been progressing in physical science and its application to mechanical construction. Mediæval Italy rivalled if it did not surpass ancient Rome, in poetry, in sculpture, in painting, and many of the fine arts. Gothic architecture reared its monuments of skill and genius throughout Europe, till the 15th century; but Gothic architecture died with the Reformation. The age of Elizabeth was the Augustan age of England. The men who lived then acquired their sentiments in a world not yet deadened and vulgarized by puritanical cant and levelling demagoguism. Since then men have arisen who have been the fashion and the go for a season, but none have appeared whose names will descend to posterity. Liberty and equality made slower advances in France. The age of Louis XIV. was the culminating point of French genius and art. It then shed but a flickering and lurid light. Frenchmen are servile copyists of Roman art, and Rome had no art of her own. She borrowed from Greece; distorted and deteriorated what she borrowed; and France imitates and falls below Roman distortions. The genius of Spain disappeared with Cervantes; and now the world seems to regard nothing as desirable except what will make money and what costs money. There is not a poet, an orator, a sculptor, or painter in the world. The tedious elaboration necessary to all the productions of high art would be ridiculed in this money-making, utilitarian, charlatan age. Nothing now but what is gaudy and costly excites admiration. The public taste is debased.

But far the worst feature of modern civilization, which is the civilization of free society, remains to be exposed. Whilst labor-saving processes have probably lessened by one half, in the last century, the amount of work needed for comfortable support, the free laborer is compelled by capital and competition to work more than he ever did before, and is less comfortable. The organization of society cheats him of his earnings, and those earnings go to swell the vulgar pomp and pageantry of the ignorant millionaires, who are the only great of the present day. These reflections might seem, at first view, to have little connexion with negro slavery; but it is well for us of the South not to be deceived by the tinsel glare and glitter of free society, and to employ ourselves in doing our duty at home, and studying the past, rather than in insidious rivalry of the expensive pleasures and pursuits of men whose sentiments and whose aims are low, sensual and grovelling.

Human progress consisting in moral and intellectual improvement, and there being no agreed and conventional standard weights or measures of moral and intellectual qualities and quantities, the question of progress can never be accurately decided. We maintain that man has not improved, because in all save the mechanic arts he reverts to the distant past for models to imitate, and he never imitates what he can excel.

We need never have white slaves in the South, because we have black ones. Our citizens, like those of Rome and Athens, are a privileged class. We should train and educate them to deserve the privileges and to perform the duties which society confers on them. Instead of, by a low demagoguism, depressing their self-respect by discourses on the equality of man, we had better excite their pride by reminding them that they do not fulfil the menial offices which white men do in other countries. Society does not feel the burden of providing for the few helpless paupers in the South. And we should recollect that here we have but half the people to educate, for half are negroes; whilst at the North they profess to educate all. It is in our power to spike this last gun of the abolitionists. We should educate all the poor. The abolitionists say that it is one of the necessary consequences of slavery that the poor are neglected. It was not so in Athens, and in Rome, and should not be so in the South. If we had less trade with and less dependence on the North, all our poor might be profitably and honorably employed in trades, professions and manufactures. Then we should have a rich and denser population. Yet we but marshal her in the way that she was going. The South is already aware of the necessity of a new policy, and has begun to act on it. Every day more and more is done for education, the mechanic arts, manufactures and internal improvements. We will soon be independent of the North.

We deem this peculiar question of negro slavery of very little importance. The issue is made throughout the world on the general subject of slavery in the abstract. The argument has commenced. One set of ideas will govern and control after awhile the civilized world. Slavery will every where be abolished, or every where be re-instituted. We think the opponents of practical, existing slavery, are stopped by their own admission; nay, that unconsciously, as socialists, they are the defenders and propagandists of slavery, and have furnished the only sound arguments on which its defence and justification can be rested. We have introduced the subject of negro slavery to afford us a better opportunity to disclaim the purpose of reducing the white man any where to the condition of negro slaves here. It would be very unwise and unscientific to govern white men as you would negroes. Every shade and variety of slavery has existed in the world. In some cases there has been much of legal regulation, much restraint of the master's authority; in others, none at all. The character of slavery necessary to protect the whites in Europe should be much milder than negro slavery, for slavery is only needed to protect the white man, whilst it is more necessary for the government of the negro even than for his protection. But even negro slavery should not be outlawed. We might and should have laws in Virginia, as in Louisiana, to make the master subject to presentment by the grand jury and to punishment, for any inhuman or improper treatment or neglect of his slave.

We abhor the doctrine of the "Types of Mankind;" first, because it is at war with scripture, which teaches us that the whole human race is descended from a common parentage; and, secondly, because it encourages and incites brutal masters to treat negroes, not as weak, ignorant and dependent brethren, but as wicked beasts, without the pale of humanity. This Southerner is the negro's friend, his only friend. Let no intermeddling abolitionist, no refined philosophy, dissolve this friendship.

CANNIBALS ALL!

OR,

SLAVES WITHOUT MASTERS.

BY

GEORGE FITZHUGH,

OF PORT ROYAL, CAROLINE, VA.

"His hand will be against every man, and every man's hand against him."—GEN. XVI. 12.
"Physician, heal thyself."—LUKE IV. 23.

RICHMOND, VA.
A. MORRIS, PUBLISHER.
1857.

DEDICATION.

TO THE HONORABLE HENRY A. WISE.

DEAR SIR:

I dedicate this work to you, because I am acquainted with no one who has so zealously, laboriously and successfully endeavored to Virginianise Virginia, by encouraging, through State legislation, her intellectual and physical growth and development; no one who has seen so clearly the evils of centralization from without, and worked so earnestly to cure or avert those evils, by building up centralization within.

Virginia should have her centres of Thought at her Colleges and her University, centres of Trade and Manufactures at her Seaboard and Western towns, and centres of Fashion at her Mineral Springs.

I agree with you, too, that State strength and State independence are the best guarantees of State rights; and that policy the wisest which most promotes the growth of State strength and independence.

Weakness invites aggression; strength commands respect; hence, the Union is safest when its separate members are best able to repel injury, or to live independently.

Your attachment to Virginia has not lessened your love for the Union. In urging forward to completion such works as the Covington and Ohio Road, you are trying to add to the wealth, the glory and the strength of our own State, whilst you would add equally to the wealth, the strength and perpetuity of the Union.

I cannot commit you to all the doctrines of my book, for you will not see it until it is published.

With very great respect,
Your obedient servant,
GEO. FITZHUGH.

Port Royal, Aug. 22, 1856.

PREFACE.

I HAVE endeavored, in this work, to treat the subjects of Liberty and Slavery in a more rigidly analytical manner than in "Sociology for the South;" and, at the same time, to furnish the reader with abundance of facts, authorities and admissions, whereby to test the truth of my views.

My chief aim has been to shew, that *Labor makes values, and Wit exploitates and accumulates them;* and hence to deduce the conclusion that the unrestricted exploitation of so-called free society, is more oppressive to the laborer than domestic slavery.

In making a distinct onslaught on the popular doctrines of Modern Ethics, I must share the credit or censure with my corresponding acquaintance and friend, Professor H* of Virginia.

Our acquaintance commenced by his congratulating me, by letter, on the announcement that I was occupied with a treatise vindicating the institution of Slavery in the abstract, and by his suggestion, that he foresaw, from what he had read of my communications to the papers, that I should be compelled to make a general assault on the prevalent political and moral philosophy. This letter, and others subsequent to it, together with the reception of my Book by the Southern Public, have induced me in the present work to avow the full breadth and scope of my purpose. I am sure it will be easier to convince the world that the customary theories of our Modern Ethical Philosophy, whether utilitarian or sentimental, are so fallacious or so false in their premises and their deductions as to deserve rejection, than to persuade it that the social forms under which it lives, and attempts to justify and approve, are equally erroneous, and should be re-placed by others

* George Frederick Holmes of the University of Virginia.

founded on a broader philosophical system and more Christian principles.

Yet, I believe that, under the banners of Socialism and, more dangerous, because more delusive, Semi-Socialism, society is insensibly, and often unconsciously, marching to the utter abandonment of the most essential institutions —religion, family ties, property, and the restraints of justice. The present profession is, indeed, to stop at the half-way house of No-Government and Free Love; but we are sure that it cannot halt and encamp in such quarters. Society will work out erroneous doctrines to their logical consequences, and detect error only by the experience of mischief. The world will only fall back on domestic slavery when all other social forms have failed and been exhausted. That hour may not be far off.

Mr. H. will not see this work before its publication, and would dissent from many of its details, from the unrestricted latitude of its positions, and from its want of precise definition. The time has not yet arrived, in my opinion, for such precision, nor will it arrive until the present philosophy is seen to be untenable, and we begin to look about us for a loftier and more enlightened substitute.

INTRODUCTION.

———•◆•———

In our little work, "Sociology for the South," we said, "We may again appear in the character of writer before the public; but we shall not intrude, and would prefer that others should finish the work which we have begun." That little work has met, every where, we believe, at the South, with a favorable reception. No one has denied its theory of Free Society, nor disputed the facts on which that theory rests. Very many able co-laborers have arisen, and many books and essays are daily appearing, taking higher ground in defence of Slavery; justifying it as a normal and natural institution, instead of excusing or apologizing for it as an exceptional one. It is now treated as a positive good, not a necessary evil. The success, not the ability of our essay, may have had some influence in eliciting this new mode of defence. We have, for many years, been gradually and cautiously testing public opinion at the South, and have ascertained that it is ready to approve, and much prefers, the highest ground of defence. We have no peculiar fitness for the work we are engaged in, except the confidence that we address a public predisposed to approve our doctrines, however bold or novel. Heretofore the great difficulty in defending Slavery has arisen from the fear that the public would take offence at assaults on its long-cherished political axioms; which, nevertheless, stood in the way of that defence. It is now evident that those axioms have outlived their day—for no one, either North or South, has complained of our rather ferocious assault on them—much less attempted to reply to or refute our arguments and objections. All men begin very clearly to perceive, that the state of revolution is politically and socially abnormal and exceptional, and that the principles that would justify it are true in the particular, false in the general. "A recurrence to fundamental principles," by an oppressed people, is treason if it fails; the noblest of heroism if it eventuates in successful revolution. But a "frequent recurrence to fundamental principles" is at war with the continued existence of all government, and is a doctrine fit to be sported only by the Isms of the North and the Red Republicans of Europe. With them no principles are considered established and sacred, nor will ever be. When, in time of revolution, society is partially disbanded, disintegrated and dissolved, the doctrine of Human Equality may have a hearing, and may be useful in stimulating rebellion; but it is practically impossible, and directly conflicts with all government, all separate property, and all social existence. We cite these two examples, as instances, to shew how the wisest and best of men are sure to deduce, as general principles, what is only true as to themselves and their peculiar circumstances. Never were people blessed with such wise and noble Institutions as we; for they combine most that was good in those of Rome and Greece, of Judea, and of Mediaeval England. But the mischievous absurdity of our political axioms and principles quite equals the wisdom and conservatism of our political practices. The ready appreciation by the public of such doctrines as these, encourages us to persevere in writing. The silence of the North is far more encouraging, however, than the approbation of the South. Piqued and taunted for two years, by many Southern Presses of high standing, to deny the proposition that Free Society in Western Europe is a failure, and that it betrays premonitory symptoms of failure, even in America, the North is silent, and thus tacitly admits the charge. Challenged to compare and weigh the advantages and disadvantages of our domestic slavery with their slavery of the masses to capital and skill, it is mute, and neither accepts nor declines our challenge. The comparative evils of Slave Society and of Free Society, of slavery to human Masters and of slavery to Capital, are the issues which the South now presents, and which the North avoids. And she avoids them, because the Abolitionists, the only assailants of Southern Slavery, have, we believe, to a man, asserted the entire failure of their own social system, proposed its subversion and suggested an approximating millennium, or some system of Free Love, Communism, or Socialism, as a substitute.

The alarming extent of this state of public opinion, or, to speak more accurately, the absence of any public opinion, or common faith and conviction about anything, is not dreamed of at the South, nor fully and properly realized, even at the North. *We* cannot believe what is so entirely different from all our experience and observation, and *they* have become familiarized and inattentive to the infected social atmosphere they continually inhale. Besides, living in the midst of the isms, their situation is not favorable for comprehensive observation or calm generalization. More than a year since, we made a short trip to the North, and whilst there only associated with distinguished Abolitionists. We have corresponded much with them, before and since, and read many of their books, lectures, essays and speeches. We have neither seen nor heard any denial by them of the failure of their own social system; but, on the contrary, found that they all concurred in the necessity of radical social changes. 'Tis true, in conversation, they will say, "Our system of society is bad, but yours of the South is worse; the cause of social science is advancing, and we are ready to institute a system better than either." We could give many private anecdotes, and quote thousands of authorities, to prove that such is the exact state of opinion with the multitudinous isms of the North. The correctness of our statement will not be denied. If it is, any one may satisfy himself of its truth by reading any Abolition or Infidel paper at the North for a single month. The Liberator, of Boston, their ablest paper, gives continually the fullest exposé of their opinions, and of their wholesale destructiveness of purpose.

The neglect of the North to take issue with us, or with the Southern Press, in the new positions which we have assumed, our own observations of the working of Northern society, the alarming increase of Socialism, as evinced by its control of many Northern State Legislatures, and its majority in the lower house of Congress, are all new proofs of the truth of our doctrine. The character of that majority in Congress is displayed in full relief, by the single fact, which we saw stated in a Northern Abolition paper, that "there are a hundred Spiritual Rappers in Congress." A Northern member of Congress made a similar remark to us a few days since. 'Tis but a copy of the Hiss Legislature of Massachusetts, or the Praise-God-Barebones Parliament of England. Further study, too, of Western European Society, which has been engaged in continual revolution for twenty years, has satisfied us that Free Society every where begets isms, and that isms soon beget bloody revolutions. Until our trip to the North, we did not justly appreciate the passage which we are about to quote from Mr. Carlyle's "Latter-Day Pamphlets." Now it seems to us as if Boston, New Haven, or Western New York, had sat for the picture:

"To rectify the relation that exists between two men, is there no method, then, but that of ending it? The old relation has become unsuitable, obsolete, perhaps unjust; and the remedy is, abolish it; let there henceforth be no relation at all. From the 'sacrament of marriage' downwards, human beings used to be manifoldly related one to another, and each to all; and there was no relation among human beings, just or unjust, that had not its grievances and its difficulties, its necessities on both sides to bear and forbear. But henceforth, be it known, we have changed all that by favor of Heaven; the 'voluntary principle' has come up, which will itself do the business for us; and now let a new sacrament, that of *Divorce,* which we call emancipation, and spout of on our platforms, be universally the order of the day! Have men considered whither all this is tending, and what it certainly enough betokens? Cut every human relation that has any where grown uneasy sheer asunder; reduce whatsoever was compulsory to voluntary, whatsoever was permanent among us to the condition of the nomadic; in other words, LOOSEN BY ASSIDUOUS WEDGES, in every joint, the whole fabric of social existence, stone from stone, till at last, all lie now quite loose enough, it can, as we already see in most countries, be overset by sudden outburst of revolutionary rage; and lying as mere mountains of anarchic rubbish, solicit you to sing Fraternity, &c. over it, and rejoice in the now remarkable era of human progress we have arrived at."

Now we plant ourselves on this passage from Carlyle. We say that, as far as it goes, 'tis a faithful picture of the isms of the North. But the restraints of Law and Public Opinion are less at the North than in Europe. The isms on each side the Atlantic are equally busy with "assiduous wedges," in "loosening in every joint the whole fabric of social existence;" but whilst they dare invoke Anarchy in Europe, they dare not inaugurate New York Free Love, and Oneida Incest, and Mormon Polygamy. The moral, religious, and social heresies of the North, are more monstrous than those of Europe. The pupil has surpassed the master, unaided by the stimulants of poverty, hunger and nakedness, which urge the master forward.

Society need not fail in the North-east until the whole West is settled, and a refluent population, or excess of immigration, overstocks permanently the labor market on the Atlantic board. Till then, the despotism of skill and capital, in forcing emigration to the West, makes proprietors of those emigrants, benefits them, peoples the West, and by their return trade, enriches the East. The social forms of the North and the South are, for the present, equally promotive of growth and prosperity at home, and equally beneficial to mankind at large, by affording asylums to the oppressed, and by furnishing food and clothing to all. Northern society is a partial failure, but only because it generates isms which threaten it with overthrow and impede its progress.

Despite of appearing vain and egotistical, we cannot refrain from mentioning another circumstance that encourages us to write. At the very time when we were writing our pamphlet entitled "Slavery Justified," in which we took ground that Free Society had failed, Mr. Carlyle began to write his *"Latter Day* Pamphlets," whose very title is the assertion of the failure of Free Society. The proof derived from this coincidence becomes the stronger, when it is perceived that an ordinary man on this side the Atlantic discovered and was exposing the same social phenomena that an extraordinary one had discovered and was exposing on the other. The very titles of our works are synonymous—for the "Latter Day" is the "Failure of Society."

Mr. Carlyle, and Miss Fanny Wright (in her England the Civilizer) vindicate Slavery by shewing that each of its apparent relaxations in England has injured the laboring class. They were fully and ably represented in Parliament by their ancient masters, the Barons. Since the Throne, and the Church, and the Nobility, have been

stripped of their power, and a House of Commons, representing lands and money, rules despotically, the masses
have become outlawed. They labor under all the disadvantages of slavery, and have none of the rights of slaves.
This is the true history of the English Constitution, and
one which we intend, in the sequel, more fully to expound. This presents another reason why we again appear
before the public. Blackstone, which is read by most
American gentlemen, teaches a doctrine the exact reverse
of this, and that doctrine we shall try to refute.

Returning from the North, we procured in New York
a copy of Aristotle's "Politics and Economics." To our surprise, we found that our theory of the origin of society
was identical with his, and that we had employed not only
the same illustrations, but the very same words. We saw
at once that the true vindication of slavery must be
founded on his theory of man's social nature, as opposed
to Locke's theory of the Social Contract, on which latter
Free Society rests for support. 'Tis true we had broached
this doctrine; but with the world at large our authority
was merely repulsive, whilst the same doctrine, coming
from Aristotle, had, besides his name, two thousand years
of human approval and concurrence in its favor; for, without that concurrence and approval, his book would have
long since perished.

In addition to all this, we think we have discovered that
Moses has anticipated the Socialists, and that in prohibit-
ing "usury of money, and of victuals, and of all things
that are lent on usury," and in denouncing "increase" he
was far wiser than Aristotle, and saw that other capital or
property did not "breed" any more than money, and that
its profits were unjust exactions levied from the laboring
man. The Socialists proclaim this as a discovery of their
own. We think Moses discovered and proclaimed it more
than three thousand years ago—and that it is the only true
theory of capital and labor, the only adequate theoretical
defence of Slavery—for it proves that the profits which
capital exacts from labor makes free laborers slaves, without the rights, privileges or advantages of domestic slaves,
and capitalists their masters, with all the advantages, and
none of the burdens and obligations of the ordinary owners of slaves.

The scientific title of this work would be best expressed

by the conventional French term *"Exploitation."* We endeavor to translate by the double periphrases of "Cannibals All; or, Slaves without Masters."

We have been imprudent enough to write our Introduction first, and may fail to satisfy the expectations which we excite. Our excess of candor must, in that event, in part supply our deficiency of ability.

CANNIBALS ALL!

CHAPTER I.

THE UNIVERSAL TRADE.

WE ARE, all, North and South, engaged in the White Slave Trade, and he who succeeds best, is esteemed most respectable. It is far more cruel than the Black Slave Trade, because it exacts more of its slaves, and neither protects nor governs them. We boast, that it exacts more, when we say, "that the *profits* made from employing free labor are greater than those from slave labor." The profits, made from free labor, are the amount of the products of such labor, which the employer, by means of the command which capital or skill gives him, takes away, exacts or "exploitates" from the free laborer. The profits of slave labor are that portion of the products of such labor which the power of the master enables him to appropriate. These profits are less, because the master allows the slave to retain a larger share of the results of his own labor, than do the employers of free labor. But we not only boast that the White Slave Trade is more exacting and fraudulent (in fact, though not in intention,) than Black Slavery; but we also boast, that it is more cruel, in leaving the laborer to take care of himself and family out of the pittance which skill or capital have allowed him to retain. When the day's labor is ended, he is free, but is overburdened with the cares of family and household, which make his freedom an empty and delusive mockery. But his employer is really free, and may enjoy the profits made by others' labor, without a care, or a trouble, as to their well-being. The negro slave is free, too, when the labors of the day are over, and free in mind as well as body; for the master provides food, raiment, house, fuel, and everything else necessary to the physical well-being of himself and family. The master's labors commence just when the slave's end. No wonder men should prefer white slavery to capital, to negro slavery, since it is more profitable, and is free from all the cares and labors of black slave-holding.

Now, reader, if you wish to know yourself—to "descant on your own deformity"—read on. But if you would cherish self-conceit, self-esteem, or self-appreciation, throw down our book; for we will dispel illusions which have promoted your happiness, and shew you that what you have considered and practiced as virtue, is little better than moral Cannibalism. But you will find yourself in numerous and respectable company; for all good and respectable people are "Cannibals all," who do not labor, or who are successfully trying to live without labor, on the unrequited labor of other people:— Whilst low, bad, and disreputable people, are those who labor to support themselves, and to support said respectable people besides. Throwing the negro slaves out of the account, and society is divided in Christendom into four classes: The rich, or independent respectable people, who live well and labor not at all; the professional and skillful respectable people, who do a little light work, for enormous wages; the poor hard-working people, who support every body, and starve themselves; and the poor thieves, swindlers and sturdy beggars, who live like gentlemen, without labor, on the labor of other people. The gentlemen exploitate, which being done on a large scale, and requiring a great many victims, is highly respectable—whilst the rogues and beggars take so little from others, that they fare little better than those who labor.

But, reader, we do not wish to fire into the flock. "Thou art the man!" You are a Cannibal! and if a successful one, pride yourself on the number of your victims, quite as much as any Feejee chieftain, who breakfasts, dines and sups on human flesh.— And your conscience smites you, if you have failed to succeed, quite as much as his, when he returns from an unsuccessful foray.

Probably, you are a lawyer, or a merchant, or a doctor, who have made by your business fifty thousand dollars, and retired to live on your capital. But, mark! not to spend your capital. That would be vulgar, disreputable, criminal. That would be, to live by your own labor; for your capital is your amassed labor. That would be, to do as common working men do; for they take the pittance which their employers leave them, to live on. They live by labor; for they exchange the results of their own labor for the products of other people's labor. It is, no doubt, an honest, vulgar way of living; but not at all a respectable way. The respectable way of living is, to make other people work for you, and to pay them nothing for so doing— and to have no concern about them after their work is done. Hence, white slave-holding is much more respectable than negro slavery—for the master works nearly as hard for the negro, as he for the master. But you, my virtuous, respectable reader, exact three thousand dollars per annum from white labor, (for your income is the product of white labor,) and make not one cent of return in any form. You retain your capital, and never labor, and yet live in luxury on the labor of others. Capital commands labor, as the master does the slave. Neither pays for labor; but the master permits the slave to retain a larger allowance from the proceeds of his own labor, and hence "free labor is cheaper than slave labor." You, with the command over labor which your capital gives you, are a slave owner —a master, without the obligations of a master. They who work for you, who create your income, are slaves, without the rights of slaves. Slaves without a master! Whilst you were engaged in amassing your capital, in seeking to become independent, you were in the White Slave Trade. To become independent, is to be able to make other people support you, without being obliged to labor for *them*. Now, what man in society is not seeking to attain this situation? He who attains it, is a slave owner, in the worst sense. He who is in pursuit of it, is engaged in the slave trade. You, reader, belong to the one or other class. The men without property, in free society, are theoretically in a worse condition than slaves. Practically, their condition corresponds with this theory, as history and statistics every where demonstrate. The capitalists, in free society, live in ten times the luxury and show that Southern masters do, because the slaves to capital work harder and cost less, than negro slaves.

The negro slaves of the South are the happiest, and, in some sense, the freest people in the world. The children and the aged and infirm work not at all, and yet have all the comforts and necessaries of life provided for them. They enjoy liberty, because they are oppressed neither by care nor labor. The women do little hard work, and are

protected from the despotism of their husbands by their
masters. The negro men and stout boys work, on the average, in good weather, not more than nine hours a day.
The balance of their time is spent in perfect abandon.
Besides, they have their Sabbaths and holidays. White
men, with so much of license and liberty, would die of
ennui; but negroes luxuriate in corporeal and mental repose. With their faces upturned to the sun, they can sleep
at any hour; and quiet sleep is the greatest of human enjoyments. "Blessed be the man who invented sleep." 'Tis
happiness in itself—and results from contentment with the
present, and confident assurance of the future. We do not
know whether free laborers ever sleep. They are fools to
do so; for, whilst they sleep, the wily and watchful capitalist is devising means to ensnare and exploitate them. The
free laborer must work or starve. He is more of a slave
than the negro, because he works longer and harder for
less allowance than the slave, and has no holiday, because
the cares of life with him begin when its labors end. He
has no liberty, and not a single right. We know, 'tis often
said, air and water are common property, which all have
equal right to participate and enjoy; but this is utterly
false. The appropriation of the lands carries with it the
appropriation of all on or above the lands, *usque ad cœlum,*
aut ad inferos. A man cannot breathe the air, without a
place to breathe it from, and all places are appropriated.
All water is private property "to the middle of the stream,"
except the ocean, and that is not fit to drink.

Free laborers have not a thousandth part of the rights
and liberties of negro slaves. Indeed, they have not a
single right or a single liberty, unless it be the right or liberty to die. But the reader may think that he and other
capitalists and employers are freer than negro slaves. Your
capital would soon vanish, if you dared indulge in the liberty and abandon of negroes. You hold your wealth and
position by the tenure of constant watchfulness, care and
circumspection. You never labor; but you are never free.

Where a few own the soil, they have unlimited power
over the balance of society, until domestic slavery comes
in, to compel them to permit this balance of society to
draw a sufficient and comfortable living from "terra ma-
ter." Free society, asserts the right of a few to the earth—

slavery, maintains that it belongs, in different degrees, to all.

But, reader, well may you follow the slave trade. It is the only trade worth following, and slaves the only property worth owning. All other is worthless, a mere *caput mortuum,* except in so far as it vests the owner with the power to command the labors of others—to enslave them. Give you a palace, ten thousand acres of land, sumptuous clothes, equipage and every other luxury; and with your artificial wants, you are poorer than Robinson Crusoe, or the lowest working man, if you have no slaves to capital, or domestic slaves. Your capital will not bring you an income of a cent, nor supply one of your wants, without labor. Labor is indispensable to give value to property, and if you owned every thing else, and did not own labor, you would be poor. But fifty thousand dollars means, and is, fifty thousand dollars worth of slaves. You can command, without touching on that capital, three thousand dollars' worth of labor per annum. You could do no more were you to buy slaves with it, and then you would be cumbered with the cares of governing and providing for them. You are a slaveholder now, to the amount of fifty thousand dollars, with all the advantages, and none of the cares and responsibilities of a master.

"Property in man" is what all are struggling to obtain. Why should they not be obliged to take care of man, their property, as they do of their horses and their hounds, their cattle and their sheep. Now, under the delusive name of liberty, you work him, "from morn to dewy eve"—from infancy to old age—then turn him out to starve. You treat your horses and hounds better. Capital is a cruel master. The free slave trade, the commonest, yet the cruellest of trades.

CHAPTER II.

LABOR, SKILL AND CAPITAL.

NOTHING written on the subject of slavery from the time of Aristotle is worth reading until the days of the modern Socialists. Nobody treating of it thought it worth while to enquire from history and statistics, whether the physical and moral condition of emancipated serfs or slaves had been improved or rendered worse by emancipation. None would condescend to compare the evils of domestic slavery with the evils of liberty without property. It entered no one's head to conceive a doubt as to the actual freedom of the emancipated. The relations of capital and labor, of the property-holders to the non-property-holders, were things about which no one had thought or written. It never occurred to either the enemies or the apologists for slavery, that if no one would employ the free laborer, his condition was infinitely worse than that of actual slavery—nor did it occur to them, that if his wages were less than the allowance of the slave, he was less free after emancipation than before St. Simon, Fourier, Owen, Fanny Wright, and a few others, who discovered and proclaimed that property was not only a bad master, but an intolerable one, were treated as wicked visionaries. After the French and other revolutions in Western Europe in 1830, all men suddenly discovered that the social relations of men were false, and that social, not political, revolutions were needed. Since that period, almost the whole literature of free society is but a voice proclaiming its absolute and total failure. Hence the works of the socialists contain the true defence of slavery.

Most of the active intellect of Christendom has for the last twenty years been engaged in analyzing, detecting and exposing the existing relations of labor, skill and capital, and in vain efforts to rectify those relations. The philosophers of Europe, who have been thus engaged, have excelled all the moral philosophers that preceded them, in the former part of their pursuit, but suggested nothing but puerile absurdities, in the latter. Their destructive philosophy is profound, demonstrative, and unanswerable—their constructive theories, wild, visionary and chimerical on paper, and failures in practice. Each one of them proves clearly enough, that the present edifice of European society is out of all rule and proportion, and must soon tumble to pieces—but no two agree as to how it is to be re-built. "We must (say they all) have a new world, if we are to have any world at all!" and each has a little model Utopia or Phalanstery, for this new and better world, which, having already failed on a small experimental scale, the inventor assures us, is, therefore, the very thing to succeed on a large one. We allude to the socialists and communists, who have more or less tinged all modern literature with their doctrines. In analyzing society; in detecting, exposing, and generalizing its operations and its various phenomena, they are but grammarians or anatomists, confining philosophy to its proper sphere, and employing it for useful purposes. When they attempt to go further—and having found the present social system to be fatally diseased, propose to originate and build up another in its stead—they are as presumptuous as the anatomist, who should attempt to create a man. Social bodies, like human bodies, are the works of God, which man may dissect, and sometimes heal, but which he cannot create. Society was not always thus diseased, or socialism would have been as common in the past as it is now. We think these presumptuous philosophers had best compare it in its healthy state with what it is now, and supply deficiencies or lop off excrescencies, as the comparison may suggest. But our present business is to call attention to some valuable discoveries in the terra firma of social science, which these socialists have made in their vain voyages in search of an ever receding and illusory Utopia. Like the alchymists, although they have signally failed in the objects of their pursuits, they have incidentally hit upon truths, unregarded and unprized by themselves, which will be valuable in the hands of more practical and less sanguine men. It is remarkable, that the political economists, who generally assume labor to be the most just and correct measure of value, should not

have discovered that the profits of capital represent no labor at all. To be consistent, the political economists should
denounce as unjust all interests, rents, dividends and other
profits of capital. We mean by rents, that portion of the
rent which is strictly income. The amount annually required for repairs and ultimately to rebuild the house, is
not profit. Four per cent. will do this. A rent of ten per
cent. is in such case a profit of six per cent. The four per
cent. is but a return to the builder of his labor and capital spent in building. "The use of a thing, is only a fair
subject of change, in so far as the article used is consumed
in the use; for such consumption is the consumption of the
labor or capital of the owner, and is but the exchange of
equivalent amounts of labor."

These socialists, having discovered that skill and capital,
by means of free competition, exercise an undue mastery
over labor, propose to do away with skill, capital, and free
competition, altogether. They would heal the diseases of
society by destroying its most vital functions. Having laid
down the broad proposition, that equal amounts of labor,
or their results, should be exchanged for each other, they
get at the conclusion that as the profits of capital are not
the results of labor, the capitalist shall be denied all interest or rents, or other profits on his capital, and be compelled in all cases to exchange a part of the capital itself,
for labor, or its results. This would prevent accumulation,
or at least limit it to the procurement of the coarsest necessaries of life. They say, "the lawyer and the artist do not
work so hard and continuously as the ploughman, and
should receive less wages than he—a bushel of wheat represents as much labor as a speech or portrait, and should
be exchanged for the one or the other." Such a system
of trade and exchange would equalize conditions, but
would banish civilization. Yet do these men show, that,
by means of the taxation and oppression, which capital
and skill exercise over labor, the rich, the professional, the
trading and skillful part of society, have become the masters of the laboring masses: whose condition, already intolerable, is daily becoming worse. They point out distinctly
the character of the disease under which the patient is
laboring, but see no way of curing the disease except by
killing the patient.

In the preceding chapter, we illustrated their theory of

capital by a single example. We might give hundreds of
illustrations, and yet the subject is so difficult that few
readers will take the trouble to understand it. Let us take
two well known historical instances: England became possessed of two fine islands, Ireland and Jamaica. Englishmen took away, or defrauded, from the Irish, their lands;
but professed to leave the people free. The people, however, must have the use of land, or starve. The English
charged them, in rent, so much, that their allowance, after
deducting that rent, was not half that of Jamaica slaves.
They were compelled to labor for their landlords, by the
fear of hunger and death—forces stronger than the overseer's lash. They worked more, and did not get half so
much pay or allowance as the Jamaica negroes. All the
reports to the French and British Parliaments show that
the physical wants of the West India slaves were well supplied. The Irish became the subjects of capital—slaves,
with no masters obliged by law, self-interest or domestic
affections, to provide for them. The freest people in the
world, in the loose and common sense of words, their condition, moral, physical and religious, was far worse than
that of civilized slaves ever has been or ever can be—for
at length, after centuries of slow starvation, three hundred
thousand perished in a single season, for want of food.
Englishmen took the lands of Jamaica also, but introduced
negro slaves, whom they were compelled to support at all
seasons, and at any cost. The negroes were comfortable,
until philanthropy taxed the poor of England and Ireland
a hundred millions to free them. Now, they enjoy Irish
liberty, whilst the English hold all the good lands. They
are destitute and savage, and in all respects worse off than
when in slavery.

Public opinion unites with self-interest, domestic affection and municipal law to protect the slave. The man who
maltreats the weak and dependant, who abuses his authority over wife, children or slaves, is universally detested.
That same public opinion, which shields and protects the
slave, encourages the oppression of free laborers—for it is
considered more honorable and praiseworthy to obtain
large fees than small ones, to make good bargains than bad
ones, (and all fees and profits come ultimately from common laborers)—to live without work, by the exactions of
accumulated capital, than to labor at the plough or the

spade, for one's living. It is the interest of the capitalist and the skillful to allow free laborers the least possible portion of the fruits of their own labor; for all capital is created by labor, and the smaller the allowance of the free laborer, the greater the gains of his employer. To treat free laborers badly and unfairly, is universally inculcated as a moral duty, and the selfishness of man's nature prompts him to the most rigorous performance of this cannibalish duty. We appeal to political economy; the ethical, social, political and economic philosophy of free society, to prove the truth of our doctrines. As an ethical and social guide, that philosophy teaches, that social, individual and national competition, is a moral duty, and we have attempted to prove that all competition is but the effort to enslave others, without being encumbered with their support. As a political guide, it would simply have government 'keep the peace;' or, to define its doctrine more exactly, it teaches "that it is the whole duty of government to hold the weak whilst the strong rob them"—for it punishes crimes accompanied with force, which none but the weak-minded commit; but encourages the war of the wits, in which the strong and astute are sure to succeed, in stripping the weak and ignorant.

It is time, high time, that political economy was banished from our schools. But what would this avail in free society, where men's antagonistic relations suggest to each one, without a teacher, that "he can only be just to himself, by doing wrong to others." Aristotle, and most other ancient philosophers and statesmen, held the doctrine, "that as money would not breed, interest should not be allowed." Moses, no doubt, saw as the modern socialists do, that all other capital stood on the same grounds with money. None of it is self-creative, or will "breed." The language employed about "usury" and "increase" in 25th Leviticus, and 23d Deuteronomy, is quite broad enough to embrace and prohibit all profits of capital. Such interest or "increase," or profits, might be charged to the Heathen, but not to the Jews. The whole arrangements of Moses were obviously intended to prevent competition in the dealings of the Jews with one another, and to beget permanent equality of condition and fraternal feelings.

The socialists have done one great good. They enable us to understand and appreciate the institutions of Moses, and to see, that none but Divinity could have originated them.* The situation of Judea was, in many respects, anomalous, and we are not to suppose that its political and social relations were intended to be universal. Yet, here it is distinctly asserted, that under certain circumstances, all profits on capital are wrong.

The reformers of the present day are all teetotalists, and attempt to banish evil altogether, not to lessen or restrict it. It would be wiser to assume that there is nothing, in its essence, evil, in the moral or physical world, but only rendered so by the wrongful applications which men make of them. Science is every day discovering that the most fatal poisons, when properly employed, become the most efficacious medicines. So, what appear to be the evil passions and propensities of men, and of societies, under proper regulation, may be made to minister to the wisest and best of purposes. Civilized society has never been found without that competition begotten by man's desire to throw most of the burdens of life on others, and to enjoy the fruits of their labors without exchanging equivalent labor of his own. In all such societies, (outside the Bible,) such selfish and grasping appropriation is inculcated as a moral duty; and he who succeeds best, either by the exercise of professional skill, or by accumulation of capital, in appropriating the labor of others, without laboring in return, is considered most meritorious. It would be unfair, in treating of the relations of capital and labor, not to consider its poor-house system, the ultimate resort of the poor.

The taxes or poor rates which support this system of relief, like all other taxes and values, are derived from the labor of the poor. The able-bodied, industrious poor are

---

* Not only does Moses evince his knowledge of the despotism of capital, in forbidding its profits, but also in his injunction, not to let emancipated slaves "go away empty." Deuteronomy xv. 13, 14.

"And when thou sendest him out free from thee, thou shalt not let him go away empty. Thou shalt furnish him liberally out of thy flock, and out of thy floor, and out of thy wine-press: of that wherewith the Lord thy God hath blessed thee thou shalt give unto him."

People without property exposed to the unrestricted exactions of capital are infinitely worse off after emancipation than before. Moses prevented the exactions of capital by providing property for the new free man.

compelled by the rich and skillful to support the weak, and
too often, the idle poor. In addition to defraying the necessary expenses and the wanton luxuries of the rich, to supporting government, and supporting themselves, capital
compels them to support its poor houses. In collection of
the poor rates, in their distribution, and in the administration of the poor-house system, probably half the tax raised
for the poor is exhausted. Of the remainder, possibly another half is expended on unworthy objects. Masters, in
like manner, support the sick, infant and aged slaves from
the labor of the strong and healthy. But nothing is wasted
in collection and administration, and nothing given to unworthy objects. The master having the control of the
objects of his bounty, takes care that they shall not become burdensome by their own crimes and idleness. It is
contrary to all human customs and legal analogies, that
those who are dependent, or are likely to become so,
should not be controlled. The duty of protecting the weak
involves the necessity of enslaving them—hence, in all
countries, women and children, wards and apprentices,
have been essentially slaves, controlled, not by law, but by
the will of a superior. This is a fatal defect in the poor-
house system. Many men become paupers from their own
improvidence or misconduct, and masters alone can prevent such misconduct and improvidence. Masters treat
their sick, infant and helpless slaves well, not only from
feeling and affection, but from motives of self-interest.
Good treatment renders them more valuable. All poor
houses, are administered on the penitentiary system, in order to deter the poor from resorting to them. Besides, masters are always in place to render needful aid to the unfortunate and helpless slaves. Thousands of the poor starve
out of reach of the poor house, or other public charity.

A common charge preferred against slavery is, that it
induces idleness with the masters. The trouble, care and
labor, of providing for wife, children and slaves, and of
properly governing and administering the whole affairs of
the farm, is usually borne on small estates by the master.
On larger ones, he is aided by an overseer or manager. If
they do their duty, their time is fully occupied. If they do
not, the estate goes to ruin. The mistress, on Southern
farms, is usually more busily, usefully and benevolently
occupied than any one on the farm. She unites in her per-

son, the offices of wife, mother, mistress, housekeeper, and
sister of charity. And she fulfills all these offices admirably
well. The rich men, in free society, may, if they please,
lounge about town, visit clubs, attend the theatre, and
have no other trouble than that of collecting rents, interest
and dividends of stock. In a well constituted slave society,
there should be no idlers. But we cannot divine how the
capitalists in free society are to be put to work. The master
labors for the slave, they exchange industrial value. But
the capitalist, living on his income, gives nothing to his
subjects. He lives by mere exploitation.

It is objected that slavery permits or induces immorality
and ignorance. This is a mistake. The intercourse of the
house-servants with the white family, assimilates, in some
degree, their state of information, and their moral conduct,
to that of the whites. The house-servants, by their intercourse with the field hands, impart their knowledge to
them. The master enforces decent morality in all. Negroes
are never ignorant of the truths of Christianity, all speak
intelligible English, and are posted up in the ordinary oc-
currences of the times. The reports to the British Parliament shew, that the agricultural and mining poor of
England scarce know the existence of God, do not speak
intelligible English, and are generally depraved and ignorant. They learn nothing by intercourse with their superiors, as negroes do. They abuse wives and children, because
they have no masters to control them, and the men are
often dissipated and idle, leaving all the labor to be done
by the women and children—for the want of this same
control.

Slavery, by separating the mass of the ignorant from
each other, and bringing them in contact and daily intercourse with the well-informed, becomes an admirable educational system—no doubt a necessary one. By subjecting
them to the constant control and supervision of their superiors, interested in enforcing morality, it becomes the best
and most efficient police system; so efficient, that the ancient Romans had scarcely any criminal code whatever.

The great objections to the colonial slavery of the latter
Romans, to serfdom, and all forms of prædial slavery, are:
that the slaves are subjected to the cares as well as the labors of life; that the masters become idlers; that want of
intercourse destroys the affectionate relations between

master and slave, throws the mass of ignorant slaves into
no other association but that with the ignorant; and deprives them, as well of the instruction, as the government,
of superiors living on the same farm. Southern slavery is
becoming the best form of slavery of which we have any
history, except that of the Jews. The Jews owned but few
slaves, and with them the relation of master and slave was
truly affectionate, protective and patriarchal. The master,
wife and children were in constant intercourse with the
slaves, and formed, in practice as well as theory, affectionate, well-ordered families.

As modern civilization advances, slavery becomes daily
more necessary, because its tendency is to accumulate all
capital in a few hands, cuts off the masses from the soil,
lessen their wages and their chances of employment,
and increases the necessity for a means of certain subsistence, which slavery alone can furnish, when a few own
all the lands and other capital.

Christian morality can find little practical foothold in a
community so constituted, that to "love our neighbor as
ourself," or "to do unto others as we would they should
do unto us," would be acts of suicidal self-sacrifice. Christian morality, however, was not preached to free competitive society, but to slave society, where it is neither very
difficult nor unnatural to practice it. In the various family
relations of husband, wife, parent, child, master and slave,
the observance of these Christian precepts is often practiced, and almost always promotes the temporal well being
of those who observe it. The interests of the various members of the family circle, correctly understood, concur and
harmonize, and each member best promotes his own selfish
interest by ministering to the wants and interests of the
rest. Two great stumbling blocks are removed from the
acceptance of Scripture, when it is proved that slavery,
which it recognizes, approves and enjoins, is promotive
of men's happiness and well-being, and that the morality,
which it inculcates, although wholly impracticable in free
society, is readily practised in that form of society to which
it was addressed.

We do not conceive that there can be any other moral
law in free society, than that which teaches "that he is
most meritorious who most wrongs his fellow beings:"
for any other law would make men martyrs to their own

virtues. We see thousands of good men vainly struggling against the evil necessities of their situation, and aggravating by their charities the evils which they would cure, for charity in free society is but the tax which skill and capital levy from the working poor, too often, to bestow on the less deserving and idle poor. We know a man at the North who owns millions of dollars, and would throw every cent into the ocean to benefit mankind. But it is capital, and, place it where he will, it becomes an engine to tax and oppress the laboring poor.

It is impossible to place labor and capital in harmonious or friendly relations, except by the means of slavery, which identifies their interests. Would that gentleman lay his capital out in land and negroes, he might be sure, in whatever hands it came, that it would be employed to protect laborers, not to oppress them; for when slaves are worth near a thousand dollars a head, they will be carefully and well provided for. In any other investment he may make of it, it will be used as an engine to squeeze the largest amount of labor from the poor, for the least amount of allowance. We say allowance, not wages; for neither slaves nor free laborers get wages, in the popular sense of the term: that is, the employer or capitalist pays them from nothing of his own, but allows them a part, generally a very small part, of the proceeds of their own labor. Free laborers pay one another, for labor creates all values, and capital, after taking the lion's share by its taxing power, but pays the so-called wages of one laborer from the proceeds of the labor of another. Capital does not breed, yet remains undiminished. Its profits are but its taxing power. Men seek to become independent, in order to cease to pay labor; in order to become masters, without the cares, duties and responsibilities of masters. Capital exercises a more perfect compulsion over free laborers, than human masters over slaves: for free laborers must at all times work or starve, and slaves are supported whether they work or not. Free laborers have less liberty than slaves, are worse paid and provided for, and have no valuable rights. Slaves, with more of actual practical liberty, with ampler allowance, and constant protection, are secure in the enjoyment of all the rights, which provide for their physical comfort at all times and under all circumstances. The free laborer must be employed or starve, yet no one is obliged to employ him. The slave is taken care of, whether employed or not. Though each free laborer has no particular master, his wants and other men's capital, make him a slave without a master, or with too many masters, which is as bad as none. It were often better that he had an ascertained master, instead of an irresponsible and unascertained one.

There are some startling social phenomena connected with this subject of labor and capital, which will probably be new to most of our readers. Legislators and philosophers often puzzle their own and other people's brains, in vain discussions as to how the taxes shall be laid, so as to fall on the rich rather than the poor. It results from our theory, that as labor creates all values, laborers pay all taxes, and the rich, in the words of Gerrit Smith, "are but the conduits that pass them over to government."

Again, since labor alone creates and pays the profits of capital; increase and accumulation of capital but increase the labor of the poor, and lessen their remuneration. Thus the poor are continually forging new chains for themselves. Proudhon cites a familiar instance to prove and illustrate this theory: A tenant improves a farm or house, and enhances their rents; his labor thus becomes the means of increasing the tax, which he or some one else must pay to the capitalist. What is true in this instance, is true of the aggregate capital of the world: its increase is but an increased tax on labor. A., by trade or speculation, gets hold of an additional million of dollars, to the capital already in existence. Now his million of dollars will yield no profit, unless a number of pauper laborers, sufficient to pay its profits, are at the same time brought into existence. After supporting their families, it will require a thousand of laborers to pay the interest or profits of a million of dollars. It may, therefore, be generally assumed as true, that where a country has gained a millionaire, it has by the same process gained a thousand pauper laborers: Provided it has been made by profits on foreign trade, or by new values created at home—that is, if it be an *addition* of a million to the capital of the nation.

A nation borrows a hundred millions, at six per cent., for a hundred years. During that time it pays, in way of tax, called interest, six times the capital loaned, and then returns the capital itself. During all this time, to the amount of the interest, the people of this nation have been slaves to the lender. He has commanded, not paid, for their labor; for his capital is returned intact. In the abstract, and according to equity, "the use of an article is only a proper subject of charge, when the article is consumed in the use; for this consumption is the consumption of the labor of the lender or hirer, and is the exchange of equal amounts of labor for each other.

A., as a merchant, a lawyer, or doctor, makes twenty dollars a day; that is, exchanges each day of his own labor for twenty days of the labor of common working men, assuming that they work at a dollar a day. In twenty years, he amasses fifty thousand dollars, invests it, and settles it on his family. Without any labor, he and his heirs, retaining all this capital, continue, by its means, to levy a tax of three thousand dollars from common laborers. He and his heirs now pay nothing for labor, but command it. They have nothing to pay except their capital, and that they retain. (This is the exploitation or despotism of capital, which has taken the place of domestic slavery, and is, in fact, a much worse kind of slavery. Hence arises socialism, which proposes to reconstruct society.) Now, this capitalist is considered highly meritorious for so doing, and the poor, self-sacrificing laborers, who really created his capital, and who pays its profits, are thought contemptible, if not criminal. In the general, those men are considered the most meritorious who live in greatest splendor, with the least, or with no labor, and they most contemptible, who labor most for others, and least for themselves. In the abstract, however, that dealing appears most correct, where men exchange equal amounts of labor, bear equal burdens for others, with those that they impose on them. Such is the golden rule of Scripture, but not the approved practice of mankind.

"The worth of a thing is just what it will bring," is the common trading principle of mankind. Yet men revolt at the extreme applications of their own principle, and denunciate any gross and palpable advantage taken of the wants, position and necessities of others as *swindling*. But we should recollect, that in all instances where unequal amounts of labor are exchanged at par, advantage is really taken by him who gets in exchange the larger amount of labor, of the wants, position and necessities of him who receives the smaller amount.

We have said that laborers pay all taxes, but labor being capital in slave society, the laborers or slaves are not injured by increased taxes; and the capitalist or master has to retrench his own expenses to meet the additional tax. Capital is not taxed in free society, but *is* taxed in slave society, because, in such society, labor is capital.

The capitalists and the professional can, and do, by increased profits and fees, throw the whole burden of taxation on the laboring class. Slaveholders cannot do so; for diminished allowance to their slaves would impair their value and lessen their own capital.

Our expose of what the socialists term the exploitation of skill and capital, will not, we know, be satisfactory to slaveholders even; for, although there be much less of such exploitation, or unjust exaction, in slave society; still, too much of it remains to be agreeable to contemplate. Besides, our analysis of human nature and human pursuits, is too dark and sombre to meet with ready acceptance. We should be rejoiced to see our theory refuted. We are sure, however, that it never can be; but equally sure, that it is subject to many modifications and limitations that have not occurred to us. We have this consolation, that in rejecting as false and noxious all systems of moral philosophy, we are thrown upon the Bible, as containing the only true system of morals. We have attempted already to adduce three instances, in which the justification of slavery furnished new and additional evidence of the truth of Christianity. We will now add others.

It is notorious that infidelity appeared in the world, on an extensive scale, only co-temporaneously with the abolition of slavery, and that it is now limited to countries where no domestic slavery exists. Besides, abolitionists are commonly infidels, as their speeches, conventions, and papers daily evince. Where there is no slavery, the minds of men are unsettled on all subjects, and there is, emphatically, faith and conviction about nothing. Their moral and social world is in a chaotic and anarchical state. Order, subordination and adaptation have vanished; and with them, the belief in a Deity, the author of all order. It had often been urged, that the order observable in the moral and physical world, furnished strong evidence of a Deity, the author of that order. How vastly is this argument now strengthened, by the new fact, now first developed, that the destruction of social order generates universal scepticism. Mere political revolutions affect social order but little, and generate but little infidelity. It remained for social revolutions, like those in Europe in 1848, to bring on an infidel age; for, outside of slave society, such is the age in which we live.

If we prove that domestic slavery is, in the general, a natural and necessary institution, we remove the greatest stumbling block to belief in the Bible; for whilst texts, detached and torn from their context, may be found for any other purpose, none can be found that even militates against slavery. The distorted and forced construction of certain passages, for this purpose, by abolitionists, if employed as a common rule of construction, would reduce the Bible to a mere allegory, to be interpreted to suit every vicious taste and wicked purpose.

But we have been looking merely to one side of human nature, and to that side rendered darker by the false, antagonistic and competitive relations in which so-called liberty and equality place man.

Man is, by nature, the most social and gregarious, and, therefore, the least selfish of animals. Within the family there is little room, opportunity or temptation to selfishness—and slavery leaves but little of the world without the family. Man loves that nearest to him best. First his wife, children and parents, then his slaves, next his neighbors and fellow-countrymen. But his unselfishness does not stop here. He is ready and anxious to relieve a famine in Ireland, and shudders when he reads of a murder at the antipodes. He feels deeply for the sufferings of domestic animals, and is rendered happy by witnessing the enjoyments of the flocks, and herds, and carroling birds that surround him. He sympathizes with all external nature. A parched field distresses him, and he rejoices as he sees the groves, and the gardens, and the plains flourishing, and blooming, and smiling about him. All men are philanthropists, and would benefit their fellow-men if they could. But we cannot be sure of benefiting those whom we cannot control. Hence, all actively good men are ambitious, and would be masters, in all save the name.

Benevolence, the love of what is without, and the disposition to incur pain or inconvenience to advance the happiness and well-being of what is without self, is as universal a motive of human conduct, as mere selfishness—which is the disposition to sacrifice the good of others to our own good.

The prevalent philosophy of the day takes cognizance of but half of human nature—and that the worst half. Our happiness is so involved in the happiness and well-being of everything around us, that a mere selfish philosophy, like political economy, is a very unsafe and delusive guide.

We employ the term Benevolence to express our outward affections, sympathies, tastes and feelings; but it is inadequate to express our meaning; it is not the opposite of selfishness, and unselfishness would be too negative for our purpose. Philosophy has been so busy with the worst feature of human nature, that it has not even found a name for this, its better feature. We must fall back on Christianity, which embraces man's whole nature, and though not a code of philosophy, is something better; for it proposes to lead us through the trials and intricacies of life, not by the mere cool calculations of the head, but by the unerring instincts of a pure and regenerate heart. The problem of the Moral World is too vast and complex for the human mind to comprehend; yet the pure heart will, safely and quietly, feel its way through the mazes that confound the head.

CHAPTER III.

INTERNATIONAL EXPLOITATION.

As INDIVIDUALS possessing skill or capital exploitate, or compel other individuals in the same community to work for them for nothing, or for undue consideration, precisely in the same way do nations possessed of those advantages exploitate other nations with whom they trade, who are without them.

England lends, say, five hundred millions of dollars to governments and individuals in America. In a hundred years, she will have withdrawn from us, in interest, six times the amount loaned or advanced, and at the expiration of that time she withdraws the principal itself. We pay England a tax of at least three thousand millions of dollars in a century; for her loans to us are probably even larger than the amount assumed. She commands the results of our labor to that extent, and gives us not a cent of the results of her labor in return—for her principal loaned represents her labor, and that we return to her intact. We are, to that extent, her slaves,—"slaves without masters;" for she commands and enjoys our labor, and is under none of the obligations of a master—to protect, defend and provide for us.

Her superior skill in the mechanic arts, by means of free trade, taxes or exploitates us quite as much as her capital. She exchanges her comparatively light and skillful labor, for our hard, exposed and unintellectual labor; and, in the general, compels us to labor three hours for her, when she labors one for us. Thus, after deducting the cost of the material, a yard of her cloth will exchange for an amount of our cotton, corn or meat, that cost three times as much labor to produce as her yard of cloth.

As in society, the skillful and professional tax or ex-

ploitate the common laborer, by exchanging one hour of
their light labor for many of the common workingman's
hard labor; as lawyers, doctors, merchants and mechanics
deal with day laborers, so England and New England treat
us of the South. This theory, and this alone, accounts for
England's ability to pay the interest on her national debt,
and yet increase her wealth. She effects it all by the immense profits of the exploitation of her skill and capital; by
the power which they give her to command labor, and appropriate its results, without consideration, or for a very
partial consideration. She trades with the world, and exploitates it all, except France. France sets the fashion, and
this enables her to exploitate England. England, in her
trade with France, has to pay for French fashions as well
as French labor. In other words, France possesses superior skill, and exploitates England by means of it. Labor,
not skill, is the just and equitable measure of values.

America sends her cotton, her surplus grain and meats,
and other agricultural products, and her California gold,
to England, and gets worse than nothing in return; for if
she were compelled to produce at home what she procures
from England, she must cultivate a thousand skillful and
intellectual pursuits, instead of being, as she too much is,
confined to the coarse drudgery of common labor. The
Southern States of this Union are exploitated of their labor
and their brains, in their trade with England and New
England. They produce nothing which we had not better
produce at home. Northern trade exploitates us. Trade further South would enrich us and enlighten us; for we would
manufacture for the far South. We should become exploi-
tators, instead of being exploitated.

When we were in New Haven, a distinguished abolitionist boasted to us that mechanics received two dollars
per day for their labor, and, by their China trade, exchanged the products of one day's labor for twenty days'
labor of the Chinese, who worked for ten cents a day. The
New England mechanic was thus the master of twenty
Chinese laborers, whose labor he commanded for one of
his own day's labor. Here was an instance of individual,
not of national exploitation. Well might China dread free
trade. It gives her task-masters, who impoverish her people and depress her civilization; for they, by their machin-

ery and superior skill, withdraw her people from a thousand mechanical pursuits that promoted civilization.

In *Sociology* [*for the South*]; we explained this subject synthetically: we have tried now to expound it analytically.

CHAPTER IV.

FREE TRADE, FASHION AND CENTRALIZATION.

LIBERTY and political economy beget and encourage free trade, as well between different localities and different nations, as between individuals of the same towns, neighborhoods or nations. The nations possessed of most skill and capital, and commercial enterprise, and cunning, gradually absorb the wealth of those nations who possess less of those qualities. The effect of international free trade, aided by the facilities of the credit system, of the mail, and speedy steam communication, is to centralize wealth in a few large cities, such as New York, Paris and London; and of social free trade to aggregate wealth in a few hands in those cities. Theoretically, the disparities of shrewdness, of skill and business capacity, between nations and individuals, would, in the commercial and trading war of the wits, rob the weak and simple, and enrich the strong and cunning. The facts of history, and of the increasing inequalities of social, individual and national wealth, under the system of free trade, stimulated by political economy, correspond with the theory. Every month brings forth its millionaire, and every day its thousands of new paupers. New York and London grow richer rapidly on the fruits of a trade that robs the less commercial and skillful people who traffic with them.

But the worst effect of free trade is, that it begets centres of opinion, thought and fashions, robs men of their nationality, and impairs their patriotism by teaching them to ape foreign manners, affect foreign dress and opinions, and despise what is domestic. Paris, as the centre of thought and fashion, wields as much power, and makes almost as much money as London, by being the centre of trade and capital. An American or Englishman will give

134

five prices for an article because it is made in Paris. Thus the want of true self-respect in America and England, makes labor produce more in Paris than elsewhere. A Virginian thinks it a disgrace to be dressed in home-spun, because home-spun is unfashionable. The Frenchman prides himself on being a Frenchman; all other people affect the cosmopolitan.

The tendency of all this is to transfer all wealth to London, New York and Paris, and reduce the civilization of Christendom to a miserable copy of French civilization, itself an indifferent copy of Roman civilization, which was an imitation, but a falling off from that of Greece.

We pay millions monthly for French silks, French wines, French brandy, and French trinkets, although we can and do make as comfortable articles for dress, and as good liquors, at home. But we despise ourselves, and admire the French, and give four hours of American labor for one of French labor, just to be in the fashion. And what is our fashion? To treat whatever is American with contempt. People who thus act are in a fair way to deserve and meet with from others that contempt which they feel for themselves. The little States of Greece each had its dialect, and cultivated it, and took pride in it. Now, dialects are vulgar and provincial. We shall have no men like the Greeks, till the manners, dress, and dialect of gentlemen, betray, like the wines of Europe, the very neighborhood whence they come. So thought Mr. Calhoun, and talked South Carolina dialect in the Senate. But for all that, it was the best English of the day. Its smack of provincialism gave it a higher flavor.

We of the South teach political economy, because it is taught in Europe. Yet political economy, and all other systems of moral science, which we derive from Europe, are tainted with abolition, and at war with our institutions. We must build up centres of trade, of thought and fashion at home. We must become national, nay, provincial, and cease to be imitative cosmopolitans. We must, especially, have good colleges and universities, where young men may learn to admire their homes, not to despise them.

The South feels the truth of all this, and after a while will begin to understand it. She has been for years earnestly and actively engaged in *promoting* the exclusive and protective policy, and preaching free trade, non-interference of government and 'let alone.' But she does not let alone. She builds roads and canals, encourages education, endows schools and colleges, improves river navigation, excludes, or taxes heavily foreign show-men, foreign pedlars, sellers of clocks, &c.; tries to build up by legislation Southern commerce, and by State legislation to multiply and encourage industrial pursuits. Protection by the State Government is her established policy—and that is the only expedient or constitutional protection. It is time for her to avow her change of policy and opinion, and to throw Adam Smith, Say, Ricardo & Co., in the fire.

We want American customs, habits, manners, dress, manufactures, modes of thought, modes of expression, and language. We should encourage national and even State peculiarities; for there are peculiarities and differences in the wants and situations of all people, that require provincial and national, not cosmopolitan, institutions and productions. Take language, for instance. It is a thing of natural growth and development, and adapts itself naturally to the changes of time and circumstance. It is never ungrammatical as spoken by children, but always expressive, practical and natural. Nature is always grammatical, and language, the child of nature, would continue so, but for the grammarians, who, with their Procrustean rules, disturb its proportions, destroy its variety and adaptation, and retard its growth. They are to language what dentists are to teeth: they more often injure it than improve it.

Grammar, lexicography, and rhetoric, applied to language, destroy its growth, variety and adaptability—stereotype it, make it at once essentially a dead language, and unfit for future use; for new localities, and changes of time and circumstances, beget new ideas, and require new words and new combinations of words. Centralization and cosmopolitanism have precisely the same effect. They would furnish a common language from the centre, which is only fully expressive and comprehensive at that centre. Walking and talking are equally natural, and talking masters and walking masters equally useless. Neither can foresee and provide for the thousands of new circumstances which make change of language, or varieties of movement necessary. Nature is never at a loss, and is the only reliable dancing master and grammar teacher. She is always graceful and appropriate, and always ready to adapt herself to changes of time, situation and circumstances.

Paris is becoming the universal model and grammar of Christendom; nothing is right unless it be a la Parisienne. Now, in truth, nothing can be right, natural, appropriate, or in good taste, outside of Paris, that is Parisienne. When will our monkey imitative world cease to sacrifice millions of money, cease to show its want of good sense and propriety, and cease to render itself ridiculous by aping what in the nature of things is unsuitable, inappropriate, and unnatural? Fashion, aided by free trade and centralization, is subjecting us to the dominion of Parisian thought; and commerce, by means of the same agencies, makes us tributaries to London. Trade and fashion conquer faster than arms.

After the Romans had conquered Greece, Athens became the school and centre of thought for the civilized world. Men had but one set of ideas, but one set of models to imitate, in the whole range of the fine arts. Inventiveness and originality ceased, and genius was subdued. The rule of Horace, *"Nullius addictus in verba magistri jurare,"* was versed, and men ceased to think for themselves, but looked to the common fountain of thought at Athens; where the teachers of mankind borrowed all their ideas from the past. Improvement and progress ceased, and imitation, chaining the present to the car of the past, soon induced rapid retrogression. Thus, we think centralization of thought occasioned the decline of civilization. Northern invaders introduced new ideas, broke up centralization, arrested imitation, and begot originality and inventiveness. Thus a start was given to a new and Christian civilization. Now, a centralization occasioned by commerce and fashion, threatens the overthrow of our civilization, as arms and conquest overthrew the ancient.

The ill effect of centralization of thought, whether its centre be the past, or some locality of the present, is apparent in the arts and literature of the Latin nations of Europe. France, Spain and Italy, though possessed of more genius, have displayed less originality than England and Germany. French art is a mere re-hash of Roman art, and very inferior to its original. The natural growth, changes and adaptation of language, are admirably described by Horace in his *De Arte Poetica*. He makes a great blunder in advising the forming and compounding words from the Greek, however; for the very want that occasions new words, shows that they cannot be supplied from the past.

CHAPTER V.

LIBERTY AND SLAVERY.

Effugit imago,
Par livibus ventis, volucri que simillima somno.

It seems to us that the vain attempts to define liberty in theory, or to secure its enjoyment in practice, proceed from the fact that man is naturally a social and gregarious animal, subject, not by contract or agreement, as Locke and his followers assume, but by birth and nature, to those restrictions of liberty which are expedient or necessary to secure the good of the human hive, to which he may belong. There is no such thing as *natural human* liberty, because it is unnatural for man to live alone and without the pale and government of society. Birds, and beasts of prey, who are not gregarious, are naturally free. Bees and herds are naturally subjects or slaves of society. Such is the theory of Aristotle, promulged more than two thousand years ago, generally considered true for two thousand years, and destined, we hope, soon again to be accepted as the only true theory of government and society.

Modern social reformers, except Mr. Carlyle, proceeding upon the theory of Locke, which is the opposite of Aristotle, propose to dissolve and disintegrate society; falsely supposing that they thereby follow nature. There is not a human tie that binds man to man that they do not propose to cut "sheer asunder." 'Tis true, after their work of destruction is finished, they see the necessity of society; but instead of that natural and historical society, which has usually existed in the world, with its gradations of rank and power, its families and its slaves, they propose wholly to disregard the natural relations of mankind, and profanely to build up states, like Fourierite Phalansteries, or Mormon and Oneida villages, where religion shall be banished, and in which property, wife and children shall

139

be held somewhat in common. These social establishments, under a self-elected despotism like that of Joe Smith, or Brigham Young, become patriarchal, and succeed so long as such despotism lasts. That is, when the association loses the character intended by its founders, and acquires a despotic head like other family associations, it works well, because it works naturally. But this success can only be temporary; for nothing but the strong rule of a Cromwell or Joe Smith can keep a society together, that wants the elements of cohesion, in the natural ties that bind man to man: and Cromwells and Joe Smiths are not to be found every day.

'Tis an historical fact, that this family association, this patriarchal government, for purposes of defence against enemies from without, gradually merges into larger associations of men under a common government or ruler. This latter is the almost universal, and we may thence infer, natural and normal condition of civilized man. In this state of society there is no liberty for the masses. Liberty has been exchanged by nature for security.

What is falsely called Free Society, is a very recent invention. It proposes to make the weak, ignorant and poor, free, by turning them loose in a world owned exclusively by the few (whom nature and education have made strong, and whom property has made stronger,) to get a living. In the fanciful state of nature, where property is unappropriated, the strong have no weapons but superior physical and mental power with which to oppress the weak. Their power of oppression is increased a thousand fold, when they become the exclusive owners of the earth and all the things thereon. They are masters without the obligations of masters, and the poor are slaves without the rights of slaves.

It is generally conceded, even by abolitionists, that the serfs of Europe were liberated because the multitude of laborers, and their competition as freemen to get employment, had rendered free labor cheaper than slave labor. But, strange to say, few seem to have seen that this is in fact asserting that they were less free after emancipation than before. Their obligation to labor was increased; for they were compelled to labor more than before to obtain a livelihood, else their free labor would not have been cheaper than their labor as slaves. They lost something in liberty, and everything in rights—for emancipation liberated or released the masters from all their burdens, cares and liabilities, whilst it increased both the labors and the cares of the liberated serf. In our chapter on the Decay of English Liberty, we show that the whole struggle in England has been to oppress the working man, pull down the powers, privileges and prerogatives of the throne, the nobility, and the church, and to elevate the property-holding class.

CHAPTER VI.

DECAY OF ENGLISH LIBERTY, AND GROWTH OF ENGLISH POOR LAWS.

BLACKSTONE, whose Commentaries have been, for half a century, a common school-book, and whose opinions on the rise, growth and full development of British liberty, are generally received as true, as well in America as in Europe, maintains a theory the very opposite of that for which we are about to contend.

He holds that the appearance of the House of Commons, about the reign of Henry the Third, was the dawn of approaching liberty. We contend that it was the origin of the capitalist and moneyed interest government, destined finally to swallow up all other powers in the State, and to bring about the most selfish, exacting and unfeeling class despotism. He thinks the emancipation of the serfs was another advance towards equality of rights and conditions. We think it aggravated inequality of conditions, and divested the liberated class of every valuable social and political right. A short history of the English Poor Laws, which we shall annex, will enable the reader to decide between us on this head. He thinks the Reformation increased the liberties of the subject. We think that, in destroying the noblest charity fund in the world, the church lands, and abolishing a priesthood, the efficient and zealous friends of the poor, the Reformation tended to diminish the liberty of the mass of the people, and to impair their moral, social and physical well-being. He thinks that the Revolution, by increasing the power of the House of Commons, and lessening the prerogative of the Crown, and the influence of the Church, promoted liberty. We think the Crown and the Church the natural friends, allies and guardians of the laboring class; the House of Commons, a moneyed firm, their natural enemies; and that the Revolution was a marked epoch in the steady decay of British liberty.

He thinks that the settlement of 1688 that successfully asserted in theory the supreme sovereignty of Parliament, but particularly the supreme sovereignty of the House of Commons, was the consummation or perfection of British liberty. We are sure, that that settlement, and the chartering of the Bank of England, which soon succeeded it, united the landed and moneyed interests, placed all the powers of government in their hands, and deprived the great laboring class of every valuable right and liberty. The nobility, the church, the king, were now powerless; and the mass of the people, wholly unrepresented in the government, found themselves exposed to the grinding and pitiless despotism of their natural and hereditary enemies. Mr. Charles Dickens, who pities the condition of the negro slaves, thus sums up, in a late speech, the worse condition of the "Slaves without Masters," in Great Britain: "Beneath all this, is a *heaving* mass of poverty, ignorance and crime." Such is English liberty for the masses. Thirty thousand men own the lands of England, three thousand those of Scotland, and fewer still those of Ireland. The great mass of the people are cut off from the soil, have no certain means of subsistence, and are trespassers upon the earth, without a single valuable or available right. Contrast their situations with that of the old villeins, and see then whether our theory of British liberty and the British constitution be true, or that of Blackstone.

All writers agree there were no beggars or paupers in England until the liberation of the serfs; and moreover admit that slaves, in all ages and in all countries, have had all their physical wants sufficiently supplied. They also concur in stating, that crime was multiplied by turning loose on society a class of men who had been accustomed to and still needed the control of masters.

Until the liberation of the villeins, every man in England had his appropriate situation and duties, and a mutual and adequate interest in the soil. Practically the lands of England were the common property of the people of England. The old Barons were not the representatives of particular classes in Parliament, but the friends, and faithful and able representatives of all classes; for the interests of all classes were identified. Monteil, a recent French author, who has written the most accurate and graphic description of social conditions during the Feudal

ages, describes the serfs as the especial pets and favorites
of the Barons. They were the most dependent, obedient,
and useful members of the feudal society, and like
younger children, became favorites. The same class now
constitute the Proletariat, the Lazzaroni, the Gypsies, the
Parias, and the "pauper banditti" of Western Europe, and
the Leperos of Mexico. As slaves, they were loved and
protected; as pretended freemen, they were execrated and
persecuted.

Mr. Lester, a New York abolitionist, after a long and
careful observation and study of the present condition of
the English laboring class, solemnly avers, in his "Glory
and Shame of England," that he would sooner subject his
child to Southern slavery, than have him to be a free laborer of England.

But it is the early history of the English Poor Laws, that
proves most conclusively that the liberation of the villeins
was a sham and a pretence, and that their situation has
been worse, their rights fewer, and their liberties less, since
emancipation than before. The Poor Laws, from the time
of Edward the Third to that of Elizabeth, were laws to
punish the poor, and to keep them at work for low wages.
Not till late in the reign of Elizabeth, was any charitable
provision made for them. Then, most of them would have
starved, as the confiscation and sales of the church lands
had deprived them of their only refuge, but for the new
system of charity. The rich must have labor, and could
not afford to let them *all* starve, although they were ready
to attempt the most stringent means to prevent their increase.

CHAPTER VII.

THE REFORMATION—THE RIGHT
OF PRIVATE JUDGMENT.

THE Reformation, like the American Revolution, was originated and conducted to successful issue by wise, good and practical men, whose intuitive judgments and sagacious instincts enabled them to feel their way through the difficulties that environed them. Wise men know that there is too much of complexity in the tangled web of human affairs to justify the attempt at once to practice and philosophise, to act and to reason. Fools and philosophers too often mar the good works of such men by pretending to see clearly, and to define accurately, the principles of action which have led to those works. A Washington, a Peel, or a Wellington, never "writes himself down an ass" by appealing to abstract principles to justify measures which are rendered necessary by a thousand minute and peculiar circumstances of the hour, which common sense and experience instinctively appreciate, but which philosophy in vain attempts to detect or to generalize. Common sense never attempts "to expel nature," but suggests and carries through a thousand useful reforms by recurrence to and comparison with the past, and by cautious experimentation.

Common sense sometimes errs by excess of conservation; but it is better to err with Pope, who thought "Whatever is, is right," than with Jefferson, whose every act and word proves that he held that "Whatever is, is *wrong*."

The Reformation was not the thought and the act of Luther, Calvin, Cranmer and Erasmus; but the thought and act of society—the vox Populi, vox Dei. Popes and cardinals are not infallible, but society is. Its harmony is its health; and to differ with it is heresy or treason, because social discord inflicts individual misery; and what disturbs and disarranges society, impairs the happiness and well-being of its members.

This doctrine of the infallibility of society, is suggested, though not expressed, in the maxim—Salus populi, est suprema lex. The Puritans, in the early days of New England, acted it out; and if they hung a few troublesome old women, the good that they achieved was more than compensated for by any errors they may have committed. Liberty of the press, liberty of speech, freedom of religion, or rather freedom from religion, and the unlimited right of private judgment, have borne no good fruits, and many bad ones. Infidels, Skeptics, Millerites, Mormons, Agrarians, Spiritual Rappers, Wakemanites, Free Negroes and Bloomers, disturb the peace of society, threaten the security of property, offend the public sense of decency, assail religion, and invoke anarchy. Society has the right, and is in duty bound, to take care of itself; and when public opinion becomes powerless, law should intervene, and punish all acts, words, or opinions, which have become criminal by becoming dangerous or injurious.

We would rejoice to see intolerance of error revived in New England. Laxity of rule and laxity of public opinion is sin of itself, and leads to thousands of sins. New England is culpable for permitting Parker and Beecher to stir up civil discord and domestic broils from the pulpit. These men deserve punishment, for they have instigated and occasioned a thousand murders in Kansas; yet they did nothing more than carry into practice the right of private judgment, liberty of speech, freedom of the press and of religion. These boasted privileges have become far more dangerous to the lives, the property and the peace of the people of this Union, than all the robbers and murderers and malefactors put together.

The Reformation was but an effort of Nature—the vis medicatrix naturæ—throwing off what was false, vicious or superfluous, and retaining what was good.

The great men of the day but show larger portions of the common thought. Men, and all other social and gregarious animals, have a community of thought, of motions, instincts and intuitions. The social body is of itself a thinking, acting, sentient being. This is eminently observable with the lower animals. Bees and herds perform their evolutions with too much rapidity and precision to leave any doubt but that one mind and one feeling, either from within or without, directs their movements. The great error of modern philosophy is the ignorance or forgetfulness of this fact. The first departure from it was not the Reformation—for that was preëminently a social idea and a social movement;—but the doctrine of the right of private judgment, which speculative philosophers and vain schismatics attempted to engraft upon it, or deduce from it. Human equality, the social contract, the let-alone and selfish doctrines of political economy, universal liberty, freedom of speech, of the press, and of religion, spring directly from this doctrine, or are only new modes of expressing it. Agrarianism, Free Love, and No Government, are its logical sequences: for the right to judge for ourself implies the right to act upon our judgments, and that can never be done in a world where the private appropriation of all capital, and the interference of government, restricts our free agency, and paralyzes our action on all sides.

We sometimes think the burning of the Alexandrian Library was a providential purification, just as the fictitious burning, by Cervantes, of Don Quixote's library ridded the world of the useless rubbish of the Middle Ages, by the ridicule so successfully attached to it. Sure we are, that a fire that would consume all the theological and other philosophical speculations of the last two centuries, would be a happy God-send.

Our Revolution, so wise in its conception and so glorious in its execution, was the mere assertion by adults of the rights of adults, and had nothing more to do with philosophy than the weaning of a calf. It was the act of a people seeking national independence, not the Utopian scheme of speculative philosophers, seeking to establish human equality and social perfection.

But the philosophers seized upon it, as they had upon the Reformation, and made it the unwilling and unnatural parent of the largest and most hideous brood of ills that had ever appeared at one birth, since the opening of the box of Pandora. Bills of Rights, Acts of Religious Freedom and Constitutions, besprinkled with doctrines directly at war with all stable government, seem to be the basis on which our institutions rest. But only seem to be; for, in truth, our laws and government are either old An-

glo-Saxon prescriptive arrangements, or else the gradual
accretions of time, circumstance and necessity. Throw our
paper platforms, preambles and resolutions, guaranties
and constitutions, into the fire, and we should be none
the worse off, provided we retained our institutions—and
the necessities that begat, and have, so far, continued
them.

All government proceeds ab extra. Neither individuals
nor societies can govern themselves, any more than the
mouse can live in the exhausted receiver, or the clown lift
himself by the lappel of his pantaloons. The South is governed by the necessity of keeping its negroes in order,
which preserves a healthy conservative public opinion.
Had the negroes votes, the necessity would be removed,
because the interest of the governing class would cease to
be conservative. The necessity, the governing power ab
extra, would be removed. The little republics of ancient
Greece were able to preserve the most artificial social arrangements, under the necessities which slavery and foreign hostile pressure from without begat. They were afraid
of change, because insurrection was dangerous.

If government on paper were really useless and harm-
less, we should say nothing about it. But it is fraught with
danger, first because we are apt to rely on it for safety and
security of rights, and secondly because it rarely suits the
occasion. Men and societies are endowed by Providence
generally with sufficient knowledge and judgment to
act correctly or prudently under circumstances as they
arise; but they cannot foresee or provide for the future,
nor lay down rules for other people's conduct. All platforms, resolutions, bills of rights and constitutions, are
true in the particular, false in the general. Hence all legislation should be repealable, and those instruments are but
laws. Fundamental principles, or the higher law, are se-
crets of nature which God keeps to himself. The vain attempt of "frequent recurrence to them," is but the act of
the child who builds card houses, for the pleasure of
knocking them down. Recurrence to fundamental principles and appeals to the higher law, are but the tocsin of
revolution that may upset everything, but which will establish nothing, because no two men are agreed as to
what the higher law, alias "fundamental principles," is.

Moses, and Lycurgus, and Solon, and Numa, built their institutions to last, enjoined it on the people never to change them, and threw around them the sanctity of religion, to ward off the sacrilegious hand of future innovation. "A frequent recurrence to fundamental principles," and the kicking down of card houses, was not part of their science of government. We have often thought, that of all the lost arts, the art of government was the only one whose loss we would deplore, or whose recovery is worth the pains of study and research.

To us it seems that "first causes," "fundamental principles," and the "higher law," mean one and the same thing: An "ignis fatuus," that it is dangerous to pursue, and hopeless to overtake.

We may be doing Mr. Jefferson injustice, in assuming that his "fundamental principles" and Mr. Seward's "higher law," mean the same thing, but the injustice can be very little, as they both mean just nothing at all, unless it be a determination to inaugurate anarchy, and to do all sorts of mischief. We refer the reader to the chapter on the Declaration of Independence," &c., in our *Sociology,* for a further dissertation on the fundamental powder-cask abstractions on which our glorious institutions *affect* to repose. We say *affect,* because we are sure neither their repose nor their permanence would be disturbed by the removal of the counterfeit foundation.

The true greatness of Mr. Jefferson was his fitness for revolution. He was the genius of innovation, the architect of ruin, the inaugurator of anarchy. His mission was to pull down, not to build up. He thought everything false as well in the physical as in the moral world. He fed his horses on potatoes, and defended harbors with gun-boats, because it was contrary to human experience and human opinion. He proposed to govern boys without the authority of masters or the control of religion, supplying their places with Laissez-faire philosophy, and morality from the pages of Lawrence Sterne. His character, like his philosophy, is exceptional—invaluable in urging on revolution, but useless, if not dangerous, in quiet times.

We would not restrict, control, or take away a single human right or liberty which experience showed was already sufficiently governed and restricted by public opinion. But we do believe that the slaveholding South is the only country on the globe, that can safely tolerate the rights and liberties which we have discussed.

The annals of revolutionary Virginia were illustrated by three great and useful men. The mighty mind of Jefferson, fitted to pull down; the plastic hand of Madison to build up, and the powerful arm of Washington to defend, sustain and conserve.

We are the friend of popular government, but only so long as conservatism is the interest of the governing class. At the South, the interests and feelings of many non-property holders are identified with those of a comparatively few property holders. It is not necessary to the security of property, that a majority of voters should own property; but where the pauper majority becomes so large as to disconnect the mass of them in feeling and interest from the property holding class, revolution and agrarianism are inevitable. We will not undertake to say that events are tending this way at the North. The absence of laws of entail and primogeniture may prevent it; yet we fear the worst; for, despite the laws of equal inheritance and distribution, wealth is accumulating in few hands, and pauperism is increasing. We shall attempt hereafter to show that a system of very small entails might correct this tendency.

CHAPTER VIII.

GOVERNMENT A THING OF FORCE, NOT OF CONSENT.

WE DO NOT agree with the authors of the Declaration of Independence that governments "derive their just powers from the consent of the governed." The women, the children, the negroes, and but few of the non-property holders were consulted, or consented to the Revolution or the governments that ensued from its success. As to these, the new governments were self-elected despotisms, and the governing class self-elected despots. Those governments originated in force, and have been continued by force. All governments must originate in force, and be continued by force. The very term, government, implies that it is carried on against the consent of the governed. Fathers do not derive their authority, as heads of families, from the consent of wife and children, nor do they govern their families by their consent. They never take the vote of the family as to the labors to be performed, the moneys to be expended, or as to anything else. Masters dare not take the vote of slaves, as to their government. If they did, constant holiday, dissipation and extravagance would be the result. Captains of ships are not appointed by the consent of the crew, and never take their vote, even in "doubling Cape Horn." If they did, the crew would generally vote to get drunk, and the ship would never weather the cape. Not even in the most democratic countries are soldiers governed by their consent, nor is their vote taken on the eve of battle. They have some how lost (or never had) the "inalienable rights of life, liberty and the pursuit of happiness;" and, whether Americans or Russians, are forced into battle, without and often against their consent. The ancient republics were governed by a small class of adult male citizens, who assumed and exercised the government, without the consent of the governed. The South is governed just as those ancient republics were. In the county in which we live, there are eighteen thousand souls, and only twelve hundred voters. But we twelve hundred, the governors, never asked and never intend to ask the consent of the sixteen thousand eight hundred whom we govern. Were we to do so, we should soon have an "organized anarchy." The governments of Europe could not exist a week without the positive force of standing armies.

They are all governments of force, not of consent. Even in our North, the women, children, and free negroes, constitute four-fifths of the population; and they are all governed without their consent. But they mean to correct this gross and glaring iniquity at the North. They hold that all men, women, and negroes, and small children, are equals, and entitled to equal rights. The widows and free negroes begin to vote in some of those States, and they will have to let all colors and sexes and ages vote soon, or give up the glorious principles of human equality and universal emancipation.

The experiment which they will make, we fear, is absurd in theory, and the symptoms of approaching anarchy and agrarianism among them, leave no doubt that its practical operation will be no better than its theory. Anti-rent-ism, "vote-myself-a-farm" ism, and all the other isms, are but the spattering drops that precede a social deluge.

Abolition ultimates in "Consent Government;" Consent Government in Anarchy, Free Love, Agrarianism, &c., &c., and "Self-elected despotism," winds up the play.

If the interests of the governors, or governing class, be not conservative, they certainly will not conserve institutions injurious to their interests. There never was and never can be an old society in which the immediate interests of a majority of human souls do not conflict with all established order, all right of property, and all existing institutions. Immediate interest is all the mass look to; and they would be sure to revolutionize government, as often as the situation of the majority was worse than that of the minority. Divide all property to-day, and a year hence the inequalities of property would provoke a re-division.

In the South, the interest of the governing class is eminently conservative, and the South is fast becoming the most conservative of nations.

Already, at the North, government vibrates and oscillates between Radicalism and Conservatism; at present, Radicalism or Black Republicanism is in the ascendant.

The number of paupers is rapidly increasing; radical and agrarian doctrines are spreading; the women and the children, and the negroes, will soon be let in to vote; and then they will try the experiment of "Consent Government and Constituted Anarchy."

It is falsely said, that revolutions never go backwards. They always go backwards, and generally farther back than where they started. The Social Revolution now going on at the North, must some day go backwards. Shall it do so now, ere it has perpetrated an infinitude of mischief, shed oceans of blood, and occasioned endless human misery; or will the Conservatives of the North let it run the length of its leather, inflict all these evils, and then rectify itself by issuing into military despotism? We think that by a kind of alliance, offensive and defensive, with the South, Northern Conservatism may now arrest and turn back the tide of Radicalism and Agrarianism. We will not presume to point out the whole means and modus operandi. They on the field of action will best see what is necessary to be done.

Whilst we hold that all government is a matter of force, we yet think the governing class should be numerous enough to understand, and so situated as to represent fairly, all interests. The Greek and Roman masters were thus situated; so were the old Barons of England, and so are the white citizens of the South. If not all masters, like Greek and Roman citizens, they all belong to the master race, have exclusive rights and privileges of citizenship, and an interest not to see this right of citizenship extended, disturbed, and rendered worthless and contemptible.

Whilst the governments of Europe are more obviously kept alive and conducted by force than at any other period, yet are they all, from necessity, watchful and regardful of Public Opinion. Opinion now rules the world, but not as expressed through the ballot-box. Governments become more popular as they become more forcible. A large governing class is not apt to mistake or disregard opinion; and, therefore, Republican institutions are best adapted to the times. Under Monarchical forms, the governments of Europe are daily becoming more Republican.

The fatal error committed in Western Europe is the wielding of government by a class who govern, but do not represent, the masses. Their interests and those of the masses are antagonistic, whilst those of masters and slaves are identical.

Looking to theory, to the examples of the Ancient Republics, and to England under the Plantagenets, we shall find that Southern institutions are far the best now existing in the world.

We think speculations as to constructing governments are little worth; for all government is the gradual accretion of Nature, time and circumstances. Yet these theories have occurred to us, and, as they are conservative, we will suggest them. In slaveholding countries all freemen should vote and govern, because their interests are conservative. In free states, the government should be in the hands of the land-owners, who are also conservative. A system of primogeniture, and entails of small parcels of land, might, in a great measure, identify the interests of all; or, at least, those who held no lands would generally be the children and kinsmen of those who did, and be taken care of by them. The frequent accumulation of large fortunes, and consequent pauperism of the masses, is the greatest evil of modern society. Would not small entails prevent this? All cannot own lands, but as many should own them as is consistent with good farming and advanced civilization. The social institutions of the Jews, as established by Moses and Joshua, most nearly fulfill our ideas of perfect government.

A word, at parting, to Northern Conservatives. A like danger threatens North and South, proceeding from the same source. Abolitionism is maturing what Political Economy began. With inexorable sequence "Let Alone" is made to usher in No-Government. North and South our danger is the same, and our remedies, though differing in degree, must in character be the same. "Let Alone" must be repudiated, if we would have any government. We must, in all sections, act upon the principle that the world is "too little governed." You of the North need not institute negro slavery; far less reduce white men to the state of negro slavery. But the masses require more of protection, and the masses and philosophers equally require more of control. Leave it to time and circumstances to suggest the necessary legislation; but, rely upon it, "Anarchy, plus the street constable," won't answer any longer. The Vigilance Committee of California is but a mob, rendered necessary by the inadequacy of the regular government. It is the "vis medicatrix naturæ," vainly attempting to discharge the office of physician. That country is "too little governed," where the best and most conservative citizens have to resolve themselves into mobs and vigilance committees to protect rights which government should, but does not, protect.

The element of force exists probably in too small a degree in our Federal Government. It has neither territory nor subjects. Kansas is better off; for she has a few citizens and a large and fertile territory. She is backing the Government out, if not whipping her. Massachusetts, too, has nullified her laws. Utah contemns her authority, and the Vigilance Committee of California sets her at successful defiance. She is an attempt at a *paper consent* government, without territory or citizens. Considered and treated as a league or treaty between separate States or Nations she may yet have a long and useful existence; for then those *Nations* or *States,* seeing that she has no means of self-enforcement, self-support, or self-conservation, may, for their mutual interests, combine to sustain and defend her. Heretofore, domestic weakness and danger from foreign foes has combined the States in sustaining the Union. Hereafter, the great advantages of friendly and mutual intercourse, trade and exchanges, may continue to produce a like result. But the prospects are alarming, and it is well that all patriots should know that the Union has little power to sustain and perpetuate itself.

There are three kinds of force that occur to us will sustain a government. First, "inside necessity," such as slavery, that occasions a few to usurp power, and to hold it forcibly, without consulting the many; secondly, the force of foreign pressure or aggression, which combines men and States together for common defence; and thirdly, the inherent force of a prescriptive or usurpative government, which sustains itself by standing armies. Such are all the governments of Western Europe. Not one of them could exist forty-eight hours, but for the standing armies. These standing armies became necessary and grew up as slavery disappeared. The old Barons kept the Ca-

naille, the Proletariat, the Sans Culottes, the Nomadic
Beggars, in order, by lashing their backs and supplying
their wants. They must be fed and kept at work. Modern
society tries to effect this (but in vain) by moral suasion
and standing armies. Riots, mobs, strikes and revolutions
are daily occurring. The mass of mankind cannot be governed by Law. More of despotic discretion, and less of
Law, is what the world wants. We take our leave by saying, "THERE IS TOO MUCH OF LAW AND TOO LITTLE OF
GOVERNMENT IN THIS WORLD."

Physical force, not moral suasion, governs the world.
The negro sees the driver's lash, becomes accustomed to
obedient, cheerful industry, and is not aware that the lash
is the force that impels him. The free citizen fulfills, "con
amore," his round of social, political and domestic duties,
and never dreams that the Law, with its fines and jails,
penitentiaries and halters, or Public Opinion, with its os-
tracism, its mobs, and its tar and feathers, help to keep him
revolving in his orbit. Yet, remove these physical forces,
and how many good citizens would shoot, like fiery comets,
from their spheres, and disturb society with their eccen-
tricities and the crimes.

Government is the life of a nation, and as no one can
foresee the various future circumstances of social, any
more than of individual life, it is absurd to define on paper, at the birth of either the nation or individual, what
they shall do and what not do. Broad construction of constitutions is as good as no constitution, for it leaves the
nation to adapt itself to circumstances; but strict construction will destroy any nation, for action is necessary to
national conservation, and constitution-makers cannot
foresee what action will be necessary. If individual or social life were passed in mere passivity, constitutions might
answer. Not in a changing and active world. Louisiana,
Florida and Texas would have been denied to the South
under strict construction and she would have been ruined.
A constitution, strictly construed, is absolutely inconsistent
with permanent national existence.

THE

IMPENDING CRISIS

OF

THE SOUTH:

HOW TO MEET IT.

BY
HINTON ROWAN HELPER,

OF NORTH CAROLINA.

COUNTRYMEN! I sue for simple justice at your hands,
Naught else I ask, nor less will have;
Act right, therefore, and yield my claim,
Or, by the great God that made all things,
I'll fight, till from my bones my flesh be hack'd!—*Shakspeare.*

The liberal deviseth liberal things,
And by liberal things shall he stand.—*Isaiah.*

NINTH THOUSAND.

NEW-YORK:
BURDICK BROTHERS, 8 SPRUCE STREET.
1857.

PREFACE.

IF MY countrymen, particularly my countrymen of the South, still more particularly those of them who are non-slaveholders, shall peruse this work, they will learn that no narrow and partial doctrines of political or social economy, no prejudices of early education have induced me to write it. If in any part of it I have actually deflected from the tone of true patriotism and nationality, I am unable to perceive the fault. What I have committed to paper is but a fair reflex of the honest and long-settled convictions of my heart.

In writing this book, it has been no part of my purpose to cast unmerited opprobrium upon slaveholders, or to display any special friendliness or sympathy for the blacks. I have considered my subject more particularly with reference to its economic aspects as regards the whites—not with reference, except in a very slight degree, to its humanitarian or religious aspects. To the latter side of the question, Northern writers have already done full and timely justice. The genius of the North has also most ably and eloquently discussed the subject in the form of novels. Yankee wives have written the most popular anti-slavery literature of the day. Against this I have nothing to say; it is all well enough for women to give the fictions of slavery; men should give the facts.

I trust that my friends and fellow-citizens of the South will read this book—nay, proud as any Southerner though I am, I entreat, I beg of them to do so. And as the work, considered with reference to its author's nativity, is a novelty—the South being my birth-place and my home, and my ancestry having resided there for more than a century —so I indulge the hope that its reception by my fellow-Southrons will also be novel; that is to say, that they will receive it, as it is offered, in a reasonable and friendly spirit, and that they will read it and reflect upon it as an honest and faithful endeavor to treat a subject of enormous import, without rancor or prejudice, by one who naturally comes within the pale of their own sympathies.

An irrepressibly active desire to do something to elevate the South to an honorable and powerful position among the enlightened quarters of the globe, has been the great leading principle that has actuated me in the preparation of the present volume; and so well convinced am I that the plan which I have proposed is the only really practical one for achieving the desired end, that I earnestly hope to see it prosecuted with energy and zeal, until the Flag of Freedom shall wave triumphantly alike over the valleys of Virginia and the mounds of Mississippi.

H. R. H.

June, 1857.

CHAPTER I.

COMPARISON BETWEEN THE FREE
AND THE SLAVE STATES.

It is not our intention in this chapter to enter into an elaborate ethnographical essay, to establish peculiarities of difference, mental, moral, and physical, in the great family of man. Neither is it our design to launch into a philosophical disquisition on the laws and principles of light and darkness, with a view of educing any additional evidence of the fact, that as a general rule, the rays of the sun are more fructifying and congenial than the shades of night. Nor yet is it our purpose, by writing a formal treatise on ethics, to draw a broad line of distinction between right and wrong, to point out the propriety of morality and its advantages over immorality, nor to waste time in pressing a universally admitted truism—that virtue is preferable to vice. Self-evident truths require no argumentative demonstration.

What we mean to do is simply this: to take a survey of the relative position and importance of the several states of this confederacy, from the adoption of the national compact; and when, of two sections of the country starting under the same auspices, and with equal natural advantages, we find the one rising to a degree of almost unexampled power and eminence, and the other sinking into a state of comparative imbecility and obscurity, it is our determination to trace out the causes which have led to the elevation of the former, and the depression of the latter, and to use our most earnest and honest endeavors to utterly extirpate whatever opposes the progress and prosperity of any portion of the union.

This survey we have already made; we have also instituted an impartial comparison between the cardinal sections of the country, north, south, east, and west; and as a true-hearted southerner, whose ancestors have resided in North Carolina between one and two hundred years, and as one who would rather have his native clime excel than be excelled, we feel constrained to confess that we are deeply abashed and chagrined at the disclosures of the comparison thus instituted. At the time of the adoption of the Constitution, in 1789, we commenced an even race with the North. All things considered, if either the North or the South had the advantage, it was the latter. In proof of this, let us introduce a few statistics, beginning with the states of

NEW YORK AND VIRGINIA.

In 1790, when the first census was taken, New York contained 340,120 inhabitants; at the same time the population of Virginia was 748,308, being more than twice the number of New York. Just sixty years afterward, as we learn from the census of 1850, New York had a population of 3,097,394; while that of Virginia was only 1,421,661, being less than half the number of New York! In 1791, the exports of New York amounted to $2,505,465; the exports of Virginia amounted to $3,130,865. In 1852, the exports of New York amounted to $87,484,456; the exports of Virginia, during the same year, amounted to only $2,724,657. In 1790, the imports of New York and Virginia were about equal; in 1853, the imports of New York amounted to the enormous sum of $178,270,999; while those of Virginia, for the same period, amounted to the pitiful sum of only $399,004. In 1850, the products of manufactures, mining and the mechanic arts in New York amounted to $237,597,249; those of Virginia amounted to only $29,705,387. At the taking of the last census, the value of real and personal property in Virginia, including negroes, was $391,646,438; that of New York, exclusive of any monetary valuation of human beings, was $1,080,- 309,216.

In August, 1856, the real and personal estate assessed in the City of New York amounted in valuation to $511,- 740,491, showing that New York City alone is worth far more than the whole State of Virginia.

What says one of Virginia's own sons? He still lives; hear him speak. Says Gov. Wise:

"It may be painful, but nevertheless profitable, to recur

occasionally to the history of the past; to listen to the admonitions of experience, and learn lessons of wisdom from the efforts and actions of those who have preceded us in the drama of human life. The records of former days show that at a period not very remote, Virginia stood preeminently the first commercial State in the Union; when her commerce exceeded in amount that of all the New England States combined; when the City of Norfolk owned more than one hundred trading ships, and her direct foreign trade exceeded that of the City of New York, now the centre of trade and the great emporium of North America. At the period of the war of independence, the commerce of Virginia was four times larger than that of New York."

The cash value of all the farms, farming implements and machinery in Virginia, in 1850, was $223,423,315; the value of the same in New York, in the same year, was $576,631,568. In about the same ratio does the value of the agricultural products and live stock of New York exceed the value of the agricultural products and live stock of Virginia. But we will pursue this humiliating comparison no further. With feelings, mingled with indignation and disgust, we turn from the picture, and will now pay our respects to

MASSACHUSETTS AND NORTH CAROLINA.

In 1790, Massachusetts contained 378,717 inhabitants; in the same year North Carolina contained 393,751; in 1850, the population of Massachusetts was 994,514, all freemen; while that of North Carolina was only 869,039, of whom 288,548 were slaves. Massachusetts has an area of only 7,800 square miles; the area of North Carolina is 50,704 square miles, which, though less than Virginia, is considerably larger than the State of New York. Massachusetts and North Carolina each have a harbor, Boston and Beaufort, which harbors, with the States that back them, are, by nature, possessed of about equal capacities and advantages for commercial and manufacturing enterprise. Boston has grown to be the second commercial city in the Union; her ships, freighted with the useful and unique inventions and manufactures of her ingenious artisans and mechanics, and bearing upon their stalwart arms the majestic flag of our country, glide triumphantly through the winds and over the waves of every ocean. She has done, and is now doing, great honor to herself, her State and the nation, and her name and fame are spoken with reverence in the remotest regions of the earth.

How is it with Beaufort, in North Carolina, whose harbor is said to be the safest and most commodious anywhere to be found on the Atlantic coast south of the harbor of New York, and but little inferior to that? Has anybody ever heard of her? Do the masts of her ships ever cast a shadow on foreign waters? Upon what distant or benighted shore have her merchants and mariners ever hoisted our national ensign, or spread the arts of civilization and peaceful industry? What changes worthy of note have taken place in the physical features of her superficies since "the evening and the morning were the third day?" But we will make no further attempt to draw a comparison between the populous, wealthy, and renowned city of Boston and the obscure, despicable little village of Beaufort, which, notwithstanding "the placid bosom of its deep and well-protected harbor," has no place in the annals or records of the country, and has scarcely ever been heard of fifty miles from home.

In 1853, the exports of Massachusetts amounted to $16,895,304, and her imports to $41,367,956; during the same time, and indeed during all the time, from the period of the formation of the government up to the year 1853, inclusive, the exports and imports of North Carolina were so utterly insignificant that we are ashamed to record them. In 1850, the products of manufactures, mining and the mechanic arts in Massachusetts, amounted to $151,-137,145; those of North Carolina, to only $9,111,245. In 1856, the products of these industrial pursuits in Massachusetts had increased to something over $288,000,000, a sum more than twice the value of the entire cotton crop of all the Southern States! In 1850, the cash value of all the farms, farming, implements and machinery in Massachusetts, was $112,285,931; the value of the same in North Carolina, in the same year, was only $71,823,298. In 1850, the value of all the real and personal estate in Massachusetts, without recognizing property in man, or setting a monetary price on the head of a single citizen, white or black, amounted to $573,342,286; the value of the same in North Carolina, including negroes, amounted to only $226,800,472. In 1856, the real and personal estate assessed in the City of Boston amounted in valuation to within a fraction of $250,000,000, showing conclusively that so far as dollars and cents are concerned, that single city could buy the whole State of North Carolina, and by right of purchase, if sanctioned by the Constitution of the United States, and by State Constitutions, hold her as a province. In 1850, there were in Massachusetts 1,861 native white and free colored persons over twenty years of age who could not read and write; in the same year, the same class of persons in North Carolina numbered 80,083; while her 288,548 slaves were, by legislative enactments, kept in a state of absolute ignorance and unconditional subordination.

Hoping, however, and believing, that a large majority of the most respectable and patriotic citizens of North Carolina have resolved, or will soon resolve, with unyielding purpose, to cast aside the great obstacle that impedes their progress, and bring into action a new policy which will lead them from poverty and ignorance to wealth and intellectual greatness, and which will shield them not only from the rebukes of their own consciences, but also from the just reproaches of the civilized world, we will, for the present, in deference to their feelings, forbear the further enumeration of these degrading disparities, and turn our attention to

PENNSYLVANIA AND SOUTH CAROLINA.

An old gentleman, now residing in Charleston, told us, but a few months since, that he had a distinct recollection of the time when Charleston imported foreign fabrics for the Philadelphia trade, and when, on a certain occasion, his mother went into a store on Market-street to select a silk dress for herself, the merchant, unable to please her fancy, persuaded her to postpone the selection for a few days, or until the arrival of a new stock of superb styles and fashions which he had recently purchased in the metropolis of South Carolina. This was all very proper. Charleston had a spacious harbor, a central position, and a mild climate; and from priority of settlement and business connections, to say nothing of other advantages, she enjoyed greater facilities for commercial transactions than Philadelphia. She had a right to get custom wherever she could find it, and in securing so valuable a customer as the Quaker City, she exhibited no small degree of laudable enterprise. But why did she not maintain her supremacy? If the answer to this query is not already in the reader's mind, it will suggest itself before he peruses the whole of this work.

A most unfortunate day was that for the Palmetto State, and indeed for the whole South, when the course of trade was changed, and she found herself the retailer of foreign and domestic goods, imported and vended by wholesale merchants at the North. Philadelphia ladies no longer look to the South for late fashions, and fine silks and satins; no Quaker dame now wears drab apparel of Charleston importation. Like all other *niggervilles* in our disreputable part of the confederacy, the commercial emporium of South Carolina is sick and impoverished; her silver cord has been loosed; her golden bowl has been broken; and her unhappy people, without proper or profitable employment, poor in pocket, and few in number, go mourning or loafing about the streets. Her annual importations are actually less now than they were a century ago, when South Carolina was the second commercial province on the continent, Virginia being the first.

In 1760, as we learn from Mr. Benton's "Thirty Years' View," the foreign imports into Charleston were $2,662,-000; in 1855, they amounted to only $1,750,000! In 1854, the imports into Philadelphia, which, in foreign trade, ranks at present but fourth among the commercial cities of the union, were $21,963,021. In 1850, the products of manufactures, mining, and the mechanic arts, in Pennsylvania, amounted to $155,044,910; the products of the same in South Carolina, amounted to only $7,063,513.

As shown by the census report of 1850, which was prepared under the superintendence of a native of South Carolina, who certainly will not be suspected of injustice to his own section of the country, the Southern states, the cash value of all the farms, farming implements, and machinery in Pennsylvania, was $422,598,640; the value of the same in South Carolina, in the same year, was only

$86,518,038. From a compendium of the same census, we
learn that the value of all the real and personal property
in Pennsylvania, actual property, no slaves, amounted to
$729,144,998; the value of the same in South Carolina,
including the estimated—we were about to say fictitious
—value of 384,925 negroes, amounted to only $288,257,-
694. We have not been able to to obtain the figures necessary to show the exact value of the real and personal estate in Philadelphia, but the amount is estimated to be not
less than $300,000,000; and as, in 1850, there were 408,-
762 free inhabitants in the single city of Philadelphia,
against 283,544 of the same class, in the whole state of
South Carolina, it is quite evident that the former is more
powerful than the latter, and far ahead of her in all the
elements of genuine and permanent superiority. In Pennsylvania, in 1850, the annual income of public schools
amounted to $1,348,249; the same in South Carolina, in
the same year, amounted to only $200,600; in the former
state there were 393 libraries other than private, in the
latter only 26; in Pennsylvania 310 newspapers and periodicals were published, circulating 84,898,672 copies
annually; in South Carolina only 46 newspapers and periodicals were published, circulating but 7,145,930 copies
per annum.

The incontrovertible facts we have thus far presented
are, we think, amply sufficient, both in number and magnitude, to bring conviction to the mind of every candid
reader, that there is something wrong, socially, politically
and morally wrong, in the policy under which the South
has so long loitered and languished. Else, how is it that
the North, under the operations of a policy directly the
opposite of ours, has surpassed us in almost everything
great and good, and left us standing before the world, an
object of merited reprehension and derision?

For one, we are heartily ashamed of the inexcusable
weakness, inertia and dilapidation everywhere so manifest
throughout our native section; but the blame properly
attaches itself to an usurping minority of the people, and
we are determined that it shall rest where it belongs. More
on this subject, however, after a brief but general survey
of the inequalities and disparities that exist between
those two grand divisions of the country, which, without

reference to the situation that any part of their territory bears to the cardinal points, are every day becoming more familiarly known by the appropriate appellation of

THE FREE AND THE SLAVE STATES.

It is a fact well known to every intelligent Southerner that we are compelled to go to the North for almost every article of utility and adornment, from matches, shoepegs and paintings up to cotton-mills, steamships and statuary; that we have no foreign trade, no princely merchants, nor respectable artists; that, in comparison with the free states, we contribute nothing to the literature, polite arts and inventions of the age; that, for want of profitable employment at home, large numbers of our native population find themselves necessitated to emigrate to the West, whilst the free states retain not only the larger proportion of those born within their own limits, but induce, annually, hundreds of thousands of foreigners to settle and remain amongst them; that almost everything produced at the North meets with ready sale, while, at the same time, there is no demand, even among our own citizens, for the productions of Southern industry; that, owing to the absence of a proper system of business amongst us, the North becomes, in one way or another, the proprietor and dispenser of all our floating wealth, and that we are dependent on Northern capitalists for the means necessary to build our railroads, canals and other public improvements; that if we want to visit a foreign country, even though it may lie directly South of us, we find no convenient way of getting there except by taking passage through a Northern port; and that nearly all the profits arising from the exchange of commodities, from insurance and shipping offices, and from the thousand and one industrial pursuits of the country, accrue to the North, and are there invested in the erection of those magnificent cities and stupendous works of art which dazzle the eyes of the South, and attest the superiority of free institutions!

The North is the Mecca of our merchants, and to it they must and do make two pilgrimages per annum—one in the spring and one in the fall. All our commercial, mechanical, manufactural, and literary supplies come from there. We want Bibles, brooms, buckets and books, and we go to the North; we want pens, ink, paper, wafers and envelopes, and we go to the North; we want shoes, hats, handkerchiefs, umbrellas and pocket knives, and we go to the North; we want furniture, crockery, glassware and pianos, and we go to the North; we want toys, primers, school books, fashionable apparel, machinery, medicines, tombstones, and a thousand other things, and we go to the North for them all. Instead of keeping our money in circulation at home, by patronizing our own mechanics, manufacturers, and laborers, we send it all away to the North, and there it remains; it never falls into our hands again.

In one way or another we are more or less subservient to the North every day of our lives. In infancy we are swaddled in Northern muslin; in childhood we are humored with Northern gewgaws; in youth we are instructed out of Northern books; at the age of maturity we sow our "wild oats" on Northern soil; in middle-life we exhaust our wealth, energies and talents in the dishonorable vocation of entailing our dependence on our children and on our children's children, and, to the neglect of our own interests and the interests of those around us, in giving aid and succor to every department of Northern power; in the decline of life we remedy our eye-sight with Northern spectacles, and support our infirmities with Northern canes; in old age we are drugged with Northern physic; and, finally, when we die, our inanimate bodies, shrouded in Northern cambric, are stretched upon the bier, borne to the grave in a Northern carriage, entombed with a Northern spade, and memorized with a Northern slab!

But it can hardly be necessary to say more in illustration of this unmanly and unnational dependence, which is so glaring that it cannot fail to be apparent to even the most careless and superficial observer. All the world sees, or ought to see, that in a commercial, mechanical, manufactural, financial, and literary point of view, we are as helpless as babes; that, in comparison with the Free States, our agricultural resources have been greatly exaggerated, misunderstood and mismanaged; and that, instead of cultivating among ourselves a wise policy of mutual assistance and co-operation with respect to individuals, and of self-reliance with respect to the South at large, instead of giving countenance and encouragement to the industrial enterprises projected in our midst, and instead of building up, aggrandizing and beautifying our own States, cities and towns, we have been spending our substance at the North, and are daily augmenting and strengthening the very power which now has us so completely under its thumb.

It thus appears, in view of the preceding statistical facts and arguments, that the South, at one time the superior of the North in almost all the ennobling pursuits and conditions of life, has fallen far behind her competitor, and now ranks more as the dependency of a mother country than as the equal confederate of free and independent States. Following the order of our task, the next duty that devolves upon us is to trace out the causes which have conspired to bring about this important change, and to place on record the reasons, as we understand them,

WHY THE NORTH HAS SURPASSED THE SOUTH.

And now that we have come to the very heart and soul of our subject, we feel no disposition to mince matters, but mean to speak plainly, and to the point, without any equivocation, mental reservation, or secret evasion whatever. The son of a venerated parent, who, while he lived, was a considerate and merciful slaveholder, a native of the South, born and bred in North Carolina, of a family whose home has been in the valley of the Yadkin for nearly a century and a half, a Southerner by instinct and by all the influences of thought, habits, and kindred, and with the desire and fixed purpose to reside permanently within the limits of the South, and with the expectation of dying there also—we feel that we have the right to express our opinion, however humble or unimportant it may be, on any and every question that affects the public good; and, so help us God, "sink or swim, live or die, survive or perish," we are determined to exercise that right with manly firmness, and without fear, favor or affection.

And now to the point. In our opinion, an opinion which has been formed from data obtained by assiduous researches, and comparisons, from laborious investigation, logical reasoning, and earnest reflection, the causes which have impeded the progress and prosperity of the South, which have dwindled our commerce, and other similar pursuits, into the most contemptible insignificance; sunk a large majority of our people in galling poverty and ignorance, rendered a small minority conceited and tyrannical, and driven the rest away from their homes; entailed upon us a humiliating dependence on the Free States; disgraced us in the recesses of our own souls, and brought us under reproach in the eyes of all civilized and enlightened nations—may all be traced to one common source, and there find solution in the most hateful and horrible word that was ever incorporated into the vocabulary of human economy—*Slavery!*

Reared amidst the institution of slavery, believing it to be wrong both in principle and in practice, and having seen and felt its evil influences upon individuals, communities and states, we deem it a duty, no less than a privilege, to enter our protest against it, and to use our most strenuous efforts to overturn and abolish it! Then we are an abolitionist? Yes! not merely a freesoiler, but an abolitionist, in the fullest sense of the term.

And here we may remark that the statistics which we propose to offer, like those already given, have been obtained from official sources, and may, therefore, be relied on as correct. The object we have in view in making a free use of facts and figures, if not already apparent, will soon be understood. It is not so much in its moral and religious aspects that we propose to discuss the question of slavery, as in its social and political character and influences. To say nothing of the sin and the shame of slavery, we believe it is a most expensive and unprofitable institution; and if our brethren of the South will but throw aside their unfounded prejudices and preconceived opinions, and give us a fair and patient hearing, we feel confident that we can bring them to the same conclusion. Indeed, we believe we shall be enabled—not alone by our own contributions, but with the aid of incontestable facts and arguments which we shall introduce from other sources—to convince all true-hearted, candid and intelligent Southerners, who may chance to read our book, (and we hope their name may be legion) that slavery, and nothing but slavery, has retarded the progress and prosperity of our portion of the Union; depopulated and impoverished our cities by forcing the more industrious and enterprising natives of the soil to emigrate to the free states; brought our domain under a sparse and inert population by preventing foreign

immigration; made us tributary to the North, and reduced us to the humiliating condition of mere provincial
subjects in fact, though not in name. We believe, moreover, that every patriotic Southerner thus convinced will
feel it a duty he owes to himself, to his country, and to
his God, to become a thorough, inflexible, practical abolitionist. So mote it be!

By taking a sort of inventory of the agricultural products
of the free and slave States in 1850, we now propose to
correct a most extraordinary and mischievous error into
which the people of the South have unconsciously fallen.
Agriculture, it is well known, is the sole boast of the
South; and, strange to say, many pro-slavery Southerners,
who, in our latitude, pass for intelligent men, are so puffed
up with the idea of our importance in this respect, that
they speak of the North as a sterile region, unfit for cultivation, and quite dependent on the South for the neces-

TABLE NO. I.

AGRICULTURAL PRODUCTS OF THE FREE STATES—1850.

States.	Wheat, bushels.	Oats, bushels.	Indian Corn, bushels.
California	17,228		12,236
Connecticut	41,762	1,258,738	1,935,043
Illinois	9,414,575	10,087,241	57,646,984
Indiana	6,214,458	5,655,014	52,964,363
Iowa	1,530,581	1,524,345	8,656,799
Maine	296,259	2,181,037	1,750,056
Massachusetts	31,211	1,165,146	2,345,490
Michigan	4,925,889	2,866,056	5,641,420
New Hampshire . . .	185,658	973,381	1,573,670
New Jersey	1,601,190	3,378,063	8,759,704
New York	13,121,498	26,552,814	17,858,400
Ohio	14,487,351	13,472,742	59,078,695
Pennsylvania	15,367,691	21,538,156	19,835,214
Rhode Island	49	215,232	539,201
Vermont	535,955	2,307,784	2,082,896
Wisconsin	4,286,131	3,414,672	1,988,979
	72,157,486	96,590,371	242,618,650

TABLE NO. II.

AGRICULTURAL PRODUCTS OF THE SLAVE STATES——1850.

States.	Wheat, bushels.	Oats, bushels.	Indian Corn, bushels.
Alabama	294,044	2,965,696	28,754,048
Arkansas	199,639	656,183	8,893,939
Delaware	482,511	604,518	3,145,542
Florida	1,027	66,586	1,996,809
Georgia	1,088,534	3,820,044	30,080,099
Kentucky	2,142,822	8,201,311	58,672,591
Louisiana	417	89,637	10,266,873
Maryland	4,494,680	2,242,151	10,749,858
Mississippi	137,990	1,508,288	22,446,552
Missouri	2,981,652	5,278,079	36,214,537
North Carolina	2,130,102	4,052,078	27,941,051
South Carolina	1,066,277	2,322,155	16,271,454
Tennessee	1,619,386	7,703,086	52,276,223
Texas	41,729	199,017	6,028,876
Virginia	11,212,616	10,179,144	85,254,819
	27,904,476	49,882,979	348,992,282

saries of life! Such rampant ignorance ought to be knocked in the head! We can prove that the North produces greater quantities of bread-stuffs than the South! Figures shall show the facts. Properly, the South has nothing left to boast of; the North has surpassed her in everything, and is going farther and farther ahead of her every day.

So much for the boasted agricultural superiority of the South! Mark well the balance in bushels, and the difference in value! Is either in favor of the South? No! Are both in favor of the North? Yes! Here we have unquestionable proof that of all the bushel-measure products of the nation, the free states produce far more than one-half; and it is worthy of particular mention, that *the excess of Northern products is of the most valuable kind.* The account shows a balance against the South, in favor of the North, of *seventeen million four hundred and twenty-three thousand one hundred and fifty-two bushels,* and a difference in value of *forty-four million seven hundred and*

TABLE NO. III.

AGRICULTURAL PRODUCTS OF THE FREE STATES—1850.

States.	Potatoes, (I. & S.) bush.	Rye, bushels.	Barley, bushels.
California	10,292		9,712
Connecticut	2,689,805	600,893	19,099
Illinois	2,672,294	83,364	110,795
Indiana	2,285,048	78,792	45,483
Iowa	282,363	19,916	25,093
Maine	3,436,040	102,916	151,731
Massachusetts	3,585,384	481,021	112,385
Michigan	2,361,074	105,871	75,249
New Hampshire	4,307,919	183,117	70,256
New Jersey	3,715,251	1,255,578	6,492
New York	15,403,997	4,148,182	3,585,059
Ohio	5,245,760	425,918	354,358
Pennsylvania	6,032,904	4,805,160	165,584
Rhode Island	651,029	26,409	18,875
Vermont	4,951,014	176,233	42,150
Wisconsin	1,402,956	81,253	209,692
	59,033,170	12,574,623	5,002,013

eighty-two thousand six hundred and thirty-six dollars.
Please bear these facts in mind, for, in order to show positively how the free and slave States do stand upon the great and important subject of rural economy, we intend to take an account of all the other products of the soil, of the live-stock upon farms, of the animals slaughtered, and, in fact, of every item of husbandry of the two sections; and if, in bringing our tabular exercises to a close, we find slavery gaining upon freedom—a thing it has never yet been known to do—we shall, as a matter of course, see that the above amount is transferred to the credit of the side to which it of right belongs.

In making up these tables we have two objects in view; the first is to open the eyes of the non-slaveholders of the South, to the system of deception, that has so long been practiced upon them, and the second is to show slave-holders themselves—we have reference only to those who

TABLE NO. IV.

AGRICULTURAL PRODUCTS OF THE SLAVE STATES—1850.

States.	Potatoes, (I. & S.) bush.	Rye, bushels.	Barley, bushels.
Alabama	5,721,205	17,261	3,958
Arkansas	981,981	8,047	177
Delaware	305,985	8,066	56
Florida	765,054	1,152	
Georgia	7,213,807	53,750	11,501
Kentucky	2,490,666	415,073	95,343
Louisiana	1,524,085	475	
Maryland	973,932	226,014	745
Mississippi	5,003,277	9,606	228
Missouri	1,274,511	44,268	9,631
North Carolina	5,716,027	229,563	2,735
South Carolina	4,478,960	43,790	4,583
Tennessee	3,845,560	89,137	2,737
Texas	1,426,803	3,108	4,776
Virginia	3,130,567	458,930	25,437
	44,847,420	1,608,240	161,907

are not too perverse, or ignorant, to perceive naked truths
—that free labor is far more respectable, profitable, and
productive, than slave labor. In the South, unfortunately,
no kind of labor is either free or respectable. Every white
man who is under the necessity of earning his bread, by
the sweat of his brow, or by manual labor, in any capacity,
no matter how unassuming in deportment, or exemplary
in morals, is treated as if he was a loathsome beast, and
shunned with the utmost disdain. His soul may be the very
seat of honor and integrity, yet without slaves—himself
a slave—he is accounted as nobody, and would be deemed
intolerably presumptuous, if he dared to open his mouth,
even so wide as to give faint utterance to a three-lettered
monosyllable, like yea or nay, in the presence of an august
knight of the whip and the lash.

There are few Southerners who will not be astonished
at the disclosures of these statistical comparisons between
the free and the slave States. That the astonishment of the

TABLE NO. V.

AGRICULTURAL PRODUCTS OF THE FREE STATES—1850.

States.	Buckwheat, bushels.	Beans & Peas, bushels.	Clov. & Grass seeds, bush.
California		2,292	
Connecticut	229,297	19,090	30,469
Illinois	184,509	82,814	17,807
Indiana	149,740	35,773	30,271
Iowa	52,516	4,475	2,438
Maine	104,523	205,541	18,311
Massachusetts	105,895	43,709	6,087
Michigan	472,917	74,254	26,274
New Hampshire	65,265	70,856	8,900
New Jersey	878,934	14,174	91,331
New York	3,183,955	741,546	184,715
Ohio	638,060	60,168	140,501
Pennsylvania	2,193,692	55,231	178,943
Rhode Island	1,245	6,846	5,036
Vermont	209,819	104,649	15,696
Wisconsin	79,878	20,657	5,486
	8,550,245	1,542,295	762,265

more intelligent and patriotic non-slaveholders will be mingled with indignation is no more than we anticipate. We confess our own surprise, and deep chagrin, at the result of our investigations. Until we examined into the matter, we thought and hoped the South was really ahead of the North in *one* particular, that of agriculture; but our thoughts have been changed, and our hopes frustrated, for instead of finding ourselves the possessors of a single advantage, we behold our dear native South stripped of every laurel, and sinking deeper and deeper in the depths of poverty and shame; while, at the same time, we see the North, our successful rival, extracting and absorbing the few elements of wealth yet remaining amongst us, and rising higher and higher in the scale of fame, fortune, and invulnerable power. Thus our disappointment gives way to a feeling of intense mortification, and our soul involuntarily, but justly, we believe, cries out for retribution

TABLE NO. VI.

AGRICULTURAL PRODUCTS OF THE SLAVE STATES—1850.

States.	Buckwheat, bushels.	Beans & Peas, bushels.	Clov. & Grass seeds, bush.
Alabama	348	892,701	685
Arkansas	175	285,738	526
Delaware	8,615	4,120	3,928
Florida	55	135,359	2
Georgia	250	1,142,011	560
Kentucky	16,097	202,574	24,711
Louisiana	3	161,732	99
Maryland	103,671	12,816	17,778
Mississippi	1,121	1,072,757	617
Missouri	23,641	46,017	4,965
North Carolina	16,704	1,584,252	1,851
South Carolina	283	1,026,900	406
Tennessee	19,427	369,321	14,214
Texas	59	179,351	10
Virginia	214,898	521,579	53,155
	405,357	7,637,227	123,517

against the treacherous, slave-driving legislators, who have
so basely and unpatriotically neglected the interests of
their poor white constituents and bargained away the
rights of posterity. Notwithstanding the fact that the white
non-slaveholders of the South, are in the majority, as five
to one, they have never yet had any part or lot in fram-
ing the laws under which they live. There is no legislation
except for the benefit of slavery, and slaveholders. As a
general rule, poor white persons are regarded with less
esteem and attention than negroes, and though the condition of the latter is wretched beyond description, vast
numbers of the former are infinitely worse off. A cun-
ningly devised mockery of freedom is guarantied to them,
and that is all. To all intents and purposes they are dis-
franchised, and outlawed, and the only privilege extended
to them is a shallow and circumscribed participation in
the political movements that usher slaveholders into office.
We have not breathed away seven and twenty years in

TABLE NO. VII.

AGRICULTURAL PRODUCTS OF THE FREE STATES—1850.

States.	Flaxseed, bushels.	Val. of Garden products.	Val. of Orchard prod'ts.
California		$75,275	$17,700
Connecticut	703	196,874	175,118
Illinois	10,787	127,494	446,049
Indiana	86,888	72,864	324,940
Iowa	1,959	8,848	8,434
Maine	580	122,387	342,865
Massachusetts	72	600,020	463,995
Michigan	519	14,738	132,650
New Hampshire	189	56,810	248,560
New Jersey	16,525	475,242	607,268
New York	57,963	912,047	1,761,950
Ohio	138,880	214,004	695,921
Pennsylvania	41,728	688,714	723,389
Rhode Island		98,298	63,994
Vermont	939	18,853	315,255
Wisconsin	1,191	32,142	4,823
	358,923	$3,714,605	$6,332,914

the South without becoming acquainted with the dema-
gogical manoeuverings of the oligarchy. Their intrigues
and tricks of legerdemain are as familiar to us as household
words; in vain might the world be ransacked for a more
precious junto of flatterers and cajolers. It is amusing to
ignorance, amazing to credulity, and insulting to intelligence, to hear them in their blattering efforts to mystify
and pervert the sacred principles of liberty, and turn the
curse of slavery into a blessing. To the illiterate poor
whites—made poor and ignorant by the system of slavery
—they hold out the idea that slavery is the very bulwark
of our liberties, and the foundation of American independence! For hours at a time, day after day, will they
expatiate upon the inexpressible beauties and excellencies
of this great, *free* and *independent* nation; and finally, with
the most extravagant gesticulations and rhetorical flour-
ishes, conclude their nonsensical ravings by attributing

TABLE NO. VIII.

AGRICULTURAL PRODUCTS OF THE SLAVE STATES—1850.

States.	Flaxseed, bushels.	Val. of Garden products.	Val. of Orchard prod'ts.
Alabama	69	$84,821	$15,408
Arkansas	321	17,150	40,141
Delaware	904	76,500	46,574
Florida		12,714	1,280
Georgia	622	8,721	92,776
Kentucky	75,801	303,120	106,230
Louisiana		148,329	22,259
Maryland	2,446	200,869	164,051
Mississippi	26	46,250	50,405
Missouri	13,696	99,454	514,711
North Carolina	38,196	39,462	34,348
South Carolina	55	47,286	85,108
Tennessee	18,904	97,183	52,894
Texas	26	12,354	12,505
Virginia	52,318	183,047	177,137
	203,484	$1,377,260	$1,355,827

all the glory and prosperity of the country, from Maine to Texas, and from Georgia to California, to the "invaluable institutions of the South!" With what patience we could command, we have frequently listened to the incoherent and truth-murdering declamations of these champions of slavery, and, in the absence of a more politic method of giving vent to our disgust and indignation, have involuntarily bit our lips into blisters.

The lords of the lash are not only absolute masters of the blacks, who are bought and sold, and driven about like so many cattle, but they are also the oracles and arbiters of all non-slaveholding whites, whose freedom is merely nominal, and whose unparalleled illiteracy and degradation is purposely and fiendishly perpetuated. How little the "poor white trash," the great majority of the Southern people, know of the real condition of the country is, indeed, sadly astonishing. The truth is, they know nothing of public measures, and little of private affairs,

RECAPITULATION—FREE STATES.

Wheat	72,157,486 bush.	@	1.50	$108,236,229
Oats	96,590,371 "	"	40	38,636,148
Indian Corn	242,618,650 "	"	60	145,571,190
Potatoes (I. & S.)	59,033,170 "	"	38	22,432,604
Rye	12,574,623 "	"	1.00	12,574,623
Barley	5,002,013 "	"	90	4,501,811
Buckwheat	8,550,245 "	"	50	4,275,122
Beans & Peas	1,542,295 "	"	1.75	2,699,015
Clov. & Grass seeds	762,265 "	"	3.00	2,286,795
Flax Seeds	358,923 "	"	1.25	448,647
Garden Products			....	3,714,605
Orchard Products			....	6,332,914

Total,.....499,190,041 bu., valued as above, at $351,709,703

RECAPITULATION—SLAVE STATES.

Wheat	27,904,476 bush.	@	1.50	$ 41,856,714
Oats	49,882,799 "	"	40	19,953,191
Indian Corn	348,992,282 "	"	60	209,395,369
Potatoes (I. & S.)	44,847,420 "	"	38	17,042,019
Rye	1,608,240 "	"	1.00	1,608,240
Barley	161,907 "	"	90	145,716
Buckwheat	405,357 "	"	50	202,678
Beans & Peas	7,637,227 "	"	1.75	13,365,147
Clov. & Grass seeds	123,517 "	"	3.00	370,551
Flax Seeds	203,484 "	"	1.25	254,355
Garden Products			....	1,377,260
Orchard Products			....	1,355,827

Total,.....481,766,889 bu., valued as above, at $306,927,067

TOTAL DIFFERENCE—BUSHEL-MEASURE PRODUCTS.

	Bushels.		Value.
Free States	499,190,041		$351,709,703
Slave States	481,766,889		306,927,067
Balance in bushels	17,423,152	Differ. in value	$44,782,636

except what their imperious masters, the slave-drivers,
condescend to tell, and that is but precious little, and even
that little, always garbled and one-sided, is never told except in public harangues; for the haughty cavaliers of

shackles and handcuffs will not degrade themselves by holding private converse with those who have neither dimes nor hereditary rights in human flesh.

Whenever it pleases, and to the extent it pleases, a slaveholder to become communicative, poor whites may hear with fear and trembling, but not speak. They must be as mum as dumb brutes, and stand in awe of their august superiors, or be crushed with stern rebukes, cruel oppressions, or downright violence. If they dare to think for themselves, their thoughts must be forever concealed. The expression of any sentiment at all conflicting with the gospel of slavery, dooms them at once in the community in which they live, and then, whether willing or unwilling, they are obliged to become heroes, martyrs, or exiles. They may thirst for knowledge, but there is no Moses among them to smite it out of the rocks of Horeb. The black veil, through whose almost impenetrable meshes light seldom gleams, has long been pendent over their eyes, and there, with fiendish jealousy, the slave-driving ruffians sedulously guard it. Non-slaveholders are not only kept in ignorance of what is transpiring at the North, but they are continually misinformed of what is going on even in the South. Never were the poorer classes of a people, and those classes so largely in the majority, and all inhabiting the same country, so basely duped, so adroitly swindled, or so damnably outraged.

It is expected that the stupid and sequacious masses, the white victims of slavery, will believe, and, as a general thing, they do believe, whatever the slaveholders tell them; and thus it is that they are cajoled into the notion that they are the freest, happiest and most intelligent people in the world, and are taught to look with prejudice and disapprobation upon every new principle or progressive movement. Thus it is that the South, woefully inert and inventionless, has lagged behind the North, and is now weltering in the cesspool of ignorance and degradation.

We have already intimated that the opinion is prevalent throughout the South that the free States are quite sterile and unproductive, and that they are mainly dependent on us for breadstuffs and other provisions. So far as the cereals, fruits, garden vegetables and esculent roots are concerned, we have, in the preceding tables, shown the utter falsity of this opinion; and we now propose to show that it is equally erroneous in other particulars, and very far from the truth in the general reckoning. We can prove, and we intend to prove, from facts in our possession, that the hay crop of the free States is worth considerably more in dollars and cents than all the cotton, tobacco, rice, hay and hemp produced in the fifteen slave States. This statement may strike some of our readers with amazement, and others may, for the moment, regard it as quite incredible; but it is true, nevertheless, and we shall soon proceed to confirm it. The single free State of New York produces more than *three times* the quantitity of hay that is produced in all the slave States. Ohio produces a larger number of tons than all the Southern and Southwestern States, and so does Pennsylvania. Vermont, little and unpretending as she is, does the same thing, with the exception of Virginia. Look at the facts as presented in the tables, and let your own eyes, physical and intellectual, confirm you in the truth.

And yet, forsooth, the slave-driving oligarchy would whip us into the belief that agriculture is not one of the leading and lucrative pursuits of the States, that the soil there is an uninterrupted barren waste, and that our Northern brethren, having the advantage in nothing except wealth, population, inland and foreign commerce, manufactures, mechanism, inventions, literature, the arts and sciences, and their concomitant branches of profitable industry,—miserable objects of charity—are dependent on us for the necessaries of life.

Next to Virginia, Maryland is the greatest Southern hay-producing State: and yet, it is the opinion of several of the most extensive hay and grain dealers in Baltimore, with whom we have conversed on the subject, that the domestic crop is scarcely equal to one-third the demand, and that the balance required for home consumption, about two-thirds, is chiefly brought from New York, Pennsylvania and Massachusetts. At this rate, Maryland receives and consumes not less than three hundred and fifteen thousand tons of Northern hay every year; and this, as we are informed by the dealers above-mentioned, at an average cost to the last purchaser, by the time it is stowed in the mow, of at least twenty-five dollars per ton; it would thus appear that this most popular and valuable provender, one of the staple commodities of the North, commands a market in a single slave State, to the amount of seven million eight hundred and seventy-five thousand dollars per annum.

In this same State of Maryland, less than one million of dollars' worth of cotton finds a market, the whole number of bales sold here in 1850 amounting to only twenty-three thousand three hundred and twenty-five, valued at seven hundred and forty-six thousand four hundred dollars. Briefly, then, and in round numbers, we may state the case thus: Maryland buys annually seven millions of dollars worth of hay from the North, and one million of dollars worth of cotton from the South. Let slaveholders and their fawning defenders read, ponder and compare.

The exact quantities of Northern hay, rye, and buckwheat flour, Irish potatoes, fruits, clover and grass seeds, and other products of the soil, received and consumed in all the slaveholding States, we have no means of ascertaining; but for all practical purposes, we can arrive sufficiently near to the amount by inference from the above data, and from what we see with our eyes and hear with our ears wherever we go. Food from the North for man or for beast, or for both, is for sale in every market in the South. Even in the most insignificant little villages in the interior of the slave States, where books, newspapers and other mediums of intelligence are unknown, where the poor whites and the negroes are alike bowed down in heathenish ignorance and barbarism, and where the news is received but once a week, and then only in a Northern-built stage-coach, drawn by horses in Northern harness, in charge of a driver dressed *cap-a-pie* in Northern habiliments, and with a Northern whip in his hand,—the agricultural products of the North, either crude, prepared, pickled or preserved, are ever to be found.

Mortifying as the acknowledgment of the fact is to us, it is our unbiased opinion—an opinion which will, we believe, be endorsed by every intelligent person who goes into a careful examination and comparison of all the facts in the case—that the profits arising to the North from the sale of provender and provisions to the South, are far greater than those arising to the South from the sale of cotton, tobacco and breadstuffs to the North. It follows, then, that the agricultural interests of the North being not only equal but actually superior to those of the South, the hundreds of millions of dollars which the commerce and manufactures of the former annually yield, is just so much clear and independent gain over the latter. It follows, also, from a corresponding train or system of deduction, and with all the foregoing facts in view, that the difference between freedom and slavery is simply the difference between sense and nonsense, wisdom and folly, good and evil, right and wrong.

Any observant American, from whatever point of the compass he may hail, who will take the trouble to pass through the Southern markets, both great and small, as we have done, and inquire where this article, that and the other came from, will be utterly astonished at the variety and quantity of Northern agricultural productions kept for sale. And this state of things is growing worse and worse every year. Exclusively agricultural as the South is in her industrial pursuits, she is barely able to support her sparse and degenerate population. Her men and her domestic animals, both dwarfed into shabby objects of commiseration under the blighting effects of slavery, are constantly feeding on the multifarious products of Northern soil. And if the whole truth must be told, we may here add, that these products, like all other articles of merchandize purchased at the North, are generally bought on a credit, and, in a great number of instances, by far too many, never paid for—not, as a general rule, because the purchasers are dishonest or unwilling to pay, but because they are impoverished and depressed by the retrogressive and deadening operations of slavery, that most unprofitable and pernicious institution under which they live.

To show how well we are sustained in our remarks upon hay and other special products of the soil, as well as to give circulation to other facts of equal significance, we quote a single passage from an address by Paul C. Cameron, before the Agricultural Society of Orange County, North Carolina. This production is, in the main, so powerfully conceived, so correct and plausible in its statements and conclusions, and so well calculated, though, perhaps, not intended, to arouse the old North State to a sense of her natural greatness and acquired shame, that we could wish to see it published in pamphlet form, and circulated throughout the length and breadth of that unfortunate and degraded heritage of slavery. Mr. Cameron says:

"I know not when I have been more humiliated, as a North Carolina farmer, than when, a few weeks ago, at a railroad depot at the very doors of our State capital, I saw wagons drawn by Kentucky mules, loading with Northern hay, for the supply not only of the town, but to be taken to the country. Such a sight at the capital of a State whose population is almost exclusively devoted to agriculture, is a most humiliating exhibition. Let us cease to use every thing, as far as it is practicable, that is not the product of our own soil and workshops—not an axe, or a broom, or bucket, from Connecticut. By every consideration of self-preservation, we are called to make better efforts to expel the Northern grocer from the State with his butter, and the Ohio and Kentucky horse, mule and hog driver, from our county at least. It is a reproach on us as farmers, and no little deduction from our wealth, that we suffer the population of our towns and villages to supply themselves with butter from another Orange County in New York."

We have promised to prove that the hay crop of the free states is worth considerably more than all the cotton, tobacco, rice, hay and hemp produced in the fifteen slave States. The compilers of the last census, as we learn from Prof. De Bow, the able and courteous superintendent, in making up the hay-tables, allowed two thousand two hundred and forty pounds to the ton. The price per ton at which we should estimate its value has puzzled us to some extent. Dealers in the article in Baltimore think it will average twenty-five dollars, in their market. Four or five months ago they sold it at thirty dollars per ton. At the very time we write, though there is less activity in the article than usual, we learn, from an examination of sundry prices-current and commercial journals, that hay is selling in Savannah at $33 per ton; in Mobile and New Orleans at $26; in Charleston at $25; in Louisville at $24; and in Cincinnati at $23. The average of these prices is *twenty-six dollars sixteen and two-third cents;* and we suppose it would be fair to employ the figures which would indicate this amount, the net value of a single ton, in calculating the total market value of the entire crop. Were we to do this—and, with the foregoing facts in view, we

submit to intelligent men whether we would not be justifiable in doing it,—the hay crop of the free states, 12,690,-
982 tons, in 1850, would amount in valuation to the
enormous sum of $331,081,695—more than four times
the value of all the cotton produced in the United States
during the same period!

But we shall not make the calculation at what we have
found to be the average value per ton throughout the
country. What rate, then, shall be agreed upon as a basis
of comparison between the value of the hay crop of the
North and that of the South, and as a means of testing the
truth of our declaration—that the former exceeds the aggregate value of all the cotton, tobacco, rice, hay and hemp
produced in the fifteen slave States? Suppose we take
$13,08⅓—just half the average value—as the multiplier
in this arithmetical exercise. This we can well afford to do;
indeed, we might reduce the amount per ton to much less
than half the average value, and still have a large margin
left for triumphant demonstration. It is not our purpose,
however, to make an overwhelming display of the incom-
parable greatness of the free States.

In estimating the value of the various agricultural products of the two great sections of the country, we have
been guided by prices emanating from the Bureau of
Agriculture in Washington; and in a catalogue of those
prices now before us, we perceive that the average value
of hay throughout the nation is supposed to be not more
than half a cent per pound—$11.20 per ton—which, as
we have seen above, is considerably less than half the
present market value;—and this, too, in the face of the
fact that prices generally rule higher than they do just
now. It will be admitted on all sides, however, that the
prices fixed upon by the Bureau of Agriculture, taken as
a whole, are as fair for one section of the country as for
the other, and that we cannot blamelessly deviate from
them in one particular without deviating from them in
another. Eleven dollars and twenty cents ($11.20) per
ton shall therefore be the price; and, notwithstanding
these greatly reduced figures, we now renew, with an addendum, our declaration and promise, that—*We can
prove, and we shall now proceed to prove, that the annual
hay crop of the free States is worth considerably more in
dollars and cents than all the cotton, tobacco, rice, hay,*

hemp and cane sugar annually produced in the fifteen slave States.

HAY CROP OF THE FREE STATES—1850.

12,690,982 tons *a* 11,20 . . . . $142,138,998

SUNDRY PRODUCTS OF THE SLAVE STATES—1850.

Cotton	2,445,779 bales	*a*	32,00	. $78,264,928
Tobacco	185,023,906 lbs.	"	10	. . 18,502,390
Rice (rough) . .	215,313,497 lbs.	"	4	. . . 8,612,539
Hay	1,137,784 tons	"	11,20	. . 12,743,180
Hemp	34,673 tons	"	112,00	. . . 3,883,376
Cane Sugar . . .	237,133,000 lbs.	"	7	. . 16,599,310

$138,605,723

RECAPITULATION.

Hay crop of the free States $142,138,998
Sundry products of the slave States 138,605,723

Balance in favor of the free States $3,533,275

There is the account; look at it, and let it stand in at-testation of the exalted virtues and surpassing powers of freedom. Scan it well, Messieurs lords of the lash, and learn from it new lessons of the utter inefficiency and despicable imbecility of slavery. Examine it minutely, liberty-loving patriots of the North, and behold in it additional evidences of the beauty, grandeur, and super-excellence of free institutions. Treasure it up in your minds, outraged friends and non-slaveholders of the South, and let the recollection of it arouse you to an inflexible determination to extirpate the monstrous enemy that stalks abroad in your land, and to recover the inalienable rights and liberties, which have been filched from you by an unprincipled oligarchy.

In deference to truth, decency and good sense, it is to be hoped that negro-driving politicians will never more have the effrontery to open their mouths in extolling the agricultural achievements of slave labor. Especially is it desirable, that, as a simple act of justice to a basely deceived populace, they may cease their stale and senseless harangues on the importance of cotton. The value of cotton to the South, to the North, to the nation, and to the

world, has been so grossly exaggerated, and so extensive
have been the evils which have resulted in consequence
of the extraordinary misrepresentations concerning it, that
we should feel constrained to reproach ourself for remiss-
ness of duty, if we failed to make an attempt to explode
the popular error. The figures above show what it is, and
what it is not. Recur to them, and learn the facts.

So hyperbolically has the importance of cotton been
magnified by certain pro-slavery politicians of the South,
that the person who would give credence to all their fus-
tian and bombast, would be under the necessity of believing that the very existence of almost everything, in the
heaven above, in the earth beneath, and in the water under the earth, depended on it. The truth is, however, that
the cotton crop is of but little value to the South. New
England and Old England, by their superior enterprise
and sagacity, turn it chiefly to their own advantage. It is
carried in their ships, spun in their factories, woven in
their looms, insured in their offices, returned again in their
own vessels, and, with double freight and cost of manufacturing added, purchased by the South at a high pre-
mium. Of all the parties engaged or interested in its transportation and manufacture, the South is the only one that
does not make a profit. Nor does she, as a general thing,
make a profit by producing it.

We are credibly informed that many of the farmers in
the immediate vicinity of Baltimore, where we now write,
have turned their attention exclusively to hay, and that
from one acre they frequently gather two tons, for which
they receive fifty dollars. Let us now inquire how many
dollars may be expected from an acre planted in cotton.
Mr. Cameron, from whose able address before the Agricultural Society of Orange County, North Carolina, we have
already gleaned some interesting particulars, informs us,
that the cotton planters in his part of the country, "have
contented themselves with a crop yielding only *ten or
twelve dollars per acre,*" and that "the summing up of a
large surface gives but a living result." An intelligent
resident of the Palmetto State, writing in De Bow's Review, not long since, advances the opinion that the cotton planters of South Carolina are not realizing more than
one per cent. on the amount of capital they have invested.
While in Virginia, very recently, an elderly slaveholder,

whose religious walk and conversation had recommended and promoted him to an eldership in the Presbyterian church, and who supports himself and family by raising niggers and tobacco, told us that, for the last eight or ten years, aside from the increase of his human chattels, he felt quite confident he had not cleared as much even as one per cent. per annum on the amount of his investment. The real and personal property of this aged *Christian* consists chiefly in a large tract of land and about thirty negroes, most of whom, according to his own confession, are more expensive than profitable. The proceeds arising from the sale of the tobacco they produce, are all absorbed in the purchase of meat and bread for home consumption, and when the crop is stunted by drought, frost, or otherwise cut short, one of the negroes must be sold to raise funds for the support of the others. Such are the agricultural achievements of slave labor; such are the results of "the sum of all villainies." The diabolical institution subsists on its own flesh. At one time children are sold to procure food for the parents, at another, parents are sold to procure food for the children. Within its pestilential atmosphere, nothing succeeds; progress and prosperity are unknown; inanition and slothfulness ensue; everything becomes dull, dismal and unprofitable; wretchedness and desolation run riot throughout the land; an aspect of most melancholy inactivity and dilapidation broods over every city and town; ignorance and prejudice sit enthroned over the minds of the people; usurping despots wield the sceptre of power; everywhere, and in everything, between Delaware Bay and the Gulf of Mexico, are the multitudinous evils of slavery apparent.

The soil itself soon sickens and dies beneath the unnatural tread of the slave. Hear what the Hon. C. C. Clay, of Alabama, has to say upon the subject. His testimony is eminently suggestive, well-timed, and truthful; and we heartily commend it to the careful consideration of every spirited Southron who loves his country, and desires to see it rescued from the fatal grasp of "the mother of harlots:" Says he:

"I can show you, with sorrow, in the older portions of Alabama, and in my native county of Madison, the sad memorials of the artless and exhausting culture of cotton. Our small planters, after taking the cream off their lands, unable to restore them by rest, manures, or otherwise, are going further West and South, in search of other virgin lands, which they may and will despoil and impoverish in like manner. Our wealthier planters, with greater means and no more skill, are buying out their poorer neighbors, extending their plantations, and adding to their slave force. The wealthy few, who are able to live on smaller profits, and to give their blasted fields some rest, are thus pushing off the many who are merely independent. Of the $20,000,000 annually realized from the sales of the cotton crop of Alabama, nearly all not expended in supporting the producers, is re-invested in land and negroes. Thus the white population has decreased and the slave increased almost *pari passu* in several counties of our State. In 1825, Madison county cast about 3,000 votes; now, she cannot cast exceeding 2,300. In traversing that county, one will discover numerous farm-houses, once the abode of industrious and intelligent freemen, now occupied by slaves, or tenantless, deserted and dilapidated; he will observe fields, once fertile, now unfenced, abandoned, and covered with those evil harbingers, fox-tail and broom-sedge; he will see the moss growing on the mouldering walls of once thrifty villages, and will find 'one only master grasps the whole domain,' that once furnished happy homes for a dozen white families. Indeed, a country in its infancy, where fifty years ago scarce a forest tree had been felled by the axe of the pioneer, is already exhibiting the painful signs of senility and decay apparent in Virginia and the Carolinas."

Some one has said that "an honest confession is good for the soul," and if the adage be true, as we have no doubt it is, we think Mr. C. C. Clay is entitled to a quiet conscience on one score at least. In the extract quoted above, he gives us a graphic description of the ruinous operations and influences of slavery in the Southwest; and we, as a native of Carolina, and a traveler through Virginia, are ready to bear testimony to the fitness of his remarks when he referred to those States as examples of senility and decay. With equal propriety, however, he might have stopped nearer home for a subject of comparison. Either of the States bordering upon Alabama, or, indeed, any other slave States would have answered his purpose quite as well as Virginia and the Carolinas. Wherever slavery exists there he may find parallels to the destruction that is sweeping with such deadly influence over his own unfortunate State.

As for examples of vigorous, industrious and thrifty communities, they can be found anywhere beyond the Upas-shadow of slavery—nowhere else. New York and Massachusetts, which, by nature, are confessedly far inferior to Virginia and the Carolinas, have, by the more liberal and equitable policy which they have pursued, in substituting liberty for slavery, attained a degree of eminence and prosperity altogether unknown in the slave States.

Amidst all the hyperbole and cajolery of slave-driving politicians who, as we have already seen, are 'the books, the arts, the academies, that show, contain, and govern all the South,' we are rejoiced to see that Mr. Clay, Mr. Cameron, and a few others, have had the boldness and honesty to step forward and proclaim the truth. All such frank admissions are to be hailed as good omens for the South. Nothing good can come from any attempt to conceal the unconcealable evidences of poverty and desolation everywhere trailing in the wake of slavery. Let the truth be told on all occasions, of the North as well as of the South, and the people will soon begin to discover the egregiousness of their errors, to draw just comparisons, to inquire into cause and effect, and to adopt the more utile measures, manners and customs of their wiser contemporaries.

In wilfully traducing and decrying everything North of Mason and Dixon's line, and in excessively magnifying the importance of everything South of it, the oligarchy have, in the eyes of all liberal and intelligent men, only made an exhibition of their uncommon folly and dishonesty. For a long time, it is true, they have succeeded in deceiving the people, in keeping them humbled in the murky sloughs of poverty and ignorance, and in instilling into their untutored minds passions and prejudices expressly calculated to strengthen and protect the accursed institution of slavery; but, thanks to heaven, their inglorious reign is fast drawing to a close; with irresistible brilliancy, and in spite of the interdict of tyrants, light from the pure fountain of knowledge is now streaming over the dark places of our land, and, ere long—mark our

words—there will ascend from Delaware, and from
Texas, and from all the intermediate States, a huzza for
Freedom and for Equal Rights, that will utterly confound
the friends of despotism, set at defiance the authority of
usurpers, and carry consternation to the heart of every
slavery-propagandist.

To undeceive the people of the South, to bring them
to a knowledge of the inferior and disreputable position
which they occupy as a component part of the Union, and
to give prominence and popularity to those plans which,
if adopted, will elevate us to an equality, socially, morally,
intellectually, industrially, politically, and financially, with
the most flourishing and refined nation in the world, and,
if possible, to place us in the van of even that, is the object
of this work. Slaveholders, either from ignorance or from
a wilful disposition to propagate error, contend that the
South has nothing to be ashamed of, that slavery has
proved a blessing to her, and that her superiority over the
North in an agricultural point of view makes amends for
all her short-comings in other respects. On the other hand,
we contend that many years of continual blushing and
severe penance would not suffice to cancel or annul the
shame and disgrace that justly attaches to the South in
consequence of slavery—the direst evil that e'er befell the
land—that the South bears nothing like even a respectable
approximation to the North in navigation, commerce, or
manufactures, and that, contrary to the opinion entertained by ninety-nine hundredths of her people, she is far
behind the free States in the only thing of which she has
ever dared to boast—agriculture. We submit the question
to the arbitration of figures, which, it is said, do not lie.
With regard to the bushel-measure products of the soil, of
which we have already taken an inventory, we have seen
that there is a balance against the South in favor of the
North of *seventeen million four hundred and twenty-three
thousand one hundred and fifty-two bushels,* and a difference in the value of the same, also in favor of the North,
of *forty-four million seven hundred and eighty-two thousand six hundred and thirty-six dollars.* It is certainly a
most novel kind of agricultural superiority that the
South claims on that score!

Our attention shall now be directed to the twelve principal pound-measure products of the free and of the slave

States—hay, cotton, butter and cheese, tobacco, cane, sugar, wool, rice, hemp, maple sugar, beeswax and honey, flax, and hops—and in taking an account of them, we shall, in order to show the exact quantity produced in each State, and for the convenience of future reference, pursue the same plan as that adopted in the preceding tables. Whether slavery will appear to better advantage on the scales than it did in the half-bushel, remains to be seen. It is possible that the rickety monster may make a better show on a new track; if it makes a more ridiculous display, we shall not be surprised. A careful examination of its precedents has taught us the folly of expecting anything good to issue from it in any manner whatever. It has no disposition to emulate the magnanimity of its betters, and as for a laudable ambition to excel, that is a characteristic altogether foreign to its nature. Languor and inertia are the insalutary viands upon which it delights to satiate its morbid appetite; and "from bad to worse" is the ill-omened motto under which, in all its feeble efforts and achievements, it ekes out a most miserable and deleterious existence.

Pray, permit us to ask—have the people of the North no interest in the United States as a *nation*, and do they not see that slavery is a great injury and disgrace to the *whole country?* Did they not, in "the days that tried men's souls," strike as hard blows to secure the independence of Georgia as they did in defending the liberties of Massachusetts, and is it not notoriously true that the Toryism of South Carolina prolonged the war two years at least? Is it not, moreover, equally true that the oligarchs of South Carolina have been unmitigated pests and bores to the General Government ever since it was organized, and that the free and conscientious people of the North are virtually excluded from her soil, in consequence of slavery? It is a well-known and incontestible fact, that the Northern States furnished about two-thirds of all the American troops engaged in the Revolutionary War; and, though they were neither more nor less brave or patriotic than their fellow-soldiers of the South, yet, inasmuch as the independence of our country was mainly secured by virtue of their numerical strength, we think they ought to consider it not only their right but their *duty* to make a firm and decisive effort to save the States which they fought to free, from falling under the yoke of a worse tyranny than that which overshadowed them under the reign of King George the Third. Freemen of the North! we earnestly entreat you to think of those things. Hitherto, as mere free-soilers, you have approached but half-way to the line of your duty; now, for your own sakes and for ours, and for the purpose of perpetuating this glorious Republic, which your fathers and our fathers founded in septennial streams of blood, we ask you, in all seriousness, to organize your-selves as *one man* under the banners of Liberty, and to aid us in *exterminating* slavery, which is the only thing that militates against our complete aggrandizement as a nation.

In this extraordinary crisis of affairs, no man can be a true patriot without first becoming an abolitionist. (A free-soiler is only a tadpole in an advanced state of transforma-tion; an abolitionist is the full and perfectly developed frog.)

We are personally acquainted with several slaveholders in North Carolina, South Carolina, Maryland and Virginia, who have unreservedly assured us that they were dis-gusted with the institution, and some of them went so far as to say they would be glad to acquiesce in the provision of a statute which would make it obligatory on them all to manumit their slaves, without the smallest shadow or substance of compensation. These, we believe, are the sentiments of all the respectable and patriotic slaveholders, who have eyes to see, and see—ears to hear, and hear; who, perceiving the impoverishing and degrading effects of slavery, are unwilling to entail it on their children, and who, on account of their undeviating adherence to truth and justice, are, like the more intelligent non-slaveholders, worthy of being regarded as gentlemen in every sense of the term. Such slaveholders were Washington, Jeffer-son, Madison, and other illustrious Virginians, who, in the language of the great chief himself, declared it among their "*first wishes* to see some plan adopted by which slav-ery, in this country, may be abolished by law." The words embraced within this quotation were used by Washing-ton, in a letter to John F. Mercer, dated September 9th, 1786—a letter from which we shall quote more freely hereafter; and we think his emphatic use of the participle *abolished,* at that early day, is proof positive that the glorious "Father of his Country" is entitled to the first place in the calendar of primitive American abolitionists.

It is against slavery on the whole, and against slaveholders as a body, that we wage an exterminating war. Those persons who, under the infamous slave-laws of the South —laws which have been correctly spoken of as a "disgrace to civilization," and which must be annulled simultaneously with the abolition of slavery—have had the vile institution entailed on them contrary to their wills, are virtually on our side; we may, therefore, very properly strike them off from the black list of three hundred and forty-seven thousand slaveholders, who, as a body, have shocked the civilized world with their barbarous conduct, and from whose conceited and presumptuous ranks are selected the officers who do all the legislation, town, county, state and national, for (against) five millions of poor outraged whites, and three millions of enslaved negroes.

Non-slaveholders of the South! farmers, mechanics and workingmen, we take this occasion to assure you that the slaveholders, the arrogant demagogues whom you have elected to offices of honor and profit, have hoodwinked you, trifled with you, and used you as mere tools for the consummation of their wicked designs. They have purposely kept you in ignorance, and have, by moulding your passions and prejudices to suit themselves, induced you to act in direct opposition to your dearest rights and interests. By a system of the grossest subterfuge and misrepresentation, and in order to avert, for a season, the vengeance that will most assuredly overtake them ere long, they have taught you to hate the abolitionists, who are your best and only true friends. Now, as one of your own number, we appeal to you to join us in our patriotic endeavors to rescue the generous soil of the South from the usurped and desolating control of these political vampires. Once and forever, at least so far as this country is concerned, the infernal question of slavery must be disposed of; a speedy and perfect abolishment of the whole institution is the true policy of the South—and this is the policy which we propose to pursue. Will you aid us, will you assist us, will you be freemen, or will you be slaves?

CHAPTER II.

HOW SLAVERY CAN BE ABOLISHED.

IN HIS present condition, we believe man exercises one of the noblest virtues with which heaven has endowed him, when, without taking any undue advantage of his fellow-men, and with a firm, unwavering purpose to confine his expenditures to the legitimate pursuits and pleasures of life, he covets money and strives to accumulate it. Entertaining this view, and having no disposition to make an improper use of money, we are free to confess that we have a greater penchant for twenty-eight dollars than for five; for ninety than for fifteen; for a thousand than for one hundred. South of Mason and Dixon's line we, the non-slaveholders, have 331,902,720 acres of land, the present average market value of which, as previously stated, is only $5,34 per acre; by abolishing slavery we expect to enhance the value to an average of at least $28,07 per acre, and thus realize an average net increase of wealth of more than *seventy-five hundred millions of dollars*. The hope of realizing smaller sums has frequently induced men to perpetrate acts of injustice; we can see no reason why the certainty of becoming immensely rich in real estate, or other property, should make us falter in the performance of a *sacred duty*.

As illustrative of our theme, a bit of personal history may not be out of place in this connection. Only a few months have elapsed since we sold to an elder brother an interest we held in an old homestead which was willed to us many years ago by our dear departed father. The tract of land, containing two hundred acres, or thereabouts, is situated two and a half miles west of Mocksville, the capital of Davie county, North Carolina, and is very nearly equally divided by Bear Creek, a small tributary of the South Yadkin. More than one-third of this tract—on

which we have plowed, and hoed, and harrowed, many a
long summer without ever suffering from the effects of
coup de soleil—is under cultivation; the remaining portion
is a well-timbered forest, in which, without being very
particular, we counted, while hunting through it not long,
since, sixty-three different kinds of indigenous trees—to
say nothing of either coppice, shrubs or plants—among
which the hickory, oak, ash, beech, birch, and black wal-
nut, were most abundant. No turpentine or rosin is produced in our part of the State; but there are, on the place
of which we speak, several species of the genus Pinus,
by the light of whose flammable knots, as radiated on the
contents of some half-dozen old books, which, by hook or
by crook, had found their way into the neighborhood, we
have been enabled to turn the long winter evenings to our
advantage, and have thus *partially* escaped from the
prison-grounds of those loathsome dungeons of illiteracy
in which it has been the constant policy of the oligarchy
to keep the masses, the non-slaveholding whites and the
negroes, forever confined. The fertility of the soil may be
inferred from the quality and variety of its natural productions; the meadow and the bottom, comprising, perhaps, an area of forty acres, are hardly surpassed by the
best lands in the valley of the Yadkin. A thorough examination of the orchard will disclose the fact that considerable attention has been paid to the selection of fruits; the
buildings are tolerable; the water is good. Altogether, to
be frank, and nothing more, it is, for its size, one of the
most desirable farms in the county, and will, at any time,
command the maximum price of land in Western Carolina.
Our brother, anxious to become the sole proprietor, readily
agreed to give us the highest market price, which we shall
publish by-and-bye. While reading the Baltimore *Sun*,
the morning after we had made the sale, our attention
was allured to a paragraph headed "Sales of Real Estate,"
from which, among other significant items, we learned that
a tract of land containing exactly two hundred acres, and
occupying a portion of one of the rural districts in the
southeastern part of Pennsylvania, near the Maryland line,
had been sold the week before, at *one hundred and five
dollars and fifty cents* per acre. Judging from the succinct
account given in the *Sun*, we are of the opinion that, with
regard to fertility of soil, the Pennsylvania tract always

has been, is now, and perhaps always will be, rather inferior to the one under special consideration. One is of the same size as the other; both are used for agricultural purposes; in all probability the only *essential* difference between them is this: one is blessed with the pure air of freedom, the other is cursed with the malaria of slavery. For our interest in the old homestead we received a nominal sum, amounting to an average of precisely *five dollars and sixty cents* per acre. No one but our brother, who was keen for the purchase, would have given us quite so much.

And, now, pray let us ask, what does this narrative teach? We shall use few words in explanation; there is an extensive void, but it can be better filled with reflection. The aggregate value of the one tract is $21,100; that of the other is only $1,120; the difference is $19,980. We contend, therefore, in view of all the circumstances detailed, that the advocates and retainers of slavery, have, to all intents and purposes, defrauded our family out of this last-mentioned sum. In like manner, and on the same basis of deduction, we contend that almost every non-slaveholder, who either is or has been the owner of real estate in the South, would, in a court of strict justice, be entitled to damages—the amount in all cases to be determined with reference to the quality of the land in question. We say this because, in violation of every principle of expediency, justice, and humanity, and in direct opposition to our solemn protests, slavery was foisted upon us, and has been thus far perpetuated, by and through the diabolical intrigues of the oligarchs, and by them alone; and furthermore, because the very best agricultural lands in the Northern States being worth from one hundred to one hundred and seventy-five dollars per acre, there is no possible reason, except slavery, why the more fertile and congenial soil of the South should not be worth at least as much. If, on this principle, we could ascertain, in the matter of real estate, the total indebtedness of the slaveholders to the non-slaveholders, we should doubtless find the sum quite equivalent to the amount estimated on a preceding page—$7,544,148,825.

We have recently conversed with two gentlemen who, to save themselves from the poverty and disgrace of slavery, left North Carolina six or seven years ago, and who are now residing in the territory of Minnesota, where they have accumulated handsome fortunes. One of them had traveled extensively in Kentucky, Missouri, Ohio, Indiana, and other adjoining States; and, according to his account, and we know him to be a man of veracity, it is almost impossible for persons at a distance, to form a proper conception of the magnitude of the difference between the current value of lands in the Free and the Slave States of the West. On one occasion, embarking at Wheeling, he sailed down the Ohio; Virginia and Kentucky on the one side, Ohio and Indiana on the other. He stopped at several places along the river, first on the right bank, then on the left, and so on, until he arrived at Evansville; continuing his trip, he sailed down to Cairo, thence up the Mississippi to the mouth of the Des Moines; having tarried at different points along the route, sometimes in Missouri, sometimes in Illinois. Wherever he landed on free soil, he found it from one to two hundred per cent. more valuable than the slave soil on the opposite bank. If, for instance, the maximum price of land was eight dollars in Kentucky, the minimum price was sixteen in Ohio; if it was seven dollars in Missouri, it was fourteen in Illinois. Furthermore, he assured us that, so far as he could learn, two years ago, when he traveled through the States of which we speak, the range of prices of agricultural lands, in Kentucky, was from three to eight dollars per acre; in Ohio, from sixteen to forty; in Missouri, from two to seven; in Illinois, from fourteen to thirty; in Arkansas, from one to four; in Iowa, from six to fifteen.

In all the old slave States, as is well known, there are vast bodies of land that can be bought for the merest trifle. We know an enterprising capitalist in Philadelphia, who owns in his individual name, in the State of Virginia, *one hundred and thirty thousand acres*, for which he paid only *thirty-seven and a half cents* per acre! Some years ago, in certain parts of North Carolina, several large tracts were purchased at the rate of *twenty-five cents* per acre!

A majority of the slaveholders with whom we are acquainted—and we happen to know a few dozen more than we care to know—own, or pretend to own, at least fifteen negroes each; some of them are the masters of more than fifty each; and we have had the *honor* (!) of an introduction to one man who is represented as the owner of sixteen hundred! It is said that if all the lands of this latter worthy were in one tract, they might be formed into two counties of more than ordinary size; he owns plantations and woodlands in three cotton-growing States.

The quantity of land owned by the slaveholder is generally in proportion to the number of negroes at his "quarter;" the master of only one or two slaves, if engaged in agriculture, seldom owns less than three hundred acres; the holder of eight or ten slaves usually owns from a thousand to fifteen hundred acres; five thousand acres are not unfrequently found in the possession of the master of fifty slaves; while in Columbia, South Carolina, about twelve months ago, a certain noted slaveholder was pointed out to us, and reported as the owner of nearly two hundred thousand acres in the State of Mississippi. How the great mass of illiterate poor whites, a majority of whom are the indescribably wretched tenants of these slavocratic landsharks, are specially imposed upon and socially outlawed, we shall, if we have time and space, take occasion to explain in a subsequent chapter.

Thus far, in giving expression to our sincere and settled opinions, we have endeavored to show, in the first place, that slavery is a great moral, social, civil, and political evil —a dire enemy to true wealth and national greatness, and an atrocious crime against both God and man; and, in the second place, that it is a paramount duty which we owe to heaven, to the earth, to America, to humanity, to our posterity, to our consciences, and to our pockets, to adopt effectual and judicious measures for its immediate abolition. The questions now arise, How can the evil be averted? What are the most prudent and practical means that can be devised for the abolition of slavery? In the solution of these problems it becomes necessary to deal with a multiplicity of stubborn realities. And yet, we can see no reason why North Carolina, in her sovereign capacity, may not, with equal ease and success, do what forty-five other States of the world have done within the last forty-five years. Nor do we believe any good reason exists why Virginia should not perform as great a deed in 1859 as did New York in 1799. Massachusetts abolished slavery in 1780; would it not be a masterly stroke of policy in Tennessee, and every other slave State, to abolish it in or before 1860?

Not long since, a slavocrat, writing on this subject, said,

apologetically, "we frankly admit that slavery is a monstrous evil; but what are we to do with an institution which has baffled the wisdom of our greatest statesmen?" Unfortunately for the South, since the days of Washington, Jefferson, Madison, and their illustrious compatriots, she has never had more than half a dozen statesmen, all told; of mere politicians, wire-pullers, and slave-driving demagogues, she has had enough, and to spare; but of statesmen, in the true sense of the term, she has had, and now has, but precious few—fewer just at this time, perhaps, than ever before. It is far from a matter of surprise to us that slavery has, for such a long period, baffled the "wisdom" of the oligarchy; but our surprise is destined to culminate in amazement, if the wisdom of the non-slaveholders does not soon baffle slavery.

From the eleventh year previous to the close of the eighteenth century down to the present moment, slaveholders and slave-breeders, who, to speak naked truth, are, as a general thing, unfit to occupy any honorable station in life, have, by chicanery and usurpation, wielded all the official power of the South; and, excepting the patriotic services of the noble abolitionists above-mentioned, the sole aim and drift of their legislation has been to aggrandize themselves, to strengthen slavery, and to keep the poor whites, the constitutional majority, bowed down in the deepest depths of degradation. We propose to subvert this entire system of oligarchal despotism. We think there should be *some* legislation for decent white men, not alone for negroes and slaveholders. Slavery lies at the root of all the shame, poverty, ignorance, tyranny and imbecility of the South; slavery must be thoroughly eradicated; let this be done, and a glorious future will await us.

The statesmen who are to abolish slavery in Kentucky, must be mainly and independently constituted by the non-slaveholders of Kentucky; so in every other slave State. Past experience has taught us the sheer folly of ever expecting voluntary justice from the slaveholders. Their illicit intercourse with "the mother of harlots" has been kept up so long, and their whole natures have, in consequence, become so depraved, that there is scarcely a spark of honor or magnanimity to be found amongst them. As well might one expect to hear highwaymen clamoring for a universal interdict against traveling, as to expect slave-

holders to pass laws for the abolition of slavery. Under all
the circumstances, it is the duty of the non-slaveholders
to mark out an independent course for themselves, to steer
entirely clear of the oligarchy, and to utterly contemn and
ignore the many vile instruments of power, animate and
inanimate, which have been so freely and so effectually
used for their enslavement. Now is the time for them to
assert their rights and liberties; never before was there
such an appropriate period to strike for Freedom in the
South.

Had it not been for the better sense, the purer patriotism, and the more practical justice of the non-slaveholders,
the Middle States and New England would still be groan-
ing and groveling under the ponderous burden of slavery;
New York would never have risen above the dishonorable
level of Virginia; Pennsylvania, trampled beneath the iron-
heel of the black code, would have remained the unpro-
gressive parallel of Georgia; Massachusetts would have
continued till the present time, and Heaven only knows
how much longer, the contemptible coequal of South Carolina.

That our plan for the abolition of slavery is the best
that can be devised, we have not the vanity to contend;
but that it is a good one, and will do to act upon until a
better shall have been suggested, we do firmly and con-
scientiously believe. Though but little skilled in the deli-
cate art of surgery, we have pretty thoroughly probed
slavery, the frightful tumor on the body politic, and have,
we think, ascertained the precise remedies requisite for a
speedy and perfect cure. Possibly the less ardent friends
of freedom may object to our prescription, on the ground
that some of its ingredients are too griping, and that it will
cost the patient a deal of most excruciating pain. But let
them remember that the patient is exceedingly refrac-
tory, that the case is a desperate one, and that drastic remedies are indispensably necessary. When they shall have
invented milder yet equally efficacious ones, it will be time
enough to discontinue the use of ours—then no one will
be readier than we to discard the infallible strong recipe
for the infallible mild. Not at the persecution of a few
thousand slaveholders, but at the restitution of natural
rights and prerogatives to several millions of non-slaveholders, do we aim.

Inscribed on the banner, which we herewith unfurl to the world, with the full and fixed determination to stand by it or die by it, unless one of more virtuous efficacy shall be presented, are the mottoes which, in substance, embody the principles, as we conceive, that should govern us in our patriotic warfare against the most subtle and insidious foe that ever menaced the inalienable rights and liberties and dearest interests of America:

1st. Thorough Organization and Independent Political Action on the part of the Non-Slaveholding whites of the South.

2nd. Ineligibility of Slaveholders—Never another vote to the Trafficker in Human Flesh.

3rd. No Co-operation with Slaveholders in Politics—No Fellowship with them in Religion—No Affiliation with them in Society.

4th. No Patronage to Slaveholding Merchants—No Guest-ship in Slave-waiting Hotels—No Fees to Slaveholding Lawyers—No Employment of Slaveholding Physicians —No Audience to Slaveholding Parsons.

5th. No Recognition of Pro-slavery Men, except as Ruffians, Outlaws, and Criminals.

6th. Abrupt Discontinuance of Subscription to Pro-slavery Newspapers.

7th. The Greatest Possible Encouragement to Free White Labor.

8th. No more Hiring of Slaves by Non-slaveholders.

9th. Immediate Death to Slavery, or if not immediate, unqualified Proscription of its Advocates during the Period of its Existence.

10th. A Tax of Sixty Dollars on every Slaveholder for each and every Negro in his Possession at the present time or at any intermediate time between now and the 4th of July, 1863—said Money to be Applied to the transportation of the Blacks to Liberia, to their Colonization in Central or South America, or to their Comfortable Settlement within the Boundaries of the United States.

11th. An additional Tax of Forty Dollars per annum to be levied annually, on every Slaveholder for each and every Negro found in his possession after the 4th of July, 1863—said Money to be paid into the hands of the

Negroes so held in Slavery, or, in cases of death, to their next of kin, and to be used by them at their own option.

This, then, is the outline of our scheme for the abolition of slavery in the Southern States. Let it be acted upon with due promptitude, and, as certain as truth is mightier than error, fifteen years will not elapse before every foot of territory, from the mouth of the Delaware to the emboguing of the Rio Grande, will glitter with the jewels of freedom. Some time during this year, next, or the year following, let there be a general convention of non-slaveholders from every slave State in the Union, to deliberate on the momentous issues now pending. First, let them adopt measures for holding in restraint the diabolical excesses of the oligarchy; secondly, in order to cast off the thraldom which the infamous slave-power has fastened upon them, and, as the first step necessary to be taken to regain the inalienable rights and liberties with which they were invested by Nature, but of which they have been divested by the accursed dealers in human flesh, let them devise ways and means for the complete annihilation of slavery; thirdly, let them put forth an equitable and comprehensive platform, fully defining their position, and inviting the active sympathy and co-operation of the millions of down-trodden non-slaveholders throughout the Southern and Southwestern States. Let all these things be done, not too hastily, but with calmness, deliberation, prudence, and circumspection; if need be, let the delegates to the convention continue in session one or two weeks; only let their labors be wisely and thoroughly performed; let them, on Wednesday morning, present to the poor whites of the South, a well-digested scheme for the reclamation of their ancient rights and prerogatives, and, on the Thursday following, slavery in the United States will be worth absolutely less than nothing; for then, besides being so vile and precarious that nobody will want it, it will be a lasting reproach to those in whose hands it is lodged.

Henceforth, let it be distinctly understood that ownership in slaves constitutes ineligibility—that it is a crime, as we verily believe it is, to vote for a slavocrat for any office whatever. Indeed, it is our honest conviction that all the pro-slavery slaveholders, who are alone responsible for the continuance of the baneful institution among us, deserve

to be at once reduced to a parallel with the basest criminals that lie fettered within the cells of our public prisons.
Beyond the power of computation is the extent of the
moral, social, civil, and political evils which they have
brought, and are still bringing, on the country. Were it
possible that the whole number could be gathered together and transformed into four equal gangs of licensed
robbers, ruffians, thieves, and murderers, society, we feel
assured, would suffer less from their atrocities then than
it does now. Let the wholesome public sentiment of the
non-slaveholders be vigilant and persevering in bringing
them down to their proper level. Long since, and in the
most unjust and cruel manner, have they socially outlawed
the non-slaveholders; now security against further oppression, and indemnity for past grievances, make it incumbent
on the non-slaveholders to cast them into the identical pit
that they dug for their betters—thus teaching them how
to catch a Tartar!

Through the most heart-sickening arrogance and brib-
ery, they have obtained control of the General Government, and all the consuls, ambassadors, envoys extraordinary and ministers plenipotentiary, who are chosen from
the South, and commissioned to foreign countries, are selected with special reference to the purity of their pro-
slavery antecedents. If credentials have ever been issued
to a single non-slaveholder of the South, we are ignorant
of both the fact and the hearsay; indeed, it would be very
strange if this much-abused class of persons were permitted to hold important offices abroad, when they are not
allowed to hold unimportant ones at home.

And, then, there is the Presidency of the United States,
which office has been held *forty-eight* years by slaveholders from the South, and only *twenty* years by non-slaveholders from the North. Nor is this the full record of
oligarchal obtrusion. On an average, the offices of Secretary of State, Secretary of the Treasury, Secretary of the
Interior, Secretary of the Navy, Secretary of War, Post-
master-General and Attorney-General, have been under
the control of slave-drivers nearly two-thirds of the time.
The Chief Justices and the Associate Justices of the
Supreme Court of the United States, the Presidents pro
tem. of the Senate, and the Speakers of the House of Representatives, have, in a large majority of instances, been

slave-breeders from the Southern side of the Potomac. Five slaveholding Presidents have been reëlected to the chief magistracy of the Republic, while no non-slaveholder has ever held the office more than a single term. Thus we see plainly that even the non-slaveholders of the North, to whose freedom, energy, enterprise, intelligence, wealth, population, power, progress, and prosperity, our country is almost exclusively indebted for its high position among the nations of the earth, have been arrogantly denied a due participation in the honors of federal office. When "the sum of all villainies" shall have ceased to exist, then the rights of the non-slaveholders of the North, of the South, of the East, and of the West, will be duly recognized and respected; not before.

With all our heart, we hope and believe it is the full and fixed determination of a majority of the more intelligent and patriotic citizens of this Republic, that the Presidential chair shall never again be filled by a slavocrat. Safely may we conclude that the doom of the oligarchy is already sealed with respect to that important and dignified station; it now behooves us to resolve, with equal firmness and effect, that, after a certain period during the next decade of years, no slaveholder shall occupy any position in the Cabinet, that no slave-breeder shall be sent as a diplomatist to any foreign country, that no slave-driver shall be permitted to bring further disgrace on either the Senate or the House of Representatives, that the chief justices, associate justices, and judges of the several courts, the governors of the States, the members of the legislatures, and all the minor functionaries of the land, shall be free from the heinous crime of ownership in man.

Until slavery and slaveholders cease to be the only favored objects of legislation in the South, the North will continue to maintain the ascendency in every important particular. With those loathsome objects out of the way, it would not take the non-slaveholders of the South more than a quarter of a century to bring her up, in all respects, to a glorious equality with the North; nor would it take them much longer to surpass the latter, which is the most vigorous and honorable rival that they have in the world. Three quarters of a century hence, if slavery is abolished within the next ten years, as it ought to be, the South will, we believe, be as much greater than the North, as the

North is now greater than the South. Three quarters of a century hence, if the South retains slavery, which God forbid! she will be to the North much the same that Poland is to Russia, that Cuba is to Spain, or that Ireland is to England.

What we want and must have, as the only sure means of attaining to a position worthy of Sovereign States in this eminently progressive and utilitarian age, is an energetic, intelligent, enterprising, virtuous, and unshackled population; an untrammeled press, and the Freedom of Speech. For ourselves, as white people, and for the negroes and other persons of whatever color or condition, we demand all the rights, interests and prerogatives, that are guaranteed to corresponding classes of mankind in the North, in England, in France, in Germany, or in any other civilized and enlightened country. Any proposition that may be offered conceding less than this demand, will be promptly and disdainfully rejected.

Speaking of the non-slaveholders of the South, George M. Weston, a zealous co-laborer in the cause of Freedom, says:—

"The non-slaveholding whites of the South, being not less than seven-tenths of the whole number of whites, would seem to be entitled to some enquiry into their actual condition; and especially, as they have no real political weight or consideration in the country, and little opportunity to speak for themselves. I have been for twenty years a reader of Southern newspapers, and a reader and hearer of Congressional debates; but, in all that time, I do not recollect ever to have seen or heard these non-slaveholding whites referred to by Southern 'gentlemen,' as constituting any part of what they call '*the South.*' When the rights of the South, or its wrongs, or its policy, or its interests, or its institutions, are spoken of, reference is always intended to the rights, wrongs, policy, interests, and institutions of the three hundred and forty-seven thousand slaveholders. Nobody gets into Congress from the South but by their direction; nobody speaks at Washington for any Southern interest except theirs. Yet there is, at the South, quite another interest than theirs; embracing from two to three times as many white people; and,

as we shall presently see, entitled to the deepest sympathy and commiseration, in view of the material, intellectual, and moral privations to which it has been
subjected, the degradation to which it has already been
reduced, and the still more fearful degradation with
which it is threatened by the inevitable operation of
existing causes and influences."

The following extract, from a paper on "Domestic
Manufactures in the South and West," published by M.
Tarver, of Missouri, may be appropriately introduced in
this connection:—

"The non-slaveholders possess, generally, but very
small means, and the land which they possess is almost
universally poor, and so sterile that a scanty subsistence is all that can be derived from its cultivation;
and the more fertile soil, being in the possession of the
slaveholders, must ever remain out of the power of
those who have none. This state of things is a great
drawback, and bears heavily upon and depresses the
moral energies of the poorer classes. The acquisition of
a respectable position in the scale of wealth appears
so difficult, that they decline the hopeless pursuit, and
many of them settle down into habits of idleness, and
become the almost passive subjects of all its consequences. And I lament to say that I have observed of
late years, that an evident deterioration is taking place
in this part of the population, the younger portion of
it being less educated, less industrious, and in every
point of view less respectable than their ancestors."

Equally worthy of attention is the testimony of Gov.
Hammond, of South Carolina, who says:—

"According to the last calculation which, in the absence of statistic facts, can be made, it is believed, that
of the three hundred thousand white inhabitants of
South Carolina, there are not less than fifty thousand
whose industry, such as it is, and compensated as it
is, is not, in the present condition of things, and does
not promise to be hereafter, adequate to procure them,
honestly, such a support as every white person is, and
feels himself, entitled to. And this, next to emigration,
is, perhaps, the heaviest of the weights that press upon

the springs of our prosperity. Most of these now follow agricultural pursuits, in feeble, yet injurious competition with slave labor. Some, perhaps, not more from inclination than from the want of due encouragement, can scarcely be said to work at all. They obtain a precarious subsistence, by occasional jobs, by hunting, by fishing, sometimes by plundering fields or folds, and too often by what is, in its effects, far worse—trading with slaves, and seducing them to plunder for their benefit."

Conjoined with the sundry plain straightforward facts which have issued from our own pen, these extracts show conclusively that immediate and independent political action on the part of the non-slaveholding whites of the South, is, with them, a matter, not only of positive duty, but also of the utmost importance. As yet, it is in their power to rescue the South from the gulf of shame and guilt, into which slavery has plunged her; but if they do not soon arouse themselves from their apathy, this power will be wrenched from them, and then, unable to resist the strong arm of the oppressor, they will be completely degraded to a social and political level with the negroes, whose condition of servitude will, in the meantime, become far more abject and forlorn than it is now.

In addition to the reasons which we have already assigned why no slavocrat should, in the future, be elected to any office whatever, there are others that deserve to be carefully considered. Among these may be mentioned the illbreeding and the ruffianism of slaveholding officials. Tedious indeed would be the task to enumerate all the homicides, duels, assaults and batteries, and other crimes, of which they are the authors in the course of a single year. To the general reader their career at the seat of government is well known; there, on frequent occasions, choking with rage at seeing their wretched sophistries scattered to the winds by the sound, logical reasoning of the champions of Freedom, they have overstepped the bounds of common decency, vacated the chair of honorable controversy, and, in the most brutal and cowardly manner, assailed their unarmed opponents with bludgeons, bowie knives and pistols. Compared with some of their barbarisms at home, however, their frenzied onslaughts at the national Capital have been but the simplest breaches of civil deportment; and it is only for the purpose of avoiding personalities that we now refrain from divulging a few instances of the unparalleled atrocities which they have perpetrated in legislative halls South of the Potomac. Nor is it alone in the national and State legislatures that they substitute brute force for genteel behavior and acuteness of intellect. Neither court-houses nor public streets, hotels nor private dwellings, rum-holes nor law-offices, are held sacred from their murderous conflicts. About certain silly abstractions that no practical business man ever allows to occupy his time or attention, they are eternally wrangling; and thus it is that rencounters, duels, homicides, and other demonstrations of personal violence, have become so popular in all slaveholding communities. A few years of entire freedom from the cares and perplexities of public life, would, we have no doubt, greatly improve both their manners and their morals; and we suggest that it is a Christian duty, which devolves on the non-slaveholders of the South, to disrobe them of the mantle of office, which they have so long worn with disgrace to themselves, injustice to their constituents, and ruin to their country.

But what shall we say of such men as Botts, Stuart, and Macfarland of Virginia; of Raynor, Morehead, Miller, Stanly, Graves, and Graham of North Carolina; of Davis and Hoffman of Maryland; of Blair and Benton of Missouri; of the Marshals of Kentucky; and of Etheridge of Tennessee? All these gentlemen, and many others of the same school, entertain, we believe, sentiments similar to those that were entertained by the immortal Fathers of the Republic—that slavery is a great moral, social, civil, and political evil, to be got rid of at the earliest practical period and if they do, in order to secure our votes, it is only necessary for them to "have the courage of their opinions," to renounce slavery, and to come out frankly, fairly and squarely, in favor of freedom. To neither of these patriotic sons of the South, nor to any one of the class to which they belong, would we give any offence whatever. In our strictures on the criminality of pro-slavery demagogues we have had heretofore, and shall have hereafter, no sort of reference to any respectable slaveholder—by which we mean, any slaveholder who admits the injustice and inhumanity of slavery, and who is not averse to the discussion of measures for its speedy and total extinction. Such slaveholders are virtually on our side, that is, on the side of the non-slaveholding whites, with whom they may very properly be classified. On this point, once for all, we desire to be distinctly understood; for it would be manifestly unjust not to discriminate between the anti-slavery proprietor who owns slaves by the law of entailment, and the pro-slavery proprietor who engages in the traffic and becomes an aider and abettor of the institution from sheer turpitude of heart; hence the propriety of this special disclaimer.

And this, by the way, is a fit occasion to call attention to the fact, that slave-driving Democrats have been the perpetrators of almost every brutal outrage that ever disgraced our halls of legislation. Of countless instances of assault and battery, affrays, and fatal rencounters, that have occurred in the court-houses, capitols, and other public buildings in the Southern States, we feel safe in saying that the aggressor, in at least nine cases out of ten, has been a negro-nursed adherent of modern, miscalled democracy. So, too, the challenger to almost every duel has been an abandoned wretch, who, on many occasions during infancy, sucked in the corrupt milk of slavery from the breasts of his father's sable concubines, and who has never been known to become weary of boasting of a fact that invariably impressed itself on the minds of his auditors or observers, the very first moment they laid their eyes upon him, namely, that *he* was a member of the Democratic party. Brute violence, however, can hardly be said to be the worst characteristic of the slave-driving Democrat; his ignorance and squalidity are proverbial; his senseless enthusiasm is disgusting.

Peculiarly illustrative of the material of which sham democracy is composed was the vote polled at the Five Points precinct, in the city of New-York, on the 4th of November, 1856, when James Buchanan was chosen President by a *minority* of the people. We will produce the figures:

Five Points Precinct, New-York City, 1856.

Votes cast for James Buchanan 574

" " " John C. Fremont 16

" " " Millard Fillmore 9

It will be recollected that Col. Fremont's majority over Buchanan, in the State of New-York, was between seventy-eight and seventy-nine thousand and that he ran ahead of the Fillmore ticket to the number of nearly one hundred and fifty-one thousand. We have not the shadow of a doubt that he is perfectly satisfied with Mr. Buchanan's triumph at the Five Points, which, with the exception of the slave-pens in Southern cities, is, perhaps, the most vile and heart-sickening locality in the United States.

One of the most noticeable and commendable features of the last general election is this: almost every State, whose inhabitants have enjoyed the advantages of free soil, free labor, free speech, free presses, and free schools, and who have, in consequence, become great in numbers, in virtue, in wealth, and in wisdom, voted for Fremont, the Republican candidate, who was pledged to use his influence for the extension of like advantages to other parts of the country. On the other hand, with a single honorable exception, all the States which "have got to hating everything with the prefix Free, from free negroes down and up through the whole catalogue—free farms, free labor, free society, free will, free thinking, free children, and free schools," and which have exposed their citizens to all the perils of numerical weakness, absolute ignorance, and hopeless poverty, voted for Buchanan, the Democratic candidate, who, in reply to the overtures of his slave-driving partisans, had signified his willingness to pursue a policy that would perpetuate and disseminate, without limit, the multitudinous evils of human bondage.

Led on by a huckstering politician, whose chief vocation, at all times, is the rallying of ragamuffins, shoulder-strikers, and liquor-house vagabonds, into the ranks of his party, and who, it is well known, receives from the agents of the slave power, regular installments of money for this infamous purpose, a Democratic procession, exceedingly motley and unrefined, marched through the streets of one of the great cities of the North, little less than a fortnight previous to the election of Mr. Buchanan to the Presidency; and the occasion gave rise, on the following day, to a communication in one of the morning papers, from which we make the following pertinent extract:

"While the Democratic procession was passing through the streets of this city, a few days since, I could not but think how significant the exultation of that ignorant multitude was of the ferocious triumphs which would be displayed if ever false Democracy should succeed in throwing the whole power of the country into the hands of the Slave Oligarchy. It is melancholy to think that every individual in that multitude, ignorant and depraved though he may be, foreign perhaps in his birth, and utterly unacquainted with the principles upon which the welfare of the country depends, and hostile it may be to those principles, if he does understand them, is equal in the power which he may exercise by his vote to the most intelligent and upright man in the community.

"Of this, indeed, it is useless to complain. We enjoy our freedom with the contingency of its loss by the acts of a numerical majority. It behooves all men, therefore, who have a regard to the common good, to look carefully at the influences which may pervert the popular mind; and this, I think, can only be done by guarding against the corruption of individual character. A man who has nothing but political business to attend to—I mean the management of elections— ought to be shunned by all honest men. If it were possible, he should have the mark of Cain put upon him, that he might be known as a plotter against the welfare of his country."

That less than *three* per cent of those who voted for Col. Fremont, that only about *five* per cent of those who gave their suffrages to Mr. Fillmore and that more than *eighteen* per cent. of those who supported Mr. Buchanan, were persons over one and twenty years of age who could not read and write, are estimates which we have no doubt are not far from the truth, and which, in the absence of reliable statistics, we venture to give, hoping, by their publicity, to draw closer attention to the fact, that the illiterate foreigners of the North, and the unlettered natives of the South, were cordially united in their suicidal adherence to the Nigger party. With few exceptions, all the intelligent non-slaveholders of the South, in concert with the more respectable slaveholders, voted for Mr. Fillmore; certain rigidly patriotic persons of the former class, whose hearts were so entirely with the gallant Fremont that they refused to vote at all—simply because they did not dare to express their preference for him—form the exceptions to which we allude.

Though the Whig, Democratic, and Know-Nothing newspapers, in all the States, free and slave, denounced Col. Fremont as an intolerant Catholic, it is now generally conceded that he was nowhere supported by the peculiar friends of Pope Pius IX. The votes polled at the Five Points precinct, which is almost exclusively inhabited by low Irish Catholics, show how powerfully the Jesuitical influence was brought to bear against him. At that delectable locality, as we have already shown, the timid Sage of Wheatland received five hundred and seventy-four votes; whereas the dauntless Finder of Empire received only sixteen.

True to their instincts for Freedom, the Germans, generally, voted the right ticket, and they will do it again, and continue to do it. With the intelligent Protestant element of the Fatherland on our side we can well afford to dispense with the ignorant Catholic element of the Emerald Isle. In the influences which they exert on society, there is so little difference between Slavery, Popery, and Negro-driving Democracy, that we are not at all surprised to see them going hand in hand in their diabolical works of inhumanity and desolation.

There is, indeed, no lack of evidence to show that the Democratic party of to-day is simply and unreservedly a sectional Nigger party. On the 15th of December, 1856, but a few weeks subsequent to the appearance of a scandalous message from an infamous governor of South Carolina, recommending the reopening of the African slave trade, Emerson Etheridge of Tennessee—honor to his name!—submitted, in the House of Representatives, the following timely resolution:—

"Resolved, That this House regard all suggestions or propositions of every kind, by whomsoever made, for a revival of the slave trade, as shocking to the moral sentiments of the enlightened portion of mankind, and that any act on the part of Congress, legislating for, conniving at, or legalizing that horrid and inhuman traffic, would justly subject the United States to the reproach and execration of all civilized and Christian people throughout the world."

Who voted *for* this resolution? and who voted *against* it? Let the yeas and nays answer; they are on record, and he who takes the trouble to examine them will find that the resolution encountered no opposition worth mentioning, except from members of the Democratic party. Scrutinize the yeas and nays on any other motion or resolution affecting the question of slavery, and the fact that a majority of the members of this party have uniformly voted for the retention and extension of the "sum of all villanies," will at once be apparent.

For many years the slave-driving Democrats of the South have labored most strenuously, both by day and by night—we regret to say how unsuccessfully—to point out abolition proclivities in the Whig and Know-Nothing parties, the latter of which is now buried, and deservedly, so deep in the depths of the dead, that it is quite preposterous to suppose it will ever see the light of resurrection.

For its truckling concessions to the slave power, the Whig party merited defeat, and defeated it was, and that, too, in the most decisive and overwhelming manner. But there is yet in this party much vitality, and if its friends will reorganize, detach themselves from the burden of slavery, espouse the cause of the white man, and hoist the fair flag of freedom, the time may come, at a day by no means remote, when their hearts will exult in triumph over the ruins of miscalled Democracy.

It is not too late, however, for the Democratic party to secure to itself a pure renown and an almost certain perpetuation of its power. Let it at once discard the worship of slavery, and do earnest battle for the principles of freedom, and it will live victoriously to a period far in the future. On the other hand, if it does not soon repudiate the fatal heresies which it has incorporated into its creed, its doom will be inevitable. Until the black flag entirely disappears from its array, we warn the non-slaveholders of the South to repulse and keep it at a distance, as they would the emblazoned skull and cross-bones that flout them from the flag of the pirate.

With regard to the sophistical reasoning which teaches that abolitionists, before abolishing slavery, should compensate the slaveholders for all or any number of the negroes in their possession, we have, perhaps, said quite enough; but wishing to brace our arguments, in every im-

portant particular, with unequivocal testimony from men
whom we are accustomed to regard as models of political
sagacity and integrity—from Southern men as far as possible—we herewith present an extract from a speech delivered in the Virginia House of Delegates, January 20,
1832, by Charles James Faulkner, whose sentiments, as
then and there expressed, can hardly fail to find a response
in the heart of every intelligent, upright man:—

"But, Sir, it is said that society having conferred this
property on the slaveholder, it cannot *now* take it from
him without an adequate compensation, by which is
meant full value. I may be singular in the opinion, but
I defy the legal research of the House to point me
to a principle recognized by the law, even in the ordinary course of its adjudications, where the community
pays for property which is removed or destroyed because it is a nuisance, and found injurious to that society. There is, I humbly apprehend, no such principle.
There is no obligation upon society to continue your
right one moment after it becomes injurious to the best
interests of society; nor to compensate you for the loss
of that, the deprivation of which is demanded by the
safety of the State, and in which general benefit you
participate as members of the community. Sir, there is
to my mind a manifest distinction between condemning private property to be applied to some beneficial
public purpose, and condemning or removing private
property which is ascertained to be a positive wrong
to society. It is a distinction which pervades the whole
genius of the law; and is founded upon the idea, that
any man who holds property injurious to the peace of
that society of which he is a member, thereby violates
the condition upon the observance of which his right
to the property is alone guaranteed. For property of the
first class condemned, there ought to be compensation;
but for property of the latter class, none can be demanded upon principle, none accorded as matter of
right.

"It is conceded that, at this precise moment of our
legislation, slaves are injurious to the interests and
threaten the subversion and ruin of this Commonwealth. Their present number, their increasing number,

all admonish us of this. In different terms, and in more measured language, the same fact has been conceded by all who have yet addressed this House. 'Something must be done,' emphatically exclaimed the gentleman from Dinwiddie; and I thought I could perceive a response to that declaration, in the countenance of a large majority of this body. And why must something be done? Because if not, says the gentleman from Campbell, the throats of all the *white* people of Virginia will be cut. No, says the gentleman from Dinwiddie—'The whites cannot be conquered—the throats of the *blacks* will be cut.' It is a trifling difference, to be sure, Sir, and matters not to the argument. For the fact is conceded, that one race or the other must be exterminated.

"Sir, such being the actual condition of this Commonwealth, I ask if we would not be justified *now,* supposing all considerations of policy and humanity concurred without even a moment's delay, in staving off this appalling and overwhelming calamity? Sir, if this immense negro population were now in arms, gathering into black and formidable masses of attack, would that man be listened to, who spoke about property, who prayed you not to direct your artillery to such or such a point, for you would destroy some of *his* property? Sir, to the eye of the Statesman, as to the eye of Omniscience, dangers pressing, and dangers that must *necessarily* press, are alike present. With a single glance he embraces Virginia now, with the elements of destruction reposing quietly upon her bosom, and Virginia is lighted from one extremity to the other with the torch of servile insurrection and massacre. It is not sufficient for him that the match is not yet applied. It is enough that the magazine is open, and the match will shortly be applied.

"Sir, it is true in national as it is in private contracts, that loss and injury to one party may constitute as fair a consideration as gain to the other. Does the Slaveholder, while he is enjoying his slaves, reflect upon the deep injury and incalculable loss which the possession of that property inflicts upon the true interests of the country? Slavery, it is admitted, is an evil—it is an institution which presses heavily against the best inter-

ests of the State. It banishes free white labor, it exter-
minates the mechanic, the artisan, the manufacturer.
It deprives them of occupation. It deprives them of
bread. It converts the energy of a community into indo-
lence, its power into imbecility, its efficiency into weakness. Sir, being thus injurious, have we not a right to
demand its extermination? shall society suffer, that the
slaveholder may continue to gather his *crop* of human
flesh? What is his mere pecuniary claim, compared
with the great interests of the common weal? Must the
country languish, droop, die, that the slaveholder may
flourish? Shall all interests be subservient to one—all
rights subordinate to those of the slaveholder? Has
not the mechanic, have not the middle classes their
rights—rights incompatible with the existence of slavery?

"Sir, so great and overshadowing are the evils of
slavery—so sensibly are they felt by those who have
traced the causes of our national decline—so percept-
ible is the poisonous operation of its principles in the
varied and diversified interests of this Commonwealth,
that all, whose minds are not warped by prejudice or
interest, must admit that the disease has now assumed
that mortal tendency, as to justify the application of
any remedy which, under the great law of State necessity, we might consider advisable."

From the abstract of our plan for the abolition of
slavery, it will be perceived that, so far from allowing
slaveholders any compensation for their slaves, we are, and
we think justly, in favor of imposing on them a tax of sixty
dollars for each and every negro now in their possession,
as also for each and every one that shall be born to them
between now and the 4th of July, 1863; after which time,
we propose that they shall be taxed forty dollars per annum, annually, for every person by them held in slavery,
without regard to age, sex, color, or condition—the
money, in both instances, to be used for the sole advantage
of the slaves. As an addendum to this proposition, we
would say that, in our opinion, if slavery is not totally abolished by the year 1869, the annual tax ought to be increased from forty to one hundred dollars; and furthermore, that if the institution does not then almost

immediately disappear under the onus of this increased taxation, the tax ought in the course of one or two years thereafter, to be augmented to such a degree as will, in harmony with other measures, prove an infallible death-blow to slavery on or before the 4th of July, 1876.

Two hundred and thirty-seven years have the negroes in America been held in inhuman bondage. During the whole of this long period they have toiled unceasingly from the gray of dawn till the dusk of eve, for their cruel task-masters, who have rewarded them with scanty allowances of the most inferior qualities of victuals and clothes, with heartless separations of the tenderest ties of kindred, with epithets, with scoldings, with execrations, and with the lash—and, not unfrequently, with the fatal bludgeon or the more deadly weapon. From the labor of their hands, and from the fruit of their loins, the human-mongers of the South have become wealthy, insolent, corrupt, and tyrannical. In reason and in conscience the slaves might claim from their masters a much larger sum than we have proposed to allow them. If they were to demand an equal share of all the property, real and personal, which has been accumulated or produced through their efforts, Heaven, we believe, would recognize them as honest claimants.

Elsewhere we have shown, by just and liberal estimates, that, on the single score of damages to lands, the slave-holders are, at this moment, indebted to the non-slave-holding whites in the extraordinary sum of $7,544,148,-825. Considered in connection with the righteous claim of wages for services which the negroes might bring against their masters, these figures are the heralds of the significant fact that, if strict justice could be meted out to all parties in the South, the slaveholders would not only be stripped of every dollar, but they would become in law as they are in reality, the hopeless debtors of the myriads of unfortunate slaves, white and black, who are now cringing, and fawning, and festering around them. In this matter, however, so far has wrong triumphed over right, that the slaveholders—a mere handful of tyrants, whose manual exercises are wholly comprised in the use they make of instruments of torture, such as whips, clubs, bowie-knives and pistols—have, as the result of a series of acts of their own villainous legislation, become the sole and niggardly proprietors of almost every important item

of Southern wealth; not only do they own all the slaves—
none of whom any really respectable person cares to own
—but they are also in possession of the more valuable
tracts of land and the appurtenances thereto belonging;
while the non-slaveholding whites and the negroes, who
compose at least nine-tenths of the entire population, and
who are the actual producers of every article of merchandize, animal, vegetable, and mineral, that is sold from the
South, are most wickedly despoiled of the fruits of their
labors, and cast into the dismal abodes of extreme ignorance, destitution and misery.

For the services of the blacks from the 20th of August,
1620, up to the 4th of July, 1863—an interval of precisely
two hundred and forty-two years ten months and fourteen
days—their masters, if unwilling, ought, in our judgment,
to be compelled to grant them their freedom, and to pay
each and every one of them at least sixty dollars cash in
hand. The aggregate sum thus raised would amount to
about two hundred and forty-five millions of dollars,
which is less than the total market value of two entire
crops of cotton—one-half of which sum would be amply
sufficient to land every negro in this country on the coast
of Liberia, whither, if we had the power, we would ship
them all within the next six months. As a means of protection against the exigencies which might arise from a sudden transition from their present homes in America to their
future homes in Africa, and for the purpose of enabling
them there to take the initiatory step in the walks of civilized life, the remainder of the sum—say about one hundred and twenty-two millions of dollars—might, very
properly, be equally distributed amongst them after their
arrival in the land of their fathers.

Dr. James Hall, the Secretary of the Maryland Colonization Society, informs us that the average cost of sending
negroes to Liberia does not exceed thirty dollars each;
and it is his opinion that arrangements might be made on
an extensive plan for conveying them thither at an average
expense of not more than twenty-five dollars each.

The American colonization movement, as now systema-
tized and conducted, is simply an American humane farce.
At present the slaves are increasing in this country at the
rate of nearly one hundred thousand per annum; within
the last ten years, as will appear below, the American

Colonization Society has sent to Liberia less than five thousand negroes.

Emigrants sent to Liberia by the American Colonization Society, during the ten years ending January 1st, 1857:

In 1847	39	
In 1848	213	
In 1849	474	
In 1850	590	
In 1851	279	
In 1852	568	Emigrants.
In 1853	583	
In 1854	783	
In 1855	207	
In 1856	544	
Total	4280	

The average of this total is precisely four hundred and twenty-eight, which may be said to be the number of negroes annually colonized by the society; while the yearly increase of slaves, as previously stated, is little less than one hundred thousand! Fiddlesticks for such colonization! Once for all, within a reasonably short period, let us make the slaveholders do something like justice to their negroes by giving each and every one of them his freedom, and sixty dollars in current money; then let us charter all the ocean steamers, packets and clipper ships that can be had on liberal terms, and keep them constantly plying between the ports of America and Africa, until all slaves shall enjoy freedom in the land of their fathers. Under a well-devised and properly conducted system of operations, but a few years would be required to redeem the United States from the monstrous curse of negro slavery.

Some few years ago, when certain ethnographical oligarchs proved to their own satisfaction that the negro was an inferior "type of mankind," they chuckled wonderfully, and avowed, in substance, that it was right for the stronger race to kidnap and enslave the weaker—that because Nature had been pleased to do a trifle more for the Caucasian race than for the African, the former, by virtue of its superiority, was perfectly justifiable in holding the latter in absolute and perpetual bondage! No system of logic could be more antagonistic to the spirit of true democracy. It is probable that the world does not contain two persons who are exactly alike in all respects; yet "*all* men are endowed by their Creator with certain *inalienable* rights, among which are life, *liberty*, and the pursuit of happiness." All mankind may or may not be the descendants of Adam and Eve. In our own humble way of thinking, we are frank to confess, we do not believe in the unity of the races. This is a matter, however, which has little or nothing to do with the great question at issue. Aside from any theory concerning the original parentage of the different races of men, facts, material and immaterial, palpable and impalpable—facts of the eyes and facts of the conscience—crowd around us on every hand, heaping proof upon proof, that slavery is a shame, a crime, and a curse—a great moral, social, civil, and political evil —an oppressive burden to the blacks, and an incalculable injury to the whites—a stumbling-block to the nation, an impediment to progress, a damper on all the nobler instincts, principles, aspirations and enterprises of man, and a dire enemy to every true interest.

Waiving all other counts, we have, we think, shown to the satisfaction of every impartial reader, that, as elsewhere stated, on the single score of damages to lands, the slaveholders are, at this moment, indebted to us, the nonslaveholding whites, in the enormous sum of nearly seventy-six hundred millions of dollars. What shall be done with this amount? It is just; shall payment be demanded? No; all the slaveholders in the country could not pay it; nor shall we ever ask them for even a moiety of the amount —no, not even for a dime, nor yet for a cent; we are willing to forfeit every farthing for the sake of freedom; for ourselves we ask no indemnification for the past: we only demand justice for the future.

But, Sirs, knights of bludgeons, chevaliers of bowie-knives and pistols, and lords of the lash, we are unwilling to allow you to swindle the slaves out of all the rights and claims to which, as human beings, they are most sacredly entitled. Not alone for ourself as an individual, but for others also—particularly for five or six millions of Southern non-slaveholding whites, whom your iniquitous statism has debarred from almost all the mental and material comforts of life—do we speak, when we say, you *must* emancipate your slaves, and pay each and every one of them at least sixty dollars cash in hand. By doing this, you will be restoring to them their natural rights, and remunerating them at the rate of less than twenty-six cents per annum for the long and cheerless period of their servitude, from the 20th of August, 1620, when, on James River, in Virginia, they became the unhappy slaves of heartless masters. Moreover, by doing this you will be performing but a simple act of justice to the non-slaveholding whites, upon whom the institution of slavery has weighed scarcely less heavily than upon the negroes themselves. You will also be applying a saving balm to your own outraged hearts and consciences, and your children—yourselves in fact—freed from the accursed stain of slavery, will become respectable, useful, and honorable members of society.

And now, Sirs, we have thus laid down our ultimatum. What are you going to do about it? Something dreadful, as a matter of course! Perhaps you will dissolve the Union *again*. Do it, if you dare! Our motto, and we would have you to understand it, is *the abolition of slavery, and the perpetuation of the American Union.* If, by any means, you do succeed in your treasonable attempts to take the South out of the Union to-day, we will bring her back to-morrow—if she goes away with you, she will return without you.

Do not mistake the meaning of the last clause of the last sentence; we could elucidate it so thoroughly that no intelligent person could fail to comprehend it; but, for reasons which may hereafter appear, we forego the task.

Henceforth there are other interests to be consulted in the South, aside from the interests of negroes and slaveholders. A profound sense of duty incites us to make the greatest possible efforts for the abolition of slavery; an equally profound sense of duty calls for a continuation of those efforts until the very last foe to freedom shall have been utterly vanquished. To the summons of the righteous monitor within, we shall endeavor to prove faithful; no opportunity for inflicting a mortal wound in the side of slavery shall be permitted to pass us unimproved. Thus, terror-engenderers of the South, have we fully and frankly defined our position; we have no modifications to propose, no compromises to offer, nothing to retract. Frown, Sirs, fret, foam, prepare your weapons, threat, strike, shoot, stab, bring on civil war, dissolve the Union, nay, annihilate the solar system if you will—do all this, more, less, better, worse, anything—do what you will, Sirs, you can neither foil nor intimidate us; our purpose is as firmly fixed as the eternal pillars of Heaven; we have determined to abolish slavery, and, so help us God, abolish it we will! Take this to bed with you tonight, Sirs, and think about it, dream over it, and let us know how you feel to-morrow morning.

CHAPTER III.

COMMERCIAL CITIES—SOUTHERN COMMERCE.

OUR theme is a city—a great Southern importing, export-
ing, and manufacturing city, to be located at some point
or port on the coast of the Carolinas, Georgia or Virginia,
where we can carry on active commerce, buy, sell, fabri-
cate, receive the profits which accrue from the exchange
of our own commodities, open facilities for direct communication with foreign countries, and establish all those col-
lateral sources of wealth, utility, and adornment, which are
the usual concomitants of a metropolis, and which add so
very materially to the interest and importance of a nation.
Without a city of this kind, the South can never develop
her commercial resources nor attain to that eminent position to which those vast resources would otherwise exalt
her. According to calculations based upon reasonable
estimates, it is owing to the lack of a great commercial city
in the South, that we are now *annually* drained of more
than One Hundred and Twenty Millions of Dollars! We
should, however, take into consideration the negative loss
as well as the positive. Especially should we think of the
influx of emigrants, of the visits of strangers and cosmop-
olites, of the patronage to hotels and public halls, of the
profits of travel and transportation, or the emoluments of
foreign and domestic trade, and of numerous other advantages which have their origin exclusively in wealthy,
enterprising, and densely populated cities.

Nothing is more evident than the fact, that our people
have never entertained a proper opinion of the importance
of home cities. Blindly, and greatly to our own injury, we
have contributed hundreds of millions of dollars towards
the erection of mammoth cities at the North, while our
own magnificent bays and harbors have been most shame-
fully disregarded and neglected. Now, instead of carrying

all our money to New York, Philadelphia, Boston, and Cincinnati, suppose we had kept it on the south side of Mason and Dixon's line—as we would have done, had it not been for slavery—and had disbursed it in the upbuilding of Norfolk, Beaufort, Charleston, or Savannah, how much richer, better, greater, would the South have been to-day! How much larger and more intelligent would have been our population. How many hundred thousand natives of the South would now be thriving at home, instead of adding to the wealth and political power of other parts of the Union. How much greater would be the number and length of our railroads, canals, turnpikes, and telegraphs. How much greater would be the extent and diversity of our manufactures. How much greater would be the grandeur, and how much larger would be the number of our churches, theatres, schools, colleges, lyceums, banks, hotels, stores, and private dwellings.

What about Southern Commerce? Is it not almost entirely tributary to the commerce of the North? Are we not dependent on New York, Philadelphia, Boston, and Cincinnati, for nearly every article of merchandise, whether foreign or domestic? Where are our ships, our mariners, our naval architects? Alas! echo answers where?

Reader! would you understand how abjectly slaveholders themselves are enslaved to the products of Northern industry? If you would, fix your mind on a Southern "gentleman"—a slave-breeder and human-flesh monger, who professes to be a Christian! Observe the routine of his daily life. See him rise in the morning from a Northern bed, and clothe himself in Northern apparel; see him walk across the floor on a Northern carpet, and perform his ablutions out of a Northern ewer and basin. See him uncover a box of Northern powders, and cleanse his teeth with a Northern brush; see him reflecting his physiognomy in a Northern mirror, and arranging his hair with a Northern comb. See him dosing himself with the mendicaments of Northern quacks, and perfuming his handkerchief with Northern cologne. See him referring to the time in a Northern watch, and glancing at the news in a Northern gazette. See him and his family sitting in Northern chairs, and singing and praying out of Northern books. See him at the breakfast table, saying grace over a Northern plate, eating with Northern cutlery, and drinking from Northern utensils. See him charmed with the melody of a Northern piano, or musing over the pages of a Northern novel. See him riding to his neighbor's in a Northern carriage, or furrowing his lands with a Northern plow. See him lighting his segar with a Northern match, and flogging his negroes with a Northern lash. See him with Northern pen and ink, writing letters on Northern paper, and sending them away in Northern envelopes, sealed with Northern wax, and impressed with a Northern stamp. Perhaps our Southern "gentleman" is a merchant; if so, see him at his store, making an unpatriotic use of his time in the miserable traffic of Northern gimcracks and haberdashery; see him when you will, where you will, he is ever surrounded with the industrial products of those whom, in the criminal inconsistency of his heart, he execrates as enemies, yet treats as friends. His labors, his talents, his influence, are all for the North, and not for the South; for the stability of slavery, and for the sake of his own personal aggrandizement, he is willing to sacrifice the dearest interests of his country.

As we see our ruinous system of commerce exemplified in the family of our Southern "gentleman," so we may see it exemplified, to a greater or less degree, in almost every other family throughout the length and breadth of the slaveholding States. We are all constantly buying, and selling, and wearing, and using Northern merchandise, at a double expense to both ourselves and our neighbors. If we but look at ourselves attentively, we shall find that we are all clothed *cap à pie* in Northern habilaments. Our hats, our caps, our cravats, our coats, our vests, our pants, our gloves, our boots, our shoes, our under-garments— all come from the North; whence, too, Southern ladies procure all their bonnets, plumes, and flowers; dresses, shawls, and scarfs; frills, ribbons, and ruffles; cuffs, capes, and collars.

True it is that the South has wonderful powers of endurance and recuperation; but she cannot forever support the reckless prodigality of her sons. We are all spendthrifts; some of us should become financiers. We must learn to take care of our money; we should withhold it from the North, and open avenues for its circulation at home. We should not run to New York, to Philadelphia, to Boston, to Cincinnati, or to any other Northern city, every time we want a shoe-string or a bedstead, a fish-hook or a hand-saw, a tooth-pick or a cotton-gin. In ease and luxury we have been lolling long enough; we should now bestir ourselves, and keep pace with the progress of the age. We must expand our energies, and acquire habits of enterprise and industry; we should arouse ourselves from the couch of lassitude, and inure our minds to thought and our bodies to action. We must begin to feed on a more substantial diet than that of pro-slavery politics; we should leave off our siestas and post-meridian naps, and employ our time in profitable vocations. Before us there is a vast work to be accomplished—a work which has been accumulating on our hands for many years. It is no less a work than that of infusing the spirit of liberty into all our systems of commerce, agriculture, manufactures, government, literature, and religion. Oligarchal despotism must be overthrown; slavery must be abolished.

For the purpose of showing how absolutely Southern "gentlemen," particularly slaveholding merchants, are lost to all sense of true honor and patriotism, we will here introduce an extract from an article which appeared more than three years ago in one of the editorial columns of the leading daily newspaper of the city of New York. It is in these words:—

"Southern merchants do indeed keep away from New York for the reason that they can't pay their debts; there is no doubt that if the jobbers of this city had not trusted Southern traders for the past three years, they would be a great deal better off than they are. * * * Already our trade with Canada is becoming as promising, sure, and profitable, as our trade with the South is uncertain, riskful, and annoying."

Now, by any body of men not utterly debased by the influences of slavery, this language would have been construed into an invitation to stay at home. But do Southern merchants stay at home? Do they build up Southern commerce? No! off they post to the North as regularly as the seasons, spring and fall, come round, and there, like cringing sycophants, flatter, beg, and scheme, for favors which they have no money to command.

The better classes of merchants, and indeed of all other people, at the North, as elsewhere, have too much genuine respect for themselves to wish to have any dealings whatever with those who make merchandise of human beings. Limited as is our acquaintance in the city of New York, we know one firm there, a large wholesale house, that makes it an invariable rule never to sell goods to a merchant from the slave States except for cash. Being well acquainted with the partners, we asked one of them, on one occasion, why he refused to trust slave-driving merchants. "Because," said he, "they are too long-winded and uncertain; when we credit them, they occasion us more loss and bother than their trade is worth." Non-slaveholders of the South! recollect that slavery is the only impediment to your progress and prosperity, that it stands diametrically opposed to all needful reforms, that it seeks to sacrifice you entirely for the benefit of others, and that it is the one great and only cause of dishonor to your country. Will you not abolish it? May Heaven help you to do your duty!

CHAPTER IV.

FACTS AND ARGUMENTS BY THE WAYSIDE.

THE ILLITERATE POOR WHITES OF THE SOUTH.

HAD we the power to sketch a true picture of life among the non-slaveholding whites of the South, every intelligent man who has a spark of philanthropy in his breast, and who should happen to gaze upon the picture, would burn with unquenchable indignation at that system of African slavery which entails unutterable miseries on the superior race. It is quite impossible, however, to describe accurately the deplorable ignorance and squalid poverty of the class to which we refer. The serfs of Russia have reason to congratulate themselves that they are neither the negroes nor the non-slaveholding whites of the South. Than the latter there can be no people in Christendom more unhappily situated. Below will be found a few extracts which will throw some light on the subject now under consideration.

Says William Gregg, in an address delivered before the South Carolina Institute, in 1851:—

> "From the best estimates that I have been able to make, I put down the white people who ought to work, and who do not, or who are so employed as to be wholly unproductive to the State, at one hundred and twenty-five thousand. Any man who is an observer of things could hardly pass through our country, without being struck with the fact that all the capital, enterprise, and intelligence, is employed in directing slave labor; and the consequence is, that a large portion of our poor white people are wholly neglected, and are suffered to while away an existence in a state but one step in advance of the Indian of the forest. It is an evil of vast magnitude, and nothing but a change

in public sentiment will effect its cure. These people must be brought into daily contact with the rich and intelligent—they must be stimulated to mental action, and taught to appreciate education and the comforts of civilized life; and this, we believe, may be effected only by the introduction of manufactures. My experience at Graniteville has satisfied me that unless our poor people can be brought together in villages, and some means of employment afforded them, it will be an utterly hopeless effort to undertake to educate them. We have collected at that place about eight hundred people, and as likely looking a set of country girls as may be found—industrious and orderly people, but deplorably ignorant, three-fourths of the adults not being able to read or to write their own names.

"It is only necessary to build a manufacturing village of shanties, in a healthy location, in any part of the State, to have crowds of these people around you, seeking employment at half the compensation given to operatives at the North. It is indeed painful to be brought in contact with such ignorance and degradation."

Again he asks:—

"Shall we pass unnoticed the thousands of poor, ignorant, degraded white people among us, who, in this land of plenty, live in comparative nakedness and starvation? Many a one is reared in *proud* South Carolina, from birth to manhood, who has never passed a month in which he has not, some part of the time, been stinted for meat. Many a mother is there who will tell you that her children are but scantily provided with bread, and much more scantily with meat; and, if they be clad with comfortable raiment, it is at the expense of these scanty allowances of food. These may be startling statements, but they are nevertheless true; and if not believed in Charleston, the members of our legislature who have traversed the State in electioneering campaigns can attest the truth."

In an article on *Manufactures in South Carolina,*" published some time ago in *DeBow's Review,* J. H. Taylor of Charleston (S. C.) says:—

"There is in some quarters, a natural jealousy of the slightest innovation upon established habits, and because an effort has been made to collect the poor and unemployed white population into our new factories, fears have arisen that some evil would grow out of the introduction of such establishments among us. * * * The poor man has a vote as well as the rich man, and in our State the number of the former will largely overbalance the latter. So long as these poor but industrious people can see no mode of living except by a degrading operation of work with the negro upon the plantation, they will be content to endure life in its most discouraging forms, satisfied that they are *above* the slave, though faring often worse than he."

Speaking in favor of manufactures, the Hon. J. H. Lumpkin, of Georgia, said in 1852:—

"It is objected that these manufacturing establishments will become the hot-beds of crime. But I am by no means ready to concede that our poor, degraded, half-fed, half-clothed, and ignorant population—without Sabbath Schools, or any other kind of instruction, mental or moral, or without any just appreciation of character—will be injured by giving them employment, which will bring them under the oversight of employers, who will inspire them with self-respect by taking an interest in their welfare."

In a paper on the *"Extension of Cotton and Wood Factories at the South,"* Mr. Steadman, of Tennessee, says:—

"In Lowell, labor is paid the fair compensation of 80 cents a day for men, and $2 a week for women, beside board, while in Tennessee the average compensation for labor does not exceed 50 cents per day for men, and $1,25 per week for women."

In the course of a speech which he delivered in Congress several years ago, Mr. T. L. Clingman, of North Carolina, said:—

"Our manufacturing establishments can obtain the raw material (cotton) at nearly two cents on the pound cheaper than the New-England establishments. Labor is likewise one hundred per cent. cheaper. In the upper parts of the State, the labor of either a free man or a slave, including board, clothing, &c., can be obtained for from $110 to $120 per annum. It will cost at least twice that sum in New-England. The difference in the cost of female labor, whether free or slave, is even greater."

The Richmond (Va.) *Dispatch* says:—

"We will only suppose that the ready-made shoes imported into this city from the North, and sold here, were manufactured in Richmond. What a great addition it would be to the means of employment! How many boys and females would find the means of earning their bread, who are now suffering for a regular supply of the necessaries of life."

A citizen of New-Orleans, writing in *DeBow's Review,* says:—

"At present the sources of employment open to females (save in menial offices) are very limited; and an inability to procure suitable occupation is an evil much to be deplored, as tending in its consequences to produce demoralization. The superior grades of female labor may be considered such as imply a necessity for education on the part of the employee, while the menial class is generally regarded as of the lowest; and in a slave State, this standard is 'in the lowest depths, a lower deep,' from the fact, that, by association, it is a reduction of the white servant to the level of their colored fellow-menials."

Black slave labor, though far less valuable, is almost invariably better paid than free white labor. The reason is this: The fiat of the oligarchy has made it *fashionable* to "have negroes around," and there are, we are grieved to say, many non-slaveholding whites (lickspittles) who, in order to retain on their premises a hired slave whom they falsely imagine secures to them not only the appearance of wealth, but also a position of high social standing in the community, keep themselves in a perpetual strait.

Last Spring we made it our special business to ascertain the ruling rates of wages paid for labor, free and slave, in

North Carolina. We found sober, energetic white men, between twenty and forty years of age, engaged in agricultural pursuits at a salary of $84 per annum—including board only; negro men, slaves, who performed little more than half the amount of labor, and who were exceedingly sluggish, awkward, and careless in all their movements, were hired out on adjoining farms at an average of about $115 per annum, including board, clothing, and medical attendance. Free white men and slaves were in the employ of the North Carolina Railroad Company; the former, whose services, in our opinion, were at least twice as valuable as the services of the latter, received only $12 per month each; the masters of the latter received $16 per month for every slave so employed. Industrious, tidy white girls, from sixteen to twenty years of age, had much difficulty in hiring themselves out as domestics in private families for $40 per annum—board only included; negro wenches, slaves, of corresponding ages, so ungraceful, stupid and filthy that no decent man would ever permit one of them to cross the threshold of his dwelling, were in brisk demand at from $65 to $70 per annum, including victuals, clothes, and medical attendance. These are facts, and in considering them, the students of political and social economy will not fail to arrive at conclusions of their own.

Notwithstanding the greater density of population in the free States, labor of every kind is, on an average, about one hundred per cent. higher there than it is in the slave States. This is another important fact, and one that every non-slaveholding white should keep registered in his mind.

Poverty, ignorance, and superstition, are the three leading characteristics of the non-slaveholding whites of the South. Many of them grow up to the age of maturity, and pass through life without ever owning as much as five dollars at any one time. Thousands of them die at an advanced age, as ignorant of the common alphabet as if it had never been invented. All are more or less impressed with a belief in witches, ghosts, and supernatural signs. Few are exempt from habits of sensuality and intemperance. None have anything like adequate ideas of the duties which they owe either to their God, to themselves, or to their fellow-men. Pitiable, indeed, in the fullest sense of the term, is their condition.

It is the almost utter lack of an education that has reduced them to their present unenviable situation. In the whole South there is scarcely a publication of any kind devoted to their interests. They are now completely under the domination of the oligarchy, and it is madness to suppose that they will ever be able to rise to a position of true manhood, until after the slave power shall have been utterly overthrown.

CHAPTER V.

SOUTHERN LITERATURE.

IT IS with some degree of hesitation that we add a chapter on Southern Literature—not that the theme is inappropriate to this work; still less, that it is an unfruitful one; but our hesitation results from our conscious inability, in the limited time and space at our command, to do the subject justice. Few, except those whose experience has taught them, have any adequate idea of the amount of preparatory labor requisite to the production of a work into which the statistical element largely enters; especially is this so, when the statistics desired are not readily accessible through public and official documents. The author who honestly aims at entire accuracy in his statements, may find himself baffled for weeks in his pursuit of a single item of information, not of much importance in itself perhaps, when separately considered, but necessary in its connection with others, to the completion of a harmonious whole.

What is the actual condition of Literature at the South? Our question includes more than simple authorship in the various departments, of letters, from the compilation of a primary reader to the production of a Scientific or Theological Treatise. We comprehend in it all the activities engaged in the creation, publication, and sale of books and periodicals, from the penny primer to the heavy folio, and from the dingy, coarse-typed weekly paper, to the large, well-filled daily.

It were unjust to deny a degree of intellectual activity to the South. It has produced a few good authors—a few competent editors, and a moderately large number of clever magazinists, paragraphists, essayists and critics. Absolutely, then, it must be conceded that the South has something that may be called a literature; it is only when we speak of her in comparison with the North, that we say, with a pardonably strong expression, "The South has no literature." This was virtually admitted by more than one speaker at the late "Southern Convention" at Savannah. Said a South Carolina orator on that occasion: "It is important that the South *should have* a literature of her own, to defend her principles and her rights;" a sufficiently plain concession that she has not, now, such a literature. But *facts* speak more significantly than the rounded periods of Convention orators. Let us look at facts, then.

First, turning our attention to the periodical literature of the South, we obtain these results: By the census of 1850, we ascertain that the entire number of periodicals, daily, semi-weekly, weekly, semi-monthly, monthly and quarterly, published in the slave States, including the District of Columbia, were seven hundred and twenty-two. These had an aggregate *yearly* circulation of ninety-two million one hundred and sixty-seven thousand one hundred and twenty-nine (92,167,129). The number of periodicals, of every class, published in the non-slave-holding States (exclusive of California) was one thousand eight hundred and ninety-three, with an aggregate yearly circulation of three hundred and thirty-three million three hundred and eighty-six thousand and eighty-one (333,-386,081).

We are aware that there may be inaccuracies in the foregoing estimates; but the compilers of the census, not we, are responsible for them. Besides, the figures are unquestionably as fair for the South as for the North; we accept them, therefore, as a just basis of our comparisons. Nearly seven years have elapsed since these statistics were taken, and these seven years have wrought an immense change in the journalism of the North, without any corresponding change in that of the South. It is noteworthy that, as a general thing, the principal journals of the free States are more comprehensive in their scope, more complete in every department, and enlist, if not a higher order of talent, at least *more* talent, than they did seven years ago. This improvement extends not only to the metropolitan, but to the country papers also. In fact, the very highest literary ability, in finance, in political economy, in science, in statism, in law, in theology, in medicine, in the belles-lettres, is laid under contribution by the journals of

the non-slaveholding States. This is true only to a very
limited degree of Southern journals. Their position, with
but few exceptions, is substantially the same that it was
ten years ago. They are neither worse nor better—the imbecility and inertia which attaches to everything which
slavery touches, clings to them now as tenaciously as it
did when Henry A. Wise thanked God for the paucity of
newspapers in the Old Dominion, and the platitudes of
"Father" Ritchie were recognized as the political gospel
of the South. They have not, so far as we can learn, increased materially in number, nor in the aggregate of their
yearly circulation. In the free States no week passes that
does not add to the number of their journals, and extend
the circle of their readers and their influence. Since the
census tables to which we have referred were prepared,
two of the many excellent weekly journals of which the
city of New York can boast, have sprung into being, and
attained an aggregate circulation more than twice as large
as that of the entire newspaper press of Virginia in 1850
—and exceeding, by some thousands, the aggregate circulation of the two hundred and fifty journals of which
Alabama, Arkansas, Kentucky, Georgia, North Carolina
and Florida, could boast at the time above-mentioned.

Throughout the non-slaveholding States, the newspaper or magazine that has *not* improved during the last
decade of years, is an exception to the general rule.
Throughout the entire slaveholding States, the newspaper
or magazine that *has* improved during that time, is no less
an exception to the general rule that there obtains. Outside of the larger cities of the South, there are not, probably, half a dozen newspapers in the whole slaveholding
region that can safely challenge a comparison with the
country-press of the North. What that country-press was
twenty years ago, the country-press of the South is now.

We do not deny that the South has produced able journalists; and that some of the newspapers of her principal
cities exhibit a degree of enterprise and talent that cannot
fail to command for them the respect of all intelligent men.
But these journals, we regret to say, are marked exceptions to the general condition of the Southern press; and
even the best of these fall far below the standard of ex-
cellence attained by the leading journals of the North.
In fact, whether our comparison embraces quantity only,

or extends to both quantity and quality, it is found to be immeasurably in favor of the non-slaveholding States, which in journalism, as in all other industrial pursuits, leave their slavery-cursed competitors at an infinite distance behind them, and thus vindicate the superiority of free institutions, which, recognizing labor as honorable, secure its rewards for all.

The literary vassalage of the South to the North constitutes in itself a most significant commentary upon the diatribes of the former concerning "a purely Southern literature." To begin at the beginning—the Alphabetical Blocks and Educational tables from which our Southern abecedarian takes his initial lesson, were projected and manufactured in the North. Going forward a step, we find the youngling intent in spelling short sentences, or gratifying his juvenile fondness for the fine arts by copying the wood-cuts from his Northern primer. Yet another step, and we discover him with his Sanders' Reader, his Mitchell's Geography, his Emerson's Arithmetic, all produced by Northern mind and Northern enterprise. There is nothing *wrong* in this; it is only a little ridiculous in view of the fulminations of the Southern proslavery press against the North. Occasionally however we are amused by the efforts of the oligarchs to make their own school-books, or to root out of all educational text-books every reference to the pestilential heresy of freedom. A "gentleman" in Charleston, S. C. is devoting his energies to the preparation of a series of pro-slavery elementary works, consisting of primers, readers, &c.—and lo! they are all printed, stitched and bound north of Mason and Dixon's line! A single *fact* like this is sufficient to overturn whole folios of *theory* concerning the divinity of slavery. The truth is, that, not school-books alone, but works of almost every class produced by the South, depend upon Northern enterprise and skill for their introduction to the public. Mr. DeBow, the eminent Statistician, publishes a Southern Review, purporting to be issued from New Orleans. It is printed and bound in the city of New York. We clip the following paragraph from a recent number of the Vicksburgh (Miss.) *Whig*:—

"SOUTHERN ENTERPRIZE.—Even the Mississippi Legislature, at its late session allowed its laws to go to

Boston to be printed, and made an appropriation of $3,000 to pay one of its members to go there and read the proof sheets instead of having it done in the State, and thereby assisting in building up a Southern publishing house. What a commentary on the Yankee-haters!"

The Greensboro (N. C.) *Patriot* thus records a similar contribution, on the part of that State, to "the creation of a purely Southern Literature:"

"We have heard it said, that those who had the control of the printing of the revised Statutes of North Carolina, in order to save a few dimes, had the work executed in Boston, in preference to giving the job to a citizen of this State. We impugn not the motives of the agents in this matter; but it is a little humiliating that no work except the commonest labor, can be done in North Carolina; that everything which requires a little skill, capital, or ingenuity, must be sent North. In the case under consideration, we have heard it remarked, that when the whole bill of expenses connected with the printing of the Revised Statutes in Boston was footed up, it only amounted to a few thousand dollars more than the job would have cost in this State. But then we have the consolation of knowing that the book *came from the North,* and that it was printed among the *abolitionists* of Boston; the *peculiar friends* of North Carolina and the South generally. —Of course we ought to be willing to pay a few extra thousands in consideration of these important facts!"

Southern divines give us elaborate "Bible Arguments;" Southern statists heap treatise upon treatise through which the Federal Constitution is tortured into all monstrous shapes; Southern novelists bore us *ad infinitum* with pictures of the beatitudes of plantation life and the negro-quarters; Southern verse-wrights drone out their drowsy dactyls or grow ventricous with their turgid heroics all in defence of slavery,—priest, politician, novelist, bardling, severally ringing the changes upon "the Biblical institution," "the conservative institution," "the humanizing institution," "the patriarchal institution"—and then—have their books printed on Northern paper, with Northern types, by Northern artizans, stitched, bound and made ready for the market by Northern industry; and yet fail to see in all this, as a true philosophical mind *must* see, an overwhelming refutation of their miserable sophisms in behalf of a system against which humanity in all its impulses and aspirations, and civilization in all its activities and triumphs, utter their perpetual protest.

From a curious article in the "American Publishers' Circular" on "Book Making in America," we give the following extracts:

> "It is somewhat alarming to know that the number of houses now actually engaged in the publishing of books, not including periodicals, amounts to more than three hundred. About three-fourths of these are engaged in Boston, New York, Philadelphia, and Baltimore—the balance being divided between Cincinnati, Buffalo, Auburn, Albany, Louisville, Chicago, St. Louis, and a few other places. There are more than three thousand booksellers who dispense the publications of these three hundred, besides six or seven thousand apothecaries, grocers, and hardware dealers, who connect literature with drugs, molasses, and nails.

> "The best printing in America is probably now done in Cambridge; the best cloth binding in Boston, and the best calf and morocco in New York and Philadelphia. In these two latter styles we are, as yet, a long distance from Heyday, the pride of London. His finish is supreme. There is nothing between it and perfection.

> "Books have multiplied to such an extent in our country, that it now takes 750 paper mills, with 2,000 engines in constant operation, to supply the printers, who work day and night, endeavoring to keep their engagements with publishers. These tireless mills produced 270,000,000 pounds of paper the past year, which immense supply has sold for about $27,000,000. A pound and a quarter of rags were required for a pound of paper, and 400,000,000 pounds were therefore consumed in this way last year. The cost of manufacturing a twelve months' supply of paper for the United States, aside from labor and rags, is computed at $4,000,000.   *   *   *

"The Harper establishment, the largest of our publishing houses, covers half an acre of ground. If old Mr. Caxton, who printed those stories of the Trojan war so long ago, could follow the Ex-Mayor of New York in one of his morning rounds in Franklin Square, he would be, to say the least, a little surprised. He would see in one room the floor loaded with the weight of 150 tons of presses. The electrotyping process would puzzle him somewhat; the drying and pressing process would startle him; the bustle would make his head ache; and the stock-room would quite finish him. An edition of Harpers' Monthly Magazine alone consists of 175,000. Few persons have any idea how large a number this is as applied to the edition of a book. It is computed that if these magazines were to rain down, and one man should attempt to pick them up like chips, it would take him a fortnight to pick up the copies of one single number, supposing him to pick up one every second, and to work ten hours a day."

"The rapidity with which books are now manufactured is almost incredible. A complete copy of one of Bulwer's novels, published across the water in three volumes, and reproduced here in one, was swept through the press in New York in fifty hours, and offered for sale smoking hot in the streets. The fabulous edifice proposed by a Yankee from Vermont, no longer seems an impossibility. 'Build the establishment according to my plan,' said he; 'drive a sheep in at one end, and he shall immediately come out at the other, four quarters of lamb, a felt hat, a leather apron, and a quarto Bible.' "

The business of the Messrs. Harper, whose establishment is referred to in the foregoing extract, is probably more generally diffused over every section of this country than that of any other publishing house. From enquiries recently made of them we learn that they issue, on an average, 3,000 bound volumes per day, throughout the year, and that each volume will average 500 pages—making a total of about one million of volumes, and not less than five hundred millions of pages per annum. This does not include the Magazine and books in pamphlet form, each of which contains as much matter as a bound volume.

—Their bills for paper exceed $300,000 annually, and as the average cost is fifteen cents per pound, they consume more than two millions of pounds—say one thousand tons of white paper.

There are regularly employed in their own premises about 550 persons, including printers, binders, engravers, and clerks. These are all paid in full once a fortnight in bankable money. Besides these, there are numerous authors and artists in every section of the country, who furnish manuscripts and illustrations, on terms generally satisfactory to all the parties interested.

The Magazine has a monthly circulation of between 175,000 and 200,000, or about two millions of copies annually. Each number of the Magazine is closed up about the fifth of the month previous to its date. Three or four days thereafter the mailing begins, commencing with more distant subscribers, all of whom are supplied before any copies are sold for delivery in New York. The intention of the publishers is, that it shall be delivered as nearly as possible on the same day in St. Louis, New-Orleans, Cincinnati, Philadelphia, Boston, and New York. It takes from ten to twelve days to dispatch the whole edition, (which weighs between four and five tons) by mail and express.

Their new periodical, "Harpers' Weekly," has, in a little more than four months, reached a sale of nearly 70,000 copies. The mailing of this commences on Tuesday night, and occupies about three days.

Ex-Mayor Harper, whom we have found to be one of the most affable and estimable gentlemen in the city of New York, informed us, sometime ago, that, though he had no means of knowing positively, he was of the opinion that about eighty per cent. of all their publications find final purchasers in the free States—the remainder, about twenty per cent., in the slave States. Yet it is probable that, with one or two exceptions, no other publishing house in the country has so large a percentage of Southern trade.

Of the "more than three hundred houses engaged in the publication of books," to which the writer in the "American Publishers' Circular" refers, upwards of nine-tenths of the number are in the non-slaveholding States, and these represent not less than ninety-nine hundredths

of the whole capital invested in the business. Baltimore
has twice as many publishers as any other Southern city;
and nearly as many as the whole South beside. The census
returns of 1850 give but twenty-four publishers for the
entire South, and ten of these were in Maryland. The
relative disproportion which then existed in this branch
of enterprise, between the North and the South, still exists;
or, if it has been changed at all, that change is in favor of
the North. So of all the capital, enterprise and industry
involved in the manufacture of the *material* that enters
into the composition of books. All the paper manufactories of the South do not produce enough to supply a
single publishing house in the city of New York.—Perhaps "a Southern Literature" does not necessarily involve
the enterprises requisite to the *manufacture* of books; but
experience has shown that there is a somewhat intimate
relation between the author, printer, paper-maker and
publisher; in other words, that the intellectual activity
which expresses itself in books, is measurable by the mechanical activities engaged in their manufacture.—Thus a
State that is fruitful in authors will almost necessarily be
fruitful in publishers; and the number of both classes will
be proportioned to the *reading* population. The poverty of
Southern literature is legitimately shown, therefore, in the
paucity of Southern publishers. We do not deny a high
degree of cultivated talent to the South; we are familiar
with the names of her sons whose genius has made them
eminent; all that we insist upon is, that the same accursed
influence which has smitten her industrial enterprises
with paralysis, and retarded indefinitely her material advancement, has exerted a corresponding influence upon
her literature. How it has done this we shall more fully
indicate before we close the chapter.

At the "Southern Convention" held some months since
at Savannah, a good deal was said about "Southern literature," and many suggestions made in reference to the
best means for its promotion. One speaker thought that
"they could get text-books at home without going to either
Old England or New England for them." Well—they can
try. The effort will not harm them; nor the North either.
The orator was confident "that the South had talent
enough to do anything that needs to be done, and independence enough to do it." The *talent* we shall not

deny; the *independence* we are ready to believe in when we see it. When she throws off the incubus of slavery under which she goes staggering like the Sailor of Bagdad under the weight of the Old Man of the Sea, she will prove her independence, and demonstrate her ability "to do anything that needs to be done." Till then she is but a fettered giant, whose vitals are torn by the dogs which her own folly has engendered.

Another speaker, on the occasion referred to, half-unconsciously it would seem, threw a gleam of light upon the subject under discussion, which, had not himself and his hearers been bat-blind, would have revealed the clue that conducts from the darkness in which they burrow to the day of redemption for the South. Said he:—

> "Northern publishers employ the talent of the South and of the whole country to write for them, and pour out thousands annually for it; but Southern men expect to get talent without paying for it. The *Southern Quarterly Review* and the *Literary Messenger* are literally struggling for existence, for want of material aid. * * *
>
> It is not the South that builds up Northern literature —*they do it themselves*. There is talent and mind and poetic genius enough in the South to build up a literature of a high order; but Southern publishers cannot get money enough to assist them in their enterprises, and, therefore, the South has no literature.

Here are truths. "Southern men expect to get talent without paying for it." A very natural expectation, considering that they have been accustomed to have all their material wants supplied by the uncompensated toil of their slaves. In this instance it may seem an absurd one, but it results legitimately from the system of slavery. That system, in fact, operates in a two-fold way against the Southern publisher: first, by its practical repudiation of the scriptural axiom that the laborer is worthy of his hire; and secondly, by restricting the circle of readers through the ignorance which it inevitably engenders. How is it that the people of the North build up their literature?— Two words reveal the secret: *intelligence—compensation.* they are *a reading people*—the poorest artizan, or day-laborer has his shelf of books, or his daily or weekly paper, whose contents he seldom fails to master before retiring at night; and *they are accustomed to pay for all the books and papers which they peruse.* Readers and payers—these are the men who insure the prosperity of publishers. Where a system of enforced servitude prevails, it is very apt to beget loose notions about the obligation of paying for anything; and many minds fail to see the distinction, morally, between compelling Sambo to pick cotton without paying him wages, or compelling Lippincott & Co. to manufacture books for the planter's pleasure or edification upon the same liberal terms. But more than this—where a system of enforced servitude prevails, a fearful degree of ignorance prevails also, as its necessary accompaniment. The enslaved masses are, of course, thrust back from the fountains of knowledge by the strong arm of law, while the poor non-slaveholding classes are almost as effectually excluded from the institutions of learning by their poverty —the sparse population of slaveholding districts being unfavorable to the maintenance of free schools, and the exigencies of their condition forbidding them to avail themselves of any more costly educational privileges.

Northern publishers can "employ the talent of the South and of the whole country to write for them, and pour out thousands annually for it," simply because a *reading* population, accustomed to *pay* for the service which it receives, enables them to do so. A similar population at the South would enable Southern publishers to do the same. Substitute free labor for slave labor, the institutions of freedom for those of slavery, and it would not long remain true that "Southern publishers cannot get money enough to assist them in their enterprises, and therefore the South has no literature." This is the discovery which the South Carolina orator from whom we quote, but narrowly escaped making, when he stood upon its very edge, and rounded his periods with the truths in whose unapprehended meanings was hidden this germ of redemption for a nation.

The self-stultification of folly, however, was never more evident than it is in the current gabble of the oligarchs about a "Southern literature." They do not mean by it a healthy, manly, normal utterance of unfettered minds, without which there can be no proper literature; but an emasculated substitute therefor, from which the element of freedom is eliminated; husks, from which the kernel has escaped—a body, from which the vitalizing spirit has fled—a literature which ignores manhood by confounding it with brutehood; or, at best, deals with all similes of freedom as treason against the "peculiar institution." There is not a single great name in the literary annals of the old or new world that could dwarf itself to the stature requisite to gain admission into the Pantheon erected by these devotees of the Inane for their Lilliputian deities. Thank God, a "Southern literature," in the sense intended by the champions of slavery, is a simple impossibility, rendered such by that exility of mind which they demand in its producers as a prerequisite to admission into the guild of Southern authorship. The tenuous thoughts of such authorlings could not survive a single breath of manly criticism. The history of the rise, progress, and decline of their literature could be easily written on a child's smooth palm, and leave space enough for its funeral oration and epitaph. The latter might appropriately be that which, in one of our rural districts, marks the grave of a still-born infant:—

> "If so early I am done for,
> I wonder what I was begun for!"

We desire to see the South bear its just proportion in the literary activities and achievements of our common country. It has never yet done so, and it never will until its own manhood is vindicated in the abolition of slavery. The impulse which such a measure would give to all industrial pursuits that deal with the elements of material prosperity, would be imparted also to the no less valuable but more intangible creations of the mind. Take from the intellect of the South the incubus which now oppresses it, and its rebound would be glorious; the era of its diviner inspirations would begin; and its triumphs would be a perpetual vindication of the superiority of free institutions over those of slavery.

To Duyckinck's "Cyclopedia of American Literature"—a sort of *Omnium-gatherum* that reminds one of Jeremiah's figs—we are indebted for the following facts: The whole number of "American authors" whose place of nativity is given, is five hundred and sixty-nine. Of these, seventy-

nine were foreign born, eighty-seven were natives of the
South, and four hundred and three—a vast majority of
the whole, first breathed the vital air in the free North.
Many of those who were born in the South, received their
education in the North, quite a number of whom became
permanent residents thereof. Still, for the purposes of this
computation, we count them on the side of the South.
Yet how significant the comparison which this computation furnishes! Throwing the foreign born (adopted citizens, mostly residents of the North) out of the reckoning, and the record stands,—Northern authors *four hundred and three;* Southern, *eighty-seven*—a difference of
three hundred and sixteen in favor of the North! And this,
probably, indicates very fairly the relative intellectual
activity of the two sections.

We accept the facts gleaned from Duyckinck's work as
a basis, simply, of our estimate: not as being absolutely
accurate in themselves, though they are doubtless reliable
in the main, and certainly as fair for the South as they are
for the North. We might dissent from the judgment of
the compiler in reference to the propriety of applying the
term "literature" to much that his compilation contains;
but as tastes have proverbially differed from the days of
the venerable dame who kissed her cow—not to extend
our researches into the condition of things anterior to that
interesting event—we will not insist upon *our* view of the
matter, but take it for granted that he has disentombed
from forgotten reviews, newspapers, pamphlets, and post-
ers, a fair relative proportion of "authors" for both North
and South, for which "American Literature" is unquestionably under infinite obligations to him!

Griswold's "Poets and Poetry of America" and Thomas
Buchanan Read's "Female Poets of America" furnish evidence, equally conclusive, of the benumbing influence of
slavery upon the intellect of a country. Of course, these
compilers say nothing about Slavery, and probably never
thought of it in connection with their respective works,
but none the less significant on that account is the testimony of the *facts* which they give. From the last edition
of Griswold's compilation (which contains the names of
none of our female writers, he having included them in a
separate volume) we find the names of one hundred and

forty-one writers of verse: of these *one* was foreign born, *seventeen* natives of the slaveholding, and *one hundred and twenty-three* of the non-slaveholding States. Of our female poets, whose nativity is given by Mr. Read, *eleven* are natives of the South; and *seventy-three* of the North! These simple arithmetical figures are God's eternal Scripture against the folly and madness of Slavery, and need no aid of rhetoric to give emphasis to the startling eloquence of their revelations.

But, after all, literature is not to be estimated by cubic feet or pounds averdupois, nor measured by the bushel or the yardstick. Quality, rather than quantity, is the true standard of estimation. The fact, however, matters little for our present purpose; for the South, we are sorry to say, is as much behind the North in the former as in the latter. We do not forget the names of Gayarre, Benton, Simms, and other eminent citizens of the Slave States, who have by their contributions to American letters conferred honor upon themselves and upon our common country, when we affirm, that those among our authors who enjoy a cosmopolitan reputation, are, with a few honorable exceptions, natives of the Free North; and that the names which most brilliantly illustrate our literature, in its every department, are those which have grown into greatness under the nurturing influence of free institutions. "Comparisons are odious," it is said; and we will not, unnecessarily, render them more so, in the present instance, by contrasting, name by name, the literary men of the South with the literary men of the North. We do not depreciate the former, nor overestimate the latter. But let us ask, whence come our geographers, our astronomers, our chemists, our meteorologists, our ethnologists, and others, who have made their names illustrious in the domain of the Natural Sciences? Not from the Slave States, certainly. In the Literature of Law, the South can furnish no name that can claim peership with those of Story and of Kent; in History, none that tower up to the altitude of Bancroft, Prescott, Hildreth, Motley and Washington Irving; in Theology, none that can challenge favorable comparison with those of Edwards, Dwight, Channing, Taylor, Bushnell, Tyler and Wayland: in Fiction, none that take rank with Cooper, and Mrs. Stowe; and but few that may do

so with even the second class novelists of the North;* in
Poetry, none that can command position with Bryant,
Halleck, and Percival, with Whittier, Longfellow, and
Lowell, with Willis, Stoddard and Taylor, with Holmes,
Saxe, and Burleigh; and—we might add twenty other
Northern names before we found their Southern peer, with
the exception of poor Poe, who, within a narrow range
of subjects, showed himself a poet of consummate art,
and occupies a sort of debatable ground between our first
and second-class writers.

We might extend this comparison to our writers in
every department of letters, from the compiler of school-
books to the author of the most profound ethical treatise,
and with precisely the same result. But we forbear. The
task is distasteful to our State pride, and would have been
entirely avoided had not a higher principle urged us to its
performance. It remains for us now to enquire,

WHAT HAS PRODUCED THIS LITERARY PAUPERISM OF THE
SOUTH? One single word, most pregnant in its terrible
meanings, answers the question. That word is—SLAVERY!
But we have been so long accustomed to the ugly thing
itself, and have become so familiar with its no less ugly
fruits, that the common mind fails to apprehend the connection between the one, as cause, and the other as effect;
and it therefore becomes necessary to give a more detailed
answer to our interrogatory.

Obviously, then, the conditions requisite to a flourishing literature are wanting at the South. These are—

I. Readers. The people of the South are not a reading
people. Many of the adult population never learned to
read; still more do not care to read. We have been impressed, during a temporary sojourn in the North, with
the difference between the middle and laboring classes in
the Free States, and the same classes in the Slave States,
in this respect. Passing along the great routes of travel in
the former, or taking our seat in the comfortable cars that
pass up and down the avenues of our great commercial
metropolis, we have not failed to contrast the employment

---

* We Southrons all glory in the literary reputation of Mr.
Simms; yet we must confess his inferiority to Cooper, and
prejudice alone will refuse to admit, that, while in the *art* of
the novelist he is the superior of Mrs. Stowe, in genius he must
take position below her.

of our fellow-passengers with that which occupies the attention of the corresponding classes on our various Southern routes of travel. In the one case, a large proportion of the passengers seem intent upon mastering the contents of the newspaper, or some recently published book. The merchant, the mechanic, the artizan, the professional man, and even the common laborer, going to or returning from their daily avocations, are busy with their morning or evening paper, or engaged in an intelligent discussion of some topic of public interest. This is their leisure hour, and it is given to the acquisition of such information as may be of immediate or ultimate use, or to the cultivation of a taste for elegant literature. In the other case, newspapers and books seem generally ignored, and noisy discussions of village and State politics, the tobacco and cotton crops, filibusterism in Cuba, Nicaragua, or Sonora, the price of negroes generally, and especially of "fine-looking wenches," the beauties of lynch-law, the delights of horse-racing, the excitement of street fights with bowie-knives and revolvers, the "manifest destiny" theory that justifies the stealing of all territory contiguous to our own, and kindred topics, constitute the warp and woof of conversation. All this is on a level with the general intelligence of the Slave States. It is true, these States have their educated men,—the majority of whom owe their literary culture to the colleges of the North. Not that there are no Southern colleges—for there are institutions, so called, in a majority of the Slave States.—Some of them, too, are not deficient in the appointments requisite to our higher educational institutions; but as a general thing, Southern colleges are colleges only in *name,* and will scarcely take rank with a third-rate Northern academy, while our academies, with a few exceptions, are immeasurably inferior to the public schools of New York, Philadelphia, and Boston. The truth is, there is a vast inert mass of stupidity and ignorance, too dense for individual effort to enlighten or remove, in all communities cursed with the institution of slavery. Disguise the unwelcome truth as we may, slavery is the parent of ignorance, and ignorance begets a whole brood of follies and of vices, and every one of these is inevitably hostile to literary culture. The masses, if they think of literature at all, think of it only as a costly luxury, to be monopolized by the few.

The proportion of white adults over twenty years of age, in each state, who cannot read and write, to the *whole* white population, is as follows:

Connecticut,	1 to every	568	Louisiana,	1 to every	38½
Vermont,	1 "	473	Maryland,	1 "	27
N. Hampshire,	1 "	310	Mississippi,	1 "	20
Massachusetts,	1 "	166	Delaware,	1 "	18
Maine,	1 "	108	South Carolina,	1 "	17
Michigan,	1 "	97	Missouri,	1 "	16
Rhode Island,	1 "	67	Alabama,	1 "	15
New Jersey,	1 "	58	Kentucky,	1 "	13½
New York,	1 "	56	Georgia,	1 "	13
Pennsylvania,	1 "	50	Virginia,	1 "	12½
Ohio,	1 "	43	Arkansas,	1 "	11½
Indiana,	1 "	18	Tennessee,	1 "	11
Illinois,	1 "	17	North Carolina,	1 "	7

In this table, Illinois and Indiana are the only Free States which, in point of education, are surpassed by any of the Slave States; and this disgraceful fact is owing, principally, to the influx of foreigners, and to immigrants from the Slave States. New York, Rhode Island, and Pennsylvania have also a large foreign element in their population, that swells very considerably this percentage of ignorance. For instance, New York shows, by the last census, a population of 98,722 who cannot read and write, and of this number 68,052 are foreigners; Rhode Island, 3,607, of whom 2,359 are foreigners; Pennsylvania, 76,-272, of whom 24,989 are foreigners. On the other hand, the ignorance of the Slave States is principally *native* ignorance, but comparatively few emigrants from Europe seeking a home upon a soil cursed with "the peculiar institution." North Carolina has a foreign population of only 340, South Carolina only 104, Arkansas only 27, Tennessee only 505, and Virginia only 1,137, who cannot read and write; while the aggregate of *native* ignorance in these five States (exclusive of the *slaves,* who are debarred all education by *law*) is 278,948! No longer ago than 1837, Governor Clarke, of Kentucky, in his message to the Legislature of that State, declared that "by the computation of those most familiar with the subject, *one-third of the adult population of the State are unable to write their names;*" and Governor Campbell, of Virginia, reported to the Legislature, that "from the returns of ninety-eight clerks, it appeared that of 4,614 applications for marriage licenses in 1837, no less than 1,047 were made by men unable to write."

In the Slave States the proportion of free white children between the ages of five and twenty, who are found at any school or college, is not quite *one-fifth* of the whole; in the Free States, the proportion is more than *three-fifths*.

We could fill our pages with facts like these to an almost indefinite extent, but it cannot be necessary. No truth is more demonstrable, nay, no truth has been more abundantly demonstrated, than this: that Slavery is hostile to general education; its strength, its very life, is in the ignorance and stolidity of the masses; it naturally and necessarily represses general literary culture. To talk, therefore, of the "creation of a purely Southern Literature," without *readers* to demand, or *writers* to produce it, is the mere babble of idiocy.

II. Another thing essential to the creation of a literature is MENTAL FREEDOM. How much of *that* is to be found in the region of Slavery? We will not say that there is *none;* but if it exists, it exists as the outlawed antagonist of human chattelhood. He who believes that the despotism of the accursed institution expends its malignant forces upon the *slave,* leaving intact the white and (so-called) free population, is the victim of a most monstrous delusion. One end of the yoke that bows the African to the dust, presses heavily upon the neck of his Anglo-Saxon master. The entire mind of the South either stultifies itself into acquiescence with Slavery, succumbs to its authority, or chafes in indignant protest against its monstrous pretensions and outrageous usurpations. A free press is an institution almost unknown at the South. Free speech is considered as treason against slavery: and when people dare neither speak nor print their thoughts, free thought itself is well nigh extinguished. All that can be said in *defence* of human bondage, may be spoken freely; but question either its morality or its policy, and the terrors of lynch law are at once invoked to put down the pestilent heresy. The legislation of the Slave States for the suppression of the freedom of speech and the press, is disgraceful and cowardly to the last degree, and can find its parallel only in the meanest and bloodiest despotisms of the Old World. No institution that could bear the light would thus sneakingly seek to burrow itself in utter darkness. Look, too, at the mobbings, lynchings, robberies, social and political proscriptions, and all manner of nameless outrages, to which men in the South have been subjected, simply upon the suspicion that they were the enemies of Slavery . We could fill page after page of this volume with the record of such atrocities. But a simple reference to them is enough. Our countrymen have not yet forgotten why John C. Underwood was, but a few months since, banished from his home in Virginia, and the accomplished Hedreck driven from his College professorship in North Carolina. They believed Slavery inimical to the best interest of the South, and for daring to give expression to this belief in moderate yet manly language, they were ostracised by the despotic Slave Power, and compelled to seek a refuge from its vengeance in States where the principles of freedom are better understood. Pending the last Presidential election, there were thousands, nay, tens of thousands of voters in the Slave States, who desired to give their suffrages for the Republican nominee, John C. Fremont, himself a Southron, but a non-slaveholder. The Constitution of the United States guaranteed to these men an expression of their preference at the ballot-box. But were they permitted such an expression? Not at all. They were denounced, threatened, overawed, by the Slave Power—and it is not too much to say that there was really no *Constitutional election,*—that is, no such free expression of political preferences as the Constitution aims to secure—in a majority of the Slave States.

From a multiplicity of facts like these, the inference is unavoidable, that Slavery tolerates no freedom of the press—no freedom of speech—no freedom of opinion. To expect that a whole-souled, manly literature can flourish under such conditions, is as absurd as it would be to look for health amid the pestilential vapors of a dungeon, or for the continuance of animal life without the aid of oxygen.

III. Mental activity—force—enterprise—are requisite to the creation of literature. Slavery tends to sluggishness —imbecility—inertia. Where free thought is treason, the masses will not long take the trouble of thinking at all. Desuetude begets incompetence—the *dare-not* soon becomes the *cannot*. The mind thus enslaved, necessarily loses its interest in the processes of other minds; and its tendency is to sink down into absolute stolidity or sottishness. Our remarks find melancholy confirmation in the abject servilism in which multitudes of the non-slaveholding whites of the South are involved. In them, ambition, pride, self-respect, hope, seem alike extinct. Their slaveholding fellows are, in some respects, in a still more unhappy condition—helpless, nerveless, ignorant, selfish; yet vainglorious, self-sufficient and brutal. Are these the chosen architects who are expected to build up "a purely Southern literature?"

The truth is, slavery destroys, or vitiates, or pollutes, whatever it touches. No interest of society escapes the influence of its clinging curse. It makes Southern religion a stench in the nostrils of Christendom—it makes Southern politics a libel upon all the principles of Republicanism—it makes Southern literature a travesty upon the honorable profession of letters. Than the better class of Southern authors themselves, none will feel more keenly the truth of our remarks. They write books, but can find for them neither publishers nor remunerative sales at the South! The executors of Calhoun seek, for his works, a Northern publisher. Benton writes history and prepares voluminous compilations, which are given to the world through a Northern publisher. Simms writes novels and poems, and they are scattered abroad from the presses of a Northern publisher. Eighty per cent. of all the copies sold are probably bought by Northern readers.

When will Southern authors understand their own interests? When will the South, as a whole, abandoning its present suicidal policy, enter upon that career of prosperity, greatness, and true renown, to which God by his word and his providences, is calling it? "If thou take away from the midst of thee the yoke, the putting forth of the finger and speaking vanity; and if thou draw out thy soul to the hungry and satisfy the afflicted soul; then shall thy light rise in obscurity and thy darkness be as the noonday: And the Lord shall guide thee continually and satisfy thy soul in drought, and make fat thy bones; and thou shalt be like a watered garden, and like a spring of water, whose waters fail not. And they that shall be of thee shall build the old waste places; thou shalt raise up the foundations of many generations; and thou shalt be called, The repairer of the breach, The restorer of paths to dwell in."

Our limits, not our materials, are exhausted. We would gladly say more, but can only, in conclusion, add as the result of our investigations in this department of our subject, that *Literature and Liberty are inseparable; the one can never have a vigorous existence without being wedded to the other.*

CONCLUSION

Our work is done. It is the voice of the non-slaveholding whites of the South, through one identified with them by interest, by feeling, by position. That voice, by whomsoever spoken, must yet be heard and heeded. The time hastens—the doom of slavery is written—the redemption of the South draws nigh.

In taking leave of our readers, we know not how we can give more forcible expression to our thoughts and intensions than by saying that, in concert with the intelligent free voters of the North, we, the non-slaveholding whites of the South, expect to elevate JOHN C. FREMONT, CASSIUS M. CLAY, JAMES G. BIRNEY, or some other Southern non-slaveholder, to the Presidency in 1860; and that the patriot thus elevated to that dignified station will, through our cordial co-operation, be succeeded by WILLIAM H. SEWARD, CHARLES SUMNER, JOHN McLEAN, or some other non-slaveholder of the North;—and furthermore, that if, in these or in any other similar cases, the oligarchs do not quietly submit to the will of a constitutional majority of the people, as expressed at the ballot-box, the first battle between freedom and slavery will be fought at home—and may God defend the right!

THE END.